Higher Education Administration

Higher Education Administration

A Guide to Legal, Ethical, and Practical Issues

Norma M. Goonen
and Rachel S. Blechman

The Greenwood Educators' Reference Collection

GREENWOOD PRESS
Westport, Connecticut • London

Library of Congress Cataloging-in-Publication Data

Goonen, Norma M.
  Higher education administration : a guide to legal, ethical, and
practical issues / Norma M. Goonen and Rachel S. Blechman.
      p.   cm.—(The Greenwood educators' reference collection,
ISSN 1056-2192)
  Includes bibliographical references (p.   ) and index.
  ISBN 0–313–30304–5 (alk. paper)
  1. Universities and colleges—United States—Administration.
2. Universities and colleges—Administration—Law and legislation—
United States.   3. Universities and colleges—Administration—Moral
and ethical aspects—United States.   I. Blechman, Rachel S., 1938–
II. Title.   III. Series.
LB2341.G573   1999
378.73—dc21   99–22144

British Library Cataloguing in Publication Data is available.

Library of Congress Catalog Card Number: 99–22144
ISBN: 0–313–30304–5
ISSN: 1056–2192

First published in 1999

Greenwood Press, 88 Post Road West, Westport, CT 06881
An imprint of Greenwood Publishing Group, Inc.
www.greenwood.com

Printed in the United States of America

The paper used in this book complies with the
Permanent Paper Standard issued by the National
Information Standards Organization (Z39.48–1984).

10 9 8 7 6 5 4 3 2 1

NMG: To my mother, Luisa Cordero Corrons, whose gentle strength smoothed the path of my life's journey.

RSB: To my loving parents, Nathan and Tobie Rudin, who gave me a solid foundation for life; and to my husband, Wil Blechman, and my law firm, Holland & Knight LLP, who provided the support and encouragement that enabled me to undertake this project.

Contents

Preface

After having worked together in our roles as academic vice president of a university and legal counsel to a university, we were acutely aware of the formidable decision-making tasks facing the academic administrator. Not only do decisions made for the university have to meet the requirements of law, but they also have to mirror the institution's values and meet the practical requirements of running a viable and stable educational enterprise.

There are a myriad of books discussing the requirements of law and how it affects academic administration. However, we found a dearth of resources on the ethical questions that arise in academic decision making and the practical considerations that impact the legal and ethical operation of the educational institution. What was needed, we decided, was a resource that raised some of the ethical issues and addressed some of the practical issues while highlighting the need for a tri-faceted approach to decisions in the academic arena. This book attempts to address certainly not all but many of the major decisions that an academic administrator is faced with on a daily basis. We decided to limit its scope to academic affairs because including student affairs would have resulted in another voluminous undertaking. We acknowledge, however, that an academic administrator may be involved in a broader spectrum of issues, and the authors would advise that a similar tri-faceted approach be employed with decisions in the student affairs realm.

The scope of decision making in academic administration revolves around relationships with faculty and students—and with others, to a lesser extent. This book, therefore, highlights the relationship between the academic administrator and faculty members relative to hiring, compensation, terminations, promotions, and other subjects covered in the first six chapters. Although many of the concepts and issues may be easily applied to relationships with other administrators and staff, the authors felt that the importance of faculty-administrator interactions merited this focus.

Similarly, two chapters are devoted to student academic matters and the relationship between academic administrators and students. Certainly, many areas of decision making regarding students remain uncovered, but we were limited by both our focus on academic administration and space constraints.

ACKNOWLEDGMENTS

Many of our colleagues reviewed all or portions of various drafts of the manuscript. They are attorneys, higher education administrators, and ethicists, all of whom had valuable insights and suggestions. We wish to give them our sincere thanks. They are: Mark G. Alexander, Susan Aprill, Joel Berman, Pamela Bernard, Isis Carvajal de Garcia, Elizabeth Chifari, Gary Feinberg, Sharon Fredda, John J. Goonen, Jr., Stephen Levitt, Richard McCray, Anne E. Mulder, Ben Mulvey, Andrew Niesiobedzki, Robin Lee Rosenberg, Don Rosenblum, and Dawn Schiller. We would also like to give special recognition to Barbara A. Lee, a distinguished author in higher education law, who reviewed the entire manuscript and gave us the benefit of her expertise.

Early in the drafting of the manuscript, we conducted a survey of a group of chief academic officers to elicit issues that they have encountered in their decision making and to ascertain that we did not miss any of the important ethical issues confronting other practicing academic administrators. We wish to thank and acknowledge them as well: Nancy J. Aumann, Lloyd Chapin, Charles M. Edmondson, E. Eugene Hall, Wayne Howard, Johnette Isham, Gary McCloskey, David Moore, Jesse S. Robertson, and several contributors who chose not to provide their names.

Finally, we acknowledge a debt of gratitude to our respective husbands, John and Wil, who were patient and always encouraging throughout the long process of nurturing this work, and to our children, family, and friends, who understood when we could not always be with them because we were working on this project. And yes, Wil, you can have the movie rights.

Higher Education
Administration

Chapter 1

A Delicate Balance: Legal, Ethical, and Practical Issues

Decision making in higher education is a complex process of balancing conflict-ing needs and interests while adhering to the law; the institution's mission, values, and standards; and the practical considerations necessary for its fiscal and operational health.

The university or college campus has various constituent bodies (the institu-tion as a whole and its directors, students, faculty, administrators, staff, alumni, and the general public), each with its own interests and concerns. Thoughtful decision making can require determining which constituency's needs should take precedence in the situation at hand, as well as measuring the decision against legal requirements, institutional values and goals, and practical consequences. The result can be a good decision for the institution that nonetheless accom-modates one group at the expense of another.

This book focuses on the academic administrator and the layered process he or she must engage in on a daily basis to make decisions for the institution's constituents that are legally and ethically sound and practically positive. *Insti-tution, college, and university*, as used in this book, unless otherwise noted, refer to public and private independent institutions above the secondary school level.

LEGAL PARAMETERS

When making decisions against a backdrop of interacting and conflicting needs, the academic administrator must first meet the requirements of law, if any. While ethical and practical considerations may be equally as important, or more so, in any particular decision, the law provides the floor below which no institutional action should fall.

The law reaches into almost every aspect of campus life, and its impact on the day-to-day decisions of the academic administrators has been increasing over the years. For example, in the academic arena, faculty members dissatisfied with promotion or tenure decisions have frequently sued the institution for discrimination in employment and/or breach of contract as well as for infringement of First Amendment rights; students have sued over grades, over academic expulsions and suspension, and over changes in the catalog offerings; and institutions have taken actions to protect the integrity of their degrees and transcripts.

The law applied to public and private institutions of higher education differs in some respects. Public institutions are deemed to be arms of the state and, as such, are subject to federal and state constitutional restrictions as well as to state and federal statutes, with their supporting administrative regulations. Private institutions, on the other hand, are not subject to constitutional requirements and the state statutes aimed at public institutions but can be subject to other federal and state statutes that may also have supporting regulations. For example, many federal laws are applicable to any public or private institution that accepts federal funds, grants, or contracts. Other statutes, such as those involving employment and student records, are generally applicable to all public and private institutions. Both public and private institutions are also subject to the common law of the state. This is the judge-made law published in case decisions that governs matters such as contracts and personal injuries. This law is applicable within the jurisdiction in which it was decided. Public and private institutions are also subject to state and federal licensing standards and accreditation standards published and enforced by accrediting bodies and may also be held to adherence to their own internal rules and regulations.

In the "Legal Parameters" section of each of the chapters of this book, the authors seek to raise some of the legal issues attendant to areas of academic decision making. The purpose of the book is not to give legal advice or to explore the law and its application to academic affairs exhaustively; rather, it is to sensitize administrators or prospective administrators to some of the legal considerations that commonly arise. Administrators who are aware of legal implications know when to consult with legal counsel and may thus avoid costly litigation or inadvertent violations of law and regulation.

ETHICAL CONSIDERATIONS

Conforming to law is mandatory if an institution wishes to avoid legal consequences. Following ethical precepts, however, can be more a matter of choice. Nonetheless, ignoring the ethics of a situation can have serious consequences for the institution. As the creator and disseminator of knowledge, and the body that certifies the competence of others, the public expects the institution to operate with high ethical standards and train the next generation to take its place in the community as knowledgeable, principled, responsible citizens. An institution that operates without allegiance to its core values cannot accomplish these tasks or retain the public's trust. Teaching ethics requires more than passing on information about ethical theories. First and foremost, it requires modeling of ethical behavior guided by a specific set of values.

For purposes of this book, therefore, we will define *ethics* as conduct based on values that guide the actions of the members of the institution. Institutional values may be formally written and disseminated or unwritten but operationalized in the customs of each institution. The systematic evaluation of conduct as a reflection of our values is *applied ethics*, or ethics in context. Our discussions throughout this book will not concern themselves with ethical theories but with applied ethics as it pertains to everyday decision making in higher education.

The word *values* is sometimes used interchangeably with the word *ethics* in the literature. Again, for purposes of our discussions, values are the standards that "guide individuals and organizations toward that which they find desirable, fulfilling, and worthwhile"[1] and lead us to make particular choices. Examples of traditional values in higher education are academic excellence, respect, honesty, fairness, caring, justice, compassion, truth, efficiency, productivity, tolerance, integrity, equity, trust, commitment to the common good, courage, responsibility, consistency, faithfulness (fidelity), citizenship, cooperation, utility, and peace. Additionally, the modern university may also subscribe to "newer" values, such as mass education, equality of access, diversity, decentralization, and openness.[2] Each institution may have its own set of values, as may various constituencies within an institution. The degree to which a college or university adheres to its stated set of values constitutes its institutional "ethos" or "culture." Decisions may be evaluated to determine their congruency and appropriateness in the context of this institutional culture. In all cases, however, awareness of values enhances the decision-making process.

To ensure congruency of institutional values and ethics, three conditions must exist: First, the institution must identify its values; second, it must assess the degree to which these values are followed in the actions of the institution; and third, it must establish a reward system that reinforces desired actions.[3] In order to avoid unethical conduct, there must be discussion of what constitutes acceptable and unacceptable behavior, and there must be a process to deal with those who will not abide by the institution's accepted standards.[4]

A relatively recent development, a *values audit* is a systematic way to identify an institution's values. It brings together all constituencies of the university community to focus on its applied ethics and to find discrepancies between explicit and implicit values and the decisions that are made in the institution. Often, the values audit measures progress against the institution's mission, vision, and value system. Consequently, a values audit may be an integral part of the strategic planning process because it focuses on a shared culture or system of values as well as on conflicts in values and how to resolve them. The process of the audit has been found to be as important as the data gathered.[5] Not an end in itself, the values audit has been known to be a catalyst in the development of a learning community, an ideal image that encompasses the search for meaning in higher education.[6] For a summary of a process that can be used to perform a values audit, see Appendix 1.

Values clarification and ethics have traditionally been taught as part of the curriculum in a variety of professional disciplines (e.g., medicine, law). Yet until recently, they were seldom included as part of the formal instruction of those who are training to become academics.[7] The irony is that academics are responsible for developing the next generation of professionals—the "essence of academic duty."[8] To partly address this need, several professional organizations have established codes of ethics, statements of professional standards, or statements of core values. A professional code of ethics is a statement or series of statements that detail and promote widely accepted ethical norms. The code can be used as a teaching tool, for the orientation of new professionals to their respective profession's core values, and as a guide for ethical and practical decision making.[9] As in the values audit and the drafting of a mission statement, the resulting code is not as important as the process. Although the mere adoption of a code does not guarantee that the members of the profession (or the institution) will engage in ethical behavior, it serves to emphasize the organization's commitment to ethics and values. The American Association of State Colleges and Universities, the American Association of Community and Junior Colleges, the National Academic Advising Association, the American Association of University Professors (AAUP), and the American Association of University Administrators (AAUA), among others, have developed codes of ethics, statements of professional standards, or statements of core values; the statements for the latter two associations are found in Appendixes 2 and 3, respectively of this book.

What can a decision maker do that will help him or her in making ethical decisions? The steps to this process, as outlined in the literature, are:

- Define the issue.
- Review alternatives and consider consequences.
- Measure each alternative against principles and ethical precepts that fit.
- Check solutions against intuitive moral judgment.
- Act on best judgment.[10]

As an additional complication to the already complex process of ethical decision making, accepted values of an institution may often be in conflict. Ethical dilemmas arise when competing and equally bona fide values are represented in a decision. As examples, an administrator must often decide between the interests and rights of the student, faculty, or staff member (values of the individual) and the interests of the institution (systemic values), or the intrinsic values espoused in a liberal arts curriculum versus the extrinsic values of a curriculum that focuses on social utility.[11] The institution may advocate all of the values on all sides of a controversy, but the decision maker must often take an action that results in placing one over the other, even though the choices are all ethical and consistent with the values of the university. Deciding between two conflicting ethical principles may be the most difficult part of decision making for the modern leader.[12]

It is unrealistic to expect to meet all needs. More reasonably, the goals of the administrator should be (1) to develop a climate on the campus where discussion of these issues with all constituencies is accepted and encouraged and (2) to make decisions on a daily basis that are internally consistent and congruent with the institution's values.

While recognizing that each institution will have its own values and priorities, for purposes of this book we have adopted a set of core values that are common to most institutions to serve as a backdrop for the ethical considerations raised. The values are truth, fairness, respect for each individual, academic excellence, fidelity, and utility. The "Ethical Considerations" section of each chapter is designed to *raise* some of the relevant *ethical questions* related to the specific topic being addressed that are based on these core values. Since institutions and decision makers have their own priorities, constituencies, and circumstances, the answers to the questions raised must be provided by each institution itself.

PRACTICAL SUGGESTIONS

The academic administrator must always be aware of the practical considerations that can make or break a decision. These include the financial ("bottom-line") considerations, as well as how to accomplish a task efficiently. Whereas the legal parameters may be a floor below which a decision maker cannot go, and the ethical issues may define and shape the institution, the practical considerations may create a ceiling above which the same decision maker cannot rise.

One of the most poignant examples of a difficult balancing act in which financial issues may prevail is the case of unwarranted litigation against the institution. Even though the institution may be legally and morally in the right, the costs of proving so in the courts may not be worth the pressing of the principles involved. In such cases, university counsel may advise the institution to settle the suit for a "nuisance" fee. Clearly, the financial considerations in this case may outweigh the others.

Political issues are also examples of practical considerations that should not, and often cannot, be ignored. However, administrators must be careful that being politically correct or astute does not compromise their individual, institutional, or even societal values. As political considerations are different from institution to institution, and possibly even within the same institution, political matters will not be reviewed in any depth in the context of the practical issues discussed and suggestions offered in this book.

A DELICATE BALANCE

Today's university is not only about the search for truth but also about the continuing search for balance. The leaders of our institutions are constantly faced with balancing conflicting needs and values. Decision making would be easy if there were one right answer; what makes decision making difficult is that oftentimes there are a number of right paths, and an administrator may only be able to choose one, negating the needs of the constituencies that embrace the other paths.

Additionally, on a daily basis, the administrator must make decisions to meet institutional needs that can survive a legal challenge, model ethical behavior, and are practically possible. It is our hope that this book will clarify the issues to be considered and help readers with this challenging "balancing act."

ILLUSTRATIVE CASE

Following the practical suggestions in Chapters 2 through 8, the authors have included a case study that illustrates the balancing of the legal, ethical, and practical dimensions of a situation related to the topic of the chapter. A description of the situation is followed by an analysis that applies the three dimensions to the issue at hand, approximating what takes place in the complex world of decision making.

NOTES

1. Richard L. Morrill, "Academic Planning: Values and Decision Making," in *Ethics and Higher Education*, ed. William W. May (New York: American Council on Education, Macmillan, 1990), 70.

2. Francis Oakley, "Apocalypse Now in U.S. Higher Education," *America* 160, no. 12 (April 1, 1989): 286–287, 308.

3. Jonathan D. Fife, foreword to *The Leadership Compass: Values and Ethics in Higher Education*, by John R. Wilcox and Susan L. Ebbs, ASHE-ERIC Higher Education Report No. 1 (Washington, DC: George Washington University, School of Education and Human Development, 1992), xvii.

4. Joseph N. Hankin, "Academic Scruples: Faculty and Personnel Issues," in *Dilemmas of Leadership: Decision Making and Ethics in the Community College*, ed. George B. Vaughan (San Francisco: Jossey-Bass, 1992), 109.

5. John R. Wilcox and Susan L. Ebbs, "Promoting an Ethical Climate on Campus: The Values Audit," *NASPA Journal* 29, no. 4 (1992): 256.

6. Wilcox and Ebbs, supra note 3, at 75.

7. Donald Kennedy, *Academic Duty* (Cambridge, MA: Harvard University Press, 1997), 21, 62.

8. Ibid., 22.

9. Roger B. Winston, Jr. and J. C. Dagley, "Ethical Standards Statements: Uses and

Limitations," in *Applied Ethics in Student Services*, ed. Harry J. Canon and Robert D. Brown (San Francisco: Jossey-Bass, 1985), 49–53.

10. Charles H. Reynolds and David C. Smith, "Academic Principles of Responsibility," in May, 45–47.

11. Lawrence K. Pettit, "Ethics in the University" (speech presented at the annual meeting of the Academic Affairs Resource Center, 1990), ED 328 169, 4.

12. James B. Tatum, "The Importance of Ethics in Good Administrative Practices," in Vaughan, 205.

Chapter 2

Hiring Issues

The hiring of competent faculty and administrators is crucial to a college's or university's success in accomplishing its primary purposes. It is the faculty who provide the teaching, service, and research that are the institution's raison d'être. In order to properly blend and focus the talents and abilities of its faculty and staff to best meet the needs of the institution, colleges and universities must seek to hire persons who not only are qualified to provide teaching, service, and research, or administration but also have personal goals and abilities that meld with those of the student body, other faculty, and the institution as a whole. The challenge of finding the right person for the job is formidable in view of these goals and the constantly changing legal, ethical, and practical constraints within which hiring choices must be made.

LEGAL PARAMETERS

College and university employees and potential employees are protected from discrimination in hiring and employment by federal, state and local statutes and regulations. Employees and potential employees of public postsecondary institutions also have constitutional protection from discriminatory treatment in employment. This section will focus on the protection against discrimination afforded by the federal statutes that predominate in the employment arena.

- **Colleges and universities hire individuals without regard to race, sex, religion, or national origin.**

Title VII Coverage

Title VII[1] is the major federal antidiscrimination in employment law. In 1972 it was made specifically applicable to colleges and universities and forbids discrimination in hiring, in termination, and in the privileges, terms, and conditions of employment based on racial, religious, sexual, or national origin. It also includes protection from harassment based on race, religion, sex, or national origin and from retaliation for filing a charge of discrimination. In addition, the prohibition on sexual discrimination includes discrimination based on pregnancy.

Educational institutions owned (in whole or substantial part), supported, controlled, or managed by a particular religion are exempted from the prohibition on discrimination on the basis of religion. Other institutions of higher education may discriminate on the basis of religion in hiring personnel for a curriculum that teaches a particular religion.[2] In such an instance, religion is deemed to be a "bona fide occupational qualification" (BFOQ).[3] Sex, age, and national origin can also be BFOQs if the employer can demonstrate that the requirement is a qualification for the position and necessary to the operation of the business.[4] Basing such a requirement on a stereotype, past experience, commonly held ideas (e.g., women are not strong enough, or a woman would not be taken seriously in this position), or the preferences of coworkers or customers will not be sufficient to conform with the law.[5] Since BFOQs constitute an exception to Title VII, they are carefully scrutinized by the courts and narrowly applied.[6] Whether a requirement is a BFOQ depends on the facts of the situation at hand. In one case, for example, based on concerns about rape, females were excluded from employment as prison guards, where they would have contact with sex offenders.[7] In an another case, however, it was decided that females as well as males could work in the male section of a jail.[8]

Title VII Enforcement. Title VII is enforced by the Equal Employment Opportunity Commission (EEOC).[9] An aggrieved individual must file a charge against the employer with the EEOC within 180 days after the discriminatory event (300 days if the claim is also within the jurisdiction of an agency enforcing a local or state law prohibiting discrimination) before pursuing the matter in court.[10] The EEOC can investigate, conciliate, and issue a "right to sue" letter to the claimant.[11] Where there has been a finding of reasonable cause to believe that Title VII was violated, the EEOC may, in individual cases or cases of systemic practices of discrimination, elect to file suit itself.[12] As part of the enforcement process, institutions of higher education, unless they are exempt religious institutions,[13] are required to keep information necessary for the completion of an EEOC-6 form and to file this form with the EEOC biennially.[14] The EEOC-6 tracks the numbers of employees in various positions in the institution by race/ethnicity and gender.

Disparate Treatment and Disparate Impact. Title VII protects employees and prospective employees from both disparate treatment and disparate impact discrimination. In disparate treatment discrimination, an individual is treated differently because of his or her membership in a particular group. In disparate impact discrimination, a facially neutral policy or procedure has a disproportionate impact on a protected group.[15] For example, having height or weight standards that are not essential to the safe performance of the job might screen out a disproportionate number of Hispanics, Asians, or women.[16]

Interviews that Conform to Title VII. Questions addressed to prospective employees on applications and in interviews should avoid eliciting information not directly related to the performance of the job and that, if used as the basis of a decision not to hire, would be discriminatory under Title VII. Obvious examples of questions to avoid include those about religious affiliations, birthplace, or plans to have children. Additionally, tests and educational requirements that are not reasonable measures of job performance can also be deemed discriminatory.[17]

Remedies. Remedies for violations of Title VII can include backpay, affirmative action measures, attorney's fees, reinstatement, and compensatory and punitive damages for disparate treatment (limited by the size of the employer), among other things. The goal of the courts is to make the injured party whole. Although courts have been reluctant to substitute judicial judgment for that of the institution in tenure and promotion issues involving academic matters and subjective judgments, when these decisions have been reached in a fair manner,[18] some courts have awarded tenure[19] and promotion[20] upon a determination of discrimination.

Title VI Coverage

Title VI of the Civil Rights Act of 1964 as amended (Title VI)[21] also prohibits colleges and universities that receive federal funds for employment (such as funds for student work-study programs) from discriminating in employment on the basis of race, color, or national origin.

The ban on discrimination under Title VI applies to the entire educational institution and not just to the program or programs receiving the federal financial support. The remedy for violation of this law is the loss of federal funding for employment. The Office of Civil Rights (OCR) enforces the prohibitions of Title VI in educational institutions.

The Equal Protection Clause

The Equal Protection Clause of the Constitution (the Fourteenth Amendment) provides employees of public institutions with additional protection from discrimination on the basis of race or gender. The discriminatory practice challenged must, however, be intentional.[22] The protection offered is most useful in areas not otherwise covered by federal statute.[23] Claimants must institute a court action to enforce this constitutional right.

Section 1981

The Civil Rights Act of 1866 (Section 1981)[24] guarantees the right to make and enforce contracts regardless of race and consequently addresses discrimination in hiring on the basis of race. This law was traditionally applied to ongoing employment as well as to the employment contract (hire). In 1989 the Supreme Court limited its application to the employment contract.[25] The Civil Rights Act of 1991, however, reestablished the application of this law to ongoing employment as well as to the initial employment contract. When applicable, plaintiffs may choose this act as a basis for a suit rather than Title VII because it provides a two-year period in which suit may be filed and it does not limit damages.

Title IX

Title IX of the Education Amendments of 1972[26] extends its protection against discrimination on the basis of sex to persons in any educational program or activity receiving federal financial assistance.[27] It currently covers the entire institution and not just the specific program receiving the federal financial assistance[28] and applies even if the aid is received indirectly.[29] Title IX is enforced by the OCR of the Department of Education.[30] The remedy in the statute is a denial of federal funding.[31] The Supreme Court has, nonetheless, held that students have an implied private right of action under Title IX[32] but has not yet addressed the question of whether employees in educational programs also have a private right to sue for discrimination in employment. Most courts that have addressed this question have held that employees charging discrimination in a private suit must bring their actions under Title VII, not Title IX,[33] unless the employee is claiming retaliation for upholding the requirements of Title IX.[34] Where a private suit is permitted, damages may be recovered.[35]

Executive Order 11246

Executive Order 11246 (EO 11246), as amended, prohibits federal contractors with contracts of $10,000 or more from discriminating on the basis of race, color, religion, national origin, sex, or disability. Federal contractors with contracts of $50,000 or more and 50 or more employees are also subject to affirmative action requirements under EO 11246. These requirements are discussed later in this chapter. EO 11246 is enforced by the Office of Federal Contract Compliance Programs (OFCCP) of the Department of Labor.

Other Statutory Protection

Under the Public Health Service Act, sex discrimination in employment in health training programs is prohibited when it would have the effect of making admissions to these health programs similarly discriminatory.[36]

Pursuant to the Emergency School Aid Act, funds can be withheld if teacher assignments have a disparate impact on racial minorities.[37]

In addition to these and other federal laws that prohibit discrimination in hiring, there are also state local laws that similarly prohibit discrimination in hiring.

- **Individuals may not be discriminated against in employment on the basis of disability. Institutions receiving federal financial assistance also have an affirmative obligation to employ and advance the employment of qualified disabled persons in programs receiving such support.**

The Americans with Disabilities Act

The Americans with Disabilities Act (ADA) of 1990,[38] which is generally applicable to employers of 15 or more, and Section 504 of the Rehabilitation Act of 1973, as amended,[39] which is applicable to certain federal contractors and recipients of federal financial assistance, prohibit discrimination in employment against handicapped/disabled individuals. To be in compliance with these laws, the highest or most demanding standard is the one that must be met. Affirmative action to recruit and hire the disabled is required of certain large federal contractors under Section 503 of the Rehabilitation Act of 1973.[40]

Under the ADA, colleges and universities may not discriminate against a qualified handicapped/disabled person in regard to employment, including application procedures and hiring practices, advancement, termination, compensation, training, and other terms, conditions, and privileges of employment.

A *disabled individual* is defined under the ADA as an individual with a physical or mental impairment that substantially limits one or more of his or her major life activities; a record of such impairment; or being regarded as having such impairment. Some impairments (i.e., cancer, AIDS [acquired immunodeficiency syndrome], dyslexia) are not visible. Temporary impairments such as flu or a broken bone are not disabilities under the law. Persons currently using illegal drugs are not protected under the ADA. However, rehabilitated drug addicts are protected as having a record of impairment. Alcoholics are considered to be disabled, but they must conform to workplace rules regarding the use or influence of alcohol and may be appropriately disciplined if they do not.

The employer must provide reasonable accommodations to assist disabled persons in the hiring process and/or employment if the accommodation permits the individual to apply for the position or perform the essential functions of the job. Consideration is given to the employer's judgment about what functions are essential to a position, and a written job description is considered evidence of the functions deemed essential. Accommodations such as providing access, obtaining or modifying equipment, or job restructuring are reasonable if they do not cause the institution undue hardship. *Undue hardship* is defined as significant difficulty or expense, determined by the practical and financial impact of the accommodation on the institution in view of its overall financial resources, the size of its workforce, and the nature of its operation.

The ADA prohibits medical examinations or inquiries about the disabilities of applicants for employment. The institution may inquire, however, about the ability of an applicant to perform the job. After an offer of employment is made, it may be conditioned on a medical examination if all entering employees are required to take this examination, and the results are filed in a separate medical file and kept confidential. The only persons who may view the medical file are (1) supervisory personnel or managers who must be advised of work restrictions or other necessary accommodations; (2) health and safety personnel, when and if special treatment is necessary; and (3) governmental officials investigating compliance with this law. Individuals who present a significant threat to the health or safety of others that cannot be ameliorated by an accommodation need not be hired. For example, someone disabled as the result of a disease that could be transmitted through food handling may be denied employment as a food handler, and someone with a muscular impairment who could not use dangerous machinery safely, even with an accommodation, could be denied a position operating that machinery.

Qualifications and standards used to hire or evaluate performance that screen out or deny a benefit to a disabled individual must be job related and a business necessity that cannot be met by the disabled individual with a reasonable accommodation.

The ADA is enforced by the EEOC.

Sections 503 and 504

Under Section 504 of the Rehabilitation Act of 1973, institutions receiving federal funds must not discriminate against qualified individuals with disabilities. This prohibition applies to the entire institution even though the funds may be directed only to certain facilities or programs.[41] Under Section 503 of the Rehabilitation Act, federal contractors with contracts worth $10,000 or more must employ and advance in employment qualified individuals with disabilities.

Enforcement. Section 503 of the Rehabilitation Act of 1973 is enforced by the OFCCP of the Department of Labor. Section 504 is enforced by the federal funding agency that provides financial assistance. For institutions of higher education, the 504 agency would be the OCR in the Department of Education. Where a complaint under Section 504 is solely for discrimination in employment and the EEOC would also have jurisdiction to investigate the discrimination under the ADA, the Department of Education must refer the matter to the EEOC unless the complainant specifically requests that the Department of Education conduct the investigation.[42]

There are also state and local laws addressing discrimination against the disabled.

- **Colleges and universities may not discriminate against individuals in employment on the basis of age.**

The Age Discrimination in Employment Act (ADEA) of 1967, as amended, protects workers age 40 and over from discrimination in employment and from mandatory retirement, with exceptions for certain executives and persons in high policy-making positions. Compulsory retirement is permitted for persons who have been employed for at least 2 years as an executive or in a high policy-making position and whose annual pension benefit will exceed $44,000 upon retirement. The applicable definition of *executive* is published in the Federal Code of Regulations for the Wage and Hour Division.[43]

Until 1993, tenured faculty were protected from mandatory retirement until the age of 70. Now this act provides unlimited protection against mandatory retirement for tenured faculty. The ADEA is enforced by the EEOC.

The Age Discrimination Act of 1975 protects employees in institutions receiving federal funds from discrimination based on age. The entire institution is covered by this protection, not just the program receiving the funds. A violation of the act may result in the withdrawal of federal funds from the institution.

There are also state and local laws that prohibit discrimination based on age.

- **Colleges and universities that are federal contractors with 50 or more employees and federal contracts of $50,000 must implement written affirmative action plans under EO 11246, the Rehabilitation Act of 1973, and the Vietnam Era Readjustment Assistance Act of 1974.**

Executive Order 11246, as amended, requires that employees of federal contractors with contracts valued at $10,000 or more be protected against discrimination based on race, color, religion, sex, and national origin. It also requires that nonconstruction contractors with 50 or more employees and contracts worth $50,000 or more write affirmative action compliance programs to ensure that individuals in protected categories are not underutilized and are provided with equal opportunity. A supporting regulation (41 C.F.R.60–1.5(a)(5) is directed at exempting religiously oriented church-related colleges and universities from the equal opportunity clause of the order.

An affirmative action program should (1) contain a statement of equal employment opportunity policy; (2) designate those responsible for the program's implementation; (3) establish procedures for internal and external dissemination; (4) include a utilization analysis to identify areas in which women and minorities are underutilized; (5) establish goals for job groups in which underutilization has been found; (6) identify problem areas; (7) implement programs to eliminate problems and reach goals; (8) audit affirmative action efforts for effectiveness; (9) monitor for compliance with sex discrimination guidelines at 41 C.F.R. Part 60–20; (10) support programs to provide equal opportunity in employment to women and minorities; (11) recruit outside the workforce for women and minorities with the requisite skills; (12) compile and maintain support data for the affirmative action program; and (13) update the program annually.[44]

The Rehabilitation Act of 1973 and the Vietnam Era Readjustment Assistance

Act of 1974 also require written affirmative action programs. These can be separate plans or integrated into other affirmative action programs. The regulations describing the requirements for these affirmative action efforts can be found at 41 C.F.R. 60–741.44(a)–7.41.44(j) and at 41 C.F.R. 60–250.44.

- **Under Title VII, courts may order affirmative action as a remedy in cases involving discrimination.**

Courts have ordered affirmative action based on race under Title VII where it was shown that the employer discriminated in the past on the basis of race.[45] Court ordered affirmative action must be narrowly tailored to accomplish its remedial objective.

- **Recent developments in the law of affirmative action in admissions as well as employment suggest an erosion of the employer's ability to undertake voluntary affirmative action. To avoid violations of Title VII and/or the Equal Protection Clause of the Constitution (in the case of public employers), race- or gender-based preferences in employment must be carefully evaluated for compliance with increasingly strict and changing requirements. Past decisions under Title VII required a private employer to demonstrate that its affirmative action addressed a manifest racial/gender imbalance in a traditionally segregated job category and that its action was temporary and did not unnecessarily trammel the rights of the nonminority population. Race-conscious affirmative action survived a challenge under the Equal Protection Clause of the Constitution when there was a compelling governmental interest, and the action chosen was narrowly tailored to address that interest. Gender-conscious affirmative action survived a challenge under the Equal Protection Clause of the Constitution when it served an important governmental interest, and the action chosen was substantially related to meeting that interest. Current cases indicate a change of attitude toward any race-conscious decisions.**

In the landmark case of *United Steelworkers v. Weber*, decided in 1979, the Supreme Court determined that voluntary affirmative action based on race did not violate Title VII where (1) there is a manifest imbalance; (2) the plan to remedy the imbalance does not unnecessarily trammel the interests of the majority employees; and (3) the plan to remedy the imbalance is temporary in nature.[46]

Based on *Weber*, a voluntary affirmative action plan by a public employer considering sex as a factor in promotion was upheld by the Supreme Court in

1987 against a Title VII challenge because there was a "manifest imbalance," even though there was no specific evidence that the public employer had discriminated in the past on the basis of sex, the plan did not trammel the rights of male applicants for promotion, and the plan was a temporary measure.[47]

Public employers' affirmative action plans can be held to constitutional standards in addition to Title VII. In *Wygant v. Jackson Board of Education*, a challenge was made under the Equal Protection Clause of the Constitution to the race-conscious affirmative action of the Jackson Board of Education, a public employer, which resulted in teacher layoffs in the majority (white) population. The Supreme Court found that affirmative action was permissible when it met a strict scrutiny standard—that is, there is a compelling governmental interest and the race-conscious affirmative action is narrowly tailored to achieve the compelling objective. The Court found that the general societal discrimination cited was not sufficiently compelling and that the matching of minority teachers to minority children, also cited, was not narrowly tailored enough to justify race-conscious layoff decisions. The layoffs were, therefore, deemed to be a violation of the Equal Protection Clause of the Constitution. The Court stated that overcoming a history of discrimination would have been deemed a sufficiently compelling objective.[48]

The Court reaffirmed the strict scrutiny standard in *City of Richmond v. J. A. Croson.*[49] Although this was not an employment case, it demonstrated the Court's approach to affirmative action issues. In this case, the City of Richmond had an affirmative action plan that provided that 30 percent of its construction contracts be set aside for minority businesses. The Court found that there was no evidence of discrimination in the city's construction industry (general societal discrimination is not sufficiently compelling), and the plan was not narrowly tailored to reach its objective.

In *United States v. Paradise*,[50] the Court upheld a lower court order for a 50 percent quota requirement on the promotion of blacks to the position of corporal in the Alabama Department of Public Safety. The pervasive, systematic, and long-standing discrimination in the Department of Public Safety was deemed a compelling interest, and the plan developed to remedy the discrimination was held to be narrowly tailored to the objective. The plan was temporary and flexible and sought a quota properly related to the numbers of blacks in the workforce. In addition, the plan did not place an unacceptable burden on white applicants for promotion. On the other hand, the Fourth Circuit found no compelling interest in an employment case based on a desire for diversity that was not essential to law enforcement.[51]

Equal Protection challenges to gender-based affirmative action plans by public employers require that the action meet an intermediate standard of scrutiny. The affirmative action must serve an important governmental objective and be substantially related to the achievement of that objective.[52]

In *Adarand Constructors, Inc. v. Pena*,[53] the Supreme Court held that racial classifications in all federal programs must meet a strict scrutiny standard to withstand a constitutional challenge. Previously, congressionally mandated preferences were held to a lower standard.

In *Taxman v. Board of Education of Township of Piscataway*,[54] the Third Circuit struck down the Board's affirmative action plan, which led to the termination of a white teacher and retention of an African American teacher where both had the same seniority and both were qualified. In light of recent cases eroding affirmative action in admissions,[55] and fearing a decision in this case that would weaken affirmative action and set a precedent, the case was settled before the Supreme Court could hear it on a petition for certiorari.[56]

The law of affirmative action for public and governmental employers is in flux. The full impact of cases in the late 1990s and the changing attitudes toward affirmative action are not yet clear.

- **Colleges and universities that are federal contractors must employ and advance qualified disabled and specially disabled veterans and veterans of the Vietnam era. Institutions may not discriminate in employment based on past, present, or future military obligations.**

Federal contractors with contracts of $10,000 or more are required to take affirmative action to employ and advance qualified disabled veterans and veterans of the Vietnam era and report annually on the numbers of each employed.[57]

Uniformed Services Employment and Reemployment Rights Act of 1994[58]

Discrimination by an employer of any size based on a person's service in the uniformed services of the United States is prohibited in hire, reemployment, retention, promotion, or a benefit of employment.

- **Deliberations and evaluations of a search and screen committee may not be shielded from discovery by the EEOC in its investigation of a complaint of discrimination.**

The deliberations of a search and screen committee, typically used in the hiring of faculty and administrators for a university, have no special protection from examination by the EEOC. If the request of the EEOC for records of the deliberations and/or decisions of the search and screen committee are relevant to a determination of discrimination in hire, they must be produced to the agency for examination.[59]

- **Under the Immigration Reform and Control Act of 1986 (IRCA), employers may not hire aliens who are not authorized to work in the United States. However, discrimination in hiring or discharge against those lawfully**

able to work on the basis of national origin or citizenship is prohibited.

Employers must verify the ability of alien employees to work legally in the United States by checking certain specified documents and attest to this verification on a form provided for this purpose by the attorney general of the United States. This form must be retained and made available for inspection. To avoid discrimination against all aliens as a result of these requirements, IRCA also prohibits discrimination in recruitment and hire, referral for a fee, or discharge. Employers of three or fewer employees are exempted. In addition, it is not a violation of the act to prefer a citizen when that is required by law or when the citizen is equally qualified.

• **An action for negligent hiring might be maintained against an institution that did not conduct a careful screening of applicants.**

Although care must be taken not to raise the specter of discrimination in hire by investigating factors with little or no relationship to job performance, it is equally important to conscientiously determine that a potential employee does not present a danger to fellow employees or students.

Case law in various state jurisdictions has established a duty of employers to protect others from employees it knew or should have known were a danger to others at the time of hire. In *Tallahassee Furniture v. Harrison*,[60] the employer did not have the employee fill out a job application. The employee had a prior criminal conviction as well as mental illness and drug abuse problems. When this employee assaulted a customer, the employer who had not made reasonable efforts to check on the employee's background was held liable.[61]

In cases in the education setting, many courts have agreed that in the proper circumstances an educational institution can be liable for negligent hiring. The Alabama Supreme Court, in examining a case where a professor murdered a student, stated that the issue for the court to determine was whether it was foreseeable that the professor would commit a murder while working for the university. The court found no substantial evidence that would have put the university on notice about the professor and consequently found in favor of the university.[62] In *Hamburg v. Cornell*,[63] the court affirmed the obligation of the institution to perform an appropriate investigation of its instructors and professors, although it, too, found that the plaintiffs had failed to show negligence on the part of the institution.

In some states, public educational institutions that are performing a function provided for by law are immune from liability for negligent hiring.[64] Also, in some jurisdictions, private institutions that are charitable corporations may be immune from liability to students for negligent hire as well as for the negligent acts of their teachers under the doctrine known as *charitable immunity*.[65] In other jurisdictions that recognize the principle of charitable immunity, negligent hire is an exception to charitable immunity for which the school could be held liable.[66]

- **Deliberations of the search and screen committee in public universities may not be confidential in states with open government laws.**

Several states have open government laws that may give the public the right to examine records of a search and screen committee in a public institution. The Florida Supreme Court held that the University of Florida was a state agency that was not exempted from the Sunshine Act by any legislative enactment. The Sunshine Act asserts that all meetings of a state agency in which official acts are taken are public meetings and must be open to the public at all times. The actions of the search and screen committee at the University of Florida were deemed official actions because this committee could eliminate candidates from consideration. Therefore, the committee's meetings had to be open to the public.[67]

- **State and local laws may extend the protection against discrimination beyond the categories protected by federal law.**

State and local laws may extend prohibited discrimination to cover categories not protected under Title VII and other federal legislation. These additional protected categories may include marital status and sexual orientation.

- **In addition to the federal, state, and local laws that regulate the employment of faculty and staff, employment is regulated by the contract between the institution and the faculty or staff member.**

The terms of a contract between the faculty or staff member and the institution will govern the employment relationship, unless the contract term is in violation of applicable law.[68] Questions arising about a contract are examined under state law and can vary to some degree from state to state.

Among others, issues have been litigated regarding whether particular oral or written statements constitute a contract or part of the contract with the employee;[69] whether institutional governance documents, policies, or guidelines are part of the contract;[70] and what was intended or what is customary where no contractual language was provided.[71]

When a written contract is provided, the courts will defer to the expressly stated terms of the contract.[72]

ETHICAL CONSIDERATIONS

In addition to the many legal requirements that must be met in the hiring process, there are many decisions that are ordered by the institution's values. The selection of staff is, by its nature, a reflection of the goals and priorities of the institution.

- **Whose interests should the selection of a new hire serve? What is the relationship of these interests to values?**

Each of the institution's major constituencies (students, faculty, administration, staff, community) may have differing priorities and preferences in hiring. For example, when selecting a new faculty member, the students may wish the person who can give the best instruction; the institution may be seeking someone of outstanding reputation and research skills; and the faculty may be most interested in finding a colleague who will be supportive or provide a specific expertise. Each hire has to be examined against a backdrop of these complementary and conflicting needs. Sometimes one set of interests will dominate; other times the choice of new hires will be based on a blending of interests. If, however, a choice between competing interests must be made, it should be based upon an assessment of the university's basic values and with a knowledge of the consequences. Examples of values that could conflict with other institutional priorities are respect for the needs of the individual versus meeting institutional needs, academic excellence versus efficiency/expediency, openness versus expediency, or commitment to the common good versus meeting the needs of an individual.

- **Should a vacancy be filled through an employment search or an appointment by an administrator of someone he or she already knows?**

Once a decision to fill a position has been made and the needs to be met by the new hire have been determined, the administrator must decide the best method for identifying and hiring a new or replacement person. In the absence of legal, collective bargaining, and/or institutional parameters regarding whether to make a "direct appointment" (a term usually used to describe a noncompetitive appointment not preceded by an open search) or to establish a "search and screen" committee and process, it is important to take into consideration the questions raised by each alternative.

A direct appointment by one or two decision makers may avoid a costly and time-consuming process and reward a deserving or long-term employee. This may certainly be the best alternative (for practical reasons) for temporary, adjunct, acting, or interim positions. It can, however, also be subject to charges of favoritism or influence or poor judgment and result in a failure to find the best person available. It also curtails input from affected constituencies who would be members of a search committee and therefore places the judgment of one person (the sole administrator making the appointment) over the collective wisdom of stakeholders who would be involved in the search. Therefore, if an institution values input from diverse perspectives and a participatory process, a direct appointment may not address those requirements. Fairness may also be at issue, as a direct appointment denies other individuals both inside and outside the institution an opportunity to compete for the position.

An open search conducted by a committee charged with finding one candidate—or a short list of candidates—for an open position (search and screen process) is less likely to be biased than an appointment. It will, however, be a more expensive and time-consuming alternative and may or may not reap the "best" person available. Search and screen committees remain a respected tradition in higher education for selecting regular faculty and administrators. Direct appointments, when acceptable under university policy, are still a viable option but could raise doubts about the fairness of the hiring procedure.

- **Should an advertised search and screen process be held for a vacant position when the inside or interim candidate is the one most likely to be chosen, provided there is no legal or regulatory requirement to conduct such a search?**

Ethical and practical questions are raised when an inside or interim candidate is almost certainly the hiring choice, but the institution goes through the motions of a search. Why search if the choice has already been made? The answer to this query may be: (1) the hiring administrator may be procedurally or legally required to implement a search; and/or (2) it may be politically expedient to do so. In these instances, a "sham" search may be implemented, often without taking the unsuspecting search and screen committee into the administrator's confidence. Sham searches raise questions of truth and fairness to the committee and candidates, as well as efficiency in the use of institutional funds that would be wasted on advertising and on the search process.

- **Should the institution reveal to outside candidates the existence of internal or "favorite" candidates?**

Other than public institutions who must adhere to open government statutes, institutions must make decisions about when and how much to reveal about the number and identity of the candidates during the selection process.

Many administrators report that once prospective candidates know that there is an inside candidate, they may be deterred from applying even if the insider is one who is not desirable and who would not get the job. Absent a direct inquiry to which a response must be made, should an institution reveal that there are inside candidates? If the institution is certain that they are ready to commit to the insider, then revealing the presence of an inside candidate may prevent misleading others. On the other hand, revealing that there is an inside candidate when there is no clear intent to hire the inside person may reduce the pool of available qualified candidates and therefore may not serve the institution or the candidates fairly.

• Should a salary range be revealed in the advertisement or posting?

A cursory scan of *The Chronicle of Higher Education* and other publications advertising faculty and administrative salaries reveals that salary ranges, although often mentioned in advertisements for faculty positions, are seldom published for administrative jobs. The reasons for not mentioning salary, or publicizing only "competitive salary" in general terms, may be practical ones. For example, there may be regulations applicable to the content of the advertisement, or salary may in many cases vary commensurate with experience, or there may be room for salary or rank negotiations between the candidate and the institution. In some cases, however, it may not be the institution's policy to divulge such information in an advertisement but rather to wait until final candidates are identified and the negotiation process has begun. Some institutions feel that since they want to attract the best candidates, publicizing a salary range may limit the range of candidates or even attract a lower-quality pool. Nonetheless, unless the institution is willing and able to go beyond the salary level set for the position, this policy may be ethically questionable. It may seriously mislead candidates and cause both the institution and the candidates to expend time, money, and effort in a search and interview process that will not succeed. Final candidates may be forced to reveal to their present employers that they are seeking employment elsewhere, not knowing that the salary available at the institution advertising the position would not be acceptable to them. Omitting salary information may be as important as omitting a part of the job description. Administrators may need to discuss the purpose and ethics of omitting any variable of the job description.

• What issues should govern decisions on the composition and duties of the search and screen committee?

A search committee that includes minorities is more likely to balance any bias or appearance of bias that might exist against minorities in hiring and act as a shield against charges of discrimination. Administrators should consider appointing a hiring committee that reflects gender, race, national origin, and religious diversity and that represents the various interest groups that may have a stake in the hire.

The number of members on the committee and the nature of the individuals (i.e., the group[s] they represent) may vary from institution to institution. This composition may be different even between institutions in the same system and just a few miles apart. For example, one institution may include a number of African Americans, whereas another whose constituency is mostly of Hispanic origin would do well to include several individuals from the latter group. Additionally, the key consideration for administrators in appointing committee members is determining who should have input into the selection decision. This determination should be guided by the degree to which the institution values openness, diversity, and equality of access. For instance, a search committee for a president could include representatives from all of the constituencies affected by that position, such as students, faculty, staff, and midlevel administrators and not just members from the board of trustees (as superordinates to the president) and vice presidents (as immediate subordinates). The inclusion of students and staff in search committees for other lower-profile but nevertheless key positions, for example, faculty and administrators, is usually a matter of choice, arrived at more often as a reflection of the institution's values than from practical considerations.

Finding individuals who can be impartial and objective should also be a goal when making selections for the search and screen committee. Individuals harboring biases or championing self-interests could compromise the process and taint the very essence of the exercise. Other qualities that should also be expected from a search committee member are competence, integrity, discretion, and availability.

- **How can the integrity of the search and screen process be protected?**

Recommendations made by the search committee or firm should carry weight with the decision makers if they are to expect that employees within the institution and candidates continue to cooperate with the search and screen process in the future. A search that reflects a commitment to truth, fairness, and consistency is one in which the expectations of the institution are clear and where the institution follows its own guidelines as well as those imposed by the external world.

- **How can the administrator balance the interests of the institution with fairness to the candidates when checking references?**

Employment references are required in order to verify the truthfulness of the candidates' assertions and to shed additional light on the qualifications, character, and performance of those applying for a position. The very act of calling references or current supervisors, however, will reveal to an institution that its employee is considering employment elsewhere. Candidates, therefore, expect that such inquiries will wait until the person becomes a final or semifinal candidate and that they would be asked if there is any reason why the hiring institution should not contact the present employer, or others, if those persons are not listed as references. Candidates who do not wish certain persons to be contacted should state the reasons, and the prospective employer must decide whether to continue their candidacy. Although there may be valid reasons for a request not to contact certain persons, candidates should supply alternatives and be willing to accept the consequences that their refusal could cause. The ethical dilemma in keeping the candidacy confidential is that it may be fair to the candidate at the cost of fairness to the candidate's present institution or to the hiring institution. This question should be discussed and resolved at the time the search and screen committee is given its charge.

When asking questions to elicit the information for the hiring institution, it is advisable to do so from an agreed-upon list so that the same questions are asked of all persons contacted, depending, of course, on their relationship to the candidate.[73] This procedure enhances fairness because it facilitates accurate comparisons among candidates.

- **How much should the job candidate be told about institutional, departmental, or personnel problems?**

As candidates seek to portray themselves in the best possible light, so should the institution. Where, however, is the line between "putting your best foot forward" and misleading the candidate to the candidate's and the institution's detriment? Administrators should carefully consider the reasons for withholding information regarding the health of the institution or the department or about personnel problems that the successful candidate will encounter upon his or her arrival at the institution.[74] Such decisions should be made after analysis of the values they reflect. Openness, or the lack thereof, at this incipient stage of the relationship between the candidate and the employer may establish a pattern for their future relationship.

- **How important is confidentiality within the search committee process?**

How much confidentiality is due the candidates? Provided there are no statutory provisions against it (such as open meetings/open records statutes), maintaining confidentiality in the search process should be a reflection of the institution's value judgment on this question.[75] If the hiring institution discloses the fact that the candidate has applied to those with no need to know or before a short list is developed, this may result in negative or embarrassing consequences to the candidate who is still employed elsewhere. However, disclosure may provide an opportunity for wider input on campus. The administrator must consider the impact of the choice made on the community, its institutional reputation with faculty and potential faculty, and its reputation for inclusiveness, among other things.

Many institutions that maintain confidentiality do so for ethical as well as practical reasons. By withholding public announcements until after the finalists are told that disclosure is imminent, the university is supportive of candidates' needs to keep their candidacy confidential until the last stages of the selection process and to advise their current supervisors regarding their candidacies before they hear the news elsewhere. On the practical side, early disclosure can scare candidates away. In certain searches, such as those for a president, a search committee leak that makes a candidate's name public may result in the withdrawal of good candidates.[76] Confidentiality can also impact the quality of the search committee discussions by allowing for more open exchanges among committee members.

Whatever position the institution takes on revealing candidates' names, general information regarding the search can be provided and serve the interests of inclusiveness and quality decision making. Information such as the type of committee or search firm utilized, approximate timetable for hiring, and the structure of the process itself could be items to be shared. It may also be advisable to solicit nominations from within the institution as well as from the outside and to provide a mechanism for general input. Examples of such input from those not on the search committee are: (1) defining qualities and skills to be listed on the job description and (2) filling out a feedback form after attending an open session to meet and hear the candidate.

Confidentiality should be a topic of discussion with the search committee or firm at the very onset of the search process.

• What are the ethical implications of hiring relatives?

Colleges and universities as well as business and industry seek to avoid *nepotism*, which is defined as favoritism based on kinship. They usually adopt policies which prohibit an individual from having supervisory status over another person who is part of his or her family. The reason for these policies is clear: They seek to discourage any favoritism or the appearance of favoritism in the workplace based on familial relationships. Nepotism raises questions about whether workload distribution is fair and equitable and whether performance evaluations are just and impartial. Some colleges and universities, however, allow husband and wife, a team of siblings, or a parent/child combination, for example, to work in the same institution unless one of them must report to the other person.

In the absence of policies or regulations on this issue, the institution should utilize caution, studying carefully the possible consequences of allowing the hiring of relatives within the same unit, either with supervisory capacity or without.

- **To what extent should keeping professional couples together be a consideration in hiring?**

A recent development in higher education, and one that occurs with increasing frequency, is the "transplanting" of the two-professional family.[77] In such cases, both husband and wife may be in higher education. If the wife, for example, is offered a position in a different institution and city, and the family does not wish to be divided by distance, she may not accept the new employment unless her spouse can also be employed in the same institution.

Some institutions are finding that a written policy regarding *preferential* hiring of spouses is needed. Should an institution create such a policy or practice? The desire to keep a family together or to get the candidate selected should be balanced against having a level playing field in the selection for the position the spouse wishes and also vis-à-vis issues raised by having family members employed by the same institution.

PRACTICAL SUGGESTIONS

An institution can prepare for conducting a lawful, ethical, and cost-effective hiring process. Among the steps the institution may take are the following.

- **Before a position is posted or advertised, an institution should review all organizational and budget considerations to ascertain the continuing need for the position. A further consideration is the practicality of hiring on an interim or acting basis if the need to fill the position is pressing.**

In order to fill a new or vacant position, the first responsibility of the institution is to ascertain that the position is needed or, in the case of a replacement, is *still* needed. In this age of necessary "reengineering" and "downsizing," an unexpected position opening may bring an opportunity to assess the structure of the department, reorganize duties among positions, or recraft entire departments and reap the cost savings the unfilled position will generate. Needless to say, strategic long-range planning should not be sacrificed for opportunities at short-term savings. The goals of the institution and department, as well as immediate practical concerns such as office space and the budget available for salary, benefits, travel, equipment, secretarial help, and other ancillary needs, must enter into a final decision that takes the "whole" into consideration, rather than a single piece out of context with the rest of the organization.

Hiring freezes have become a common practice in higher education, especially in the last ten years. Most freezes, however, make allowances for the filling of positions that are considered crucial to the operations of the institution. When a position is vacated, the hiring administrator(s) should review the organizational structure and assess the continuing need for the position, and if a hiring freeze is in place, the administrator must determine whether the position is among those considered essential.

Once the decision to fill a new or vacant position has been made, the next consideration is how long the position can remain vacant. An essential position, whether administrative or faculty, may be vacant for several months or even in excess of a year by the time a proper search and screen procedure is completed. Frequently, a search is unsuccessful, and thus the position must be readvertised and rescreened. Therefore, consideration should be given to whether or not a person should be appointed to serve on an interim or acting basis prior to establishing the search. The budgetary burden that hiring an interim individual will create may be balanced against the hardship that would befall the institution and its constituents if the functions of the position were not discharged for an indeterminate period of time. Other considerations in making an interim appointment are: Is there a qualified internal or external candidate available to perform the functions of the position on an interim basis? Will the institution allow the interim appointee to apply for the permanent position? (If this is not allowed, it should be made a condition of an individual's accepting the interim appointment.) What should the process of making the position permanent be (appointment after a period of time, or search and screen process)? Are there other issues to consider, such as morale of the unit, grant or contract requirements, or change in administrative structure?

If an interim or acting appointment is decided upon, the parameters of the job should be clearly set forth and communicated and agreed to by the candidate(s) before an appointment is made. In some cases, the institution may wish to institute a rule that acting/interim appointees are not to apply for the permanent position. This step may be taken when a governing board or administrators want to make it clear that the interim person will not be the one selected or to "free" the interim appointee to perform the duties of the acting position without having to play the politics involved in candidacy. If the decision to keep interim appointees from applying for the permanent position is made, it should be made known to the candidates for the interim position before they apply.

- **Under certain circumstances, practical considerations may justify a direct appointment in lieu of a search process.**

As mentioned in the ethics section, direct appointments without an advertised search are more cost-effective and speedy for the institution and may be an adequate method of filling adjunct or temporary positions.

Direct appointments are often used when making a temporary, interim, or acting appointment. Direct, acting, or interim appointments are more common for administrative positions than for faculty positions. Faculty positions, however, can be filled by adjunct or temporary instructors appointed on a one-academic-year contract basis. Such direct temporary appointments ensure that the functions of the positions are not interrupted and allow the department and institution, as well as the interim or temporary employee, to experience the "fit" between the person and the requirements of the position. The temporary arrangement usually reveals the level of competence and compatibility the temporary employee has with his or her colleagues, students, and the goals of the institution and department.

A temporary appointment for longer than one year may affect morale and call into question the stability of the department or institution. Interim/acting or temporary appointments may be followed by a formal or informal search and screen within a year or less, or a direct permanent appointment should be made public if the position is to be retained. However, direct permanent appointments to full-time positions, especially if made frequently, may be problematic and should be considered carefully.

- **The use of a search consultant or firm may be advisable for certain types of employment searches.**

A relatively recent development in higher education is the use of professional search consultants or firms. Numerous institutions are utilizing these services, especially for high-level administrative positions (e.g., presidents, vice presidents, deans).

The role of the professional consultant or search firm may vary. Some institutions may utilize a consultant in conjunction with an internal search and screen committee, who still deliberates and renders the recommendations for a candidate or candidates. A professional search firm may enhance the process in several ways—for example, conducting "focus groups" throughout the institution in order to elucidate the qualities really needed or desired in the position; composing the advertisement or posting; advising search and screen committees on the screening process; and recommending candidates.

The institution must make a decision to use either a search committee from within the institution to provide greater involvement by those on the inside or an outside search firm that will bring expertise that the search committee may not have. The university will need to balance the value of inclusion against the benefits and costs of hiring the outside search firm. Although the costs of retaining a professional search firm are usually clear, institutions often fail to take into consideration the time and effort expended by their own search committees. If a fair comparison is to be made, the latter must be made quantifiable. An additional consideration is the experience the search firm brings to the task versus the experience (or lack of experience) the internal search committee has in conducting effective searches. The importance/value of the position to the institution is often the deciding factor when the institution opts to spend additional dollars to achieve a more professional and smoother search process.

- **Clear job descriptions should be composed before the hiring process is begun.**

A common but potentially costly error that institutions make is the failure to develop clear job descriptions for existing and new positions. Many institutions do not keep job descriptions on file for some positions, and even when they do, they are neither clear, updated, nor comprehensive.

To enable the institution to hire a qualified disabled person who is able to perform the essential functions of the position with or without an accommodation, and to effect a good match between a candidate and the position, it is imperative to know what is expected of the person who occupies the position. In fact, a clear job description may make the difference in attracting or repelling the right candidates for the position.

Clear job descriptions have several characteristics in common. They will (1) identify the duties and functions to be performed, distinguishing between those that are essential and those that are auxiliary or optional; (2) list qualifications and experience the institution feels are reasonably necessary to perform the job; (3) identify hierarchical structures, that is, reporting relationships to and from the position; (4) specify the terms of the positions, for example, tenured, tenure- or nontenure earning, administrative with faculty or without faculty appointment, one-year or multiple-year rolling contract, position contingent upon special (such as grant or contract) funding, and so on; and (5) include a salary range and the bargaining unit (if any) by which the position would be governed.

If the position is an existing one, it is advisable to review the job description on file for that position carefully to pinpoint any changes that need to be made to conform to reality or to reflect other changes that may have occurred in the organization. Consequently, it is recommended that the date the job description was last revised be included (for internal purposes) in the document.

Even when the position is not newly created, a job analysis, identifying the skills, abilities, and knowledge necessary to perform the job, should have preceded the development or review of the job description. In fact, an annual job analysis is an advisable practice in order to prevent outdated job descriptions that could lead to denying a job or appointing a candidate based on invalid criteria.

- **Advertising considerations include when and where to advertise and how to craft a clear, concise, and informative advertisement.**

Public institutions may have internal guidelines and requirements to meet in advertising positions. Once these have been met, the institution may decide whether to simply post the position internally or whether to advertise locally, regionally, nationally, or internationally.

To maximize the possibility of obtaining numerous quality responses to an advertised position opening, a carefully crafted advertisement should be placed in the right places, at the right time. What will determine the right places will depend on the type of position opening. For example, if the opening is for a faculty position, the best places to advertise will depend on the discipline in which expertise is sought. In addition to the popular and widely read *Chronicle of Higher.Education*, the institution may choose to place an advertisement in the publication of a particular professional association representing that discipline or in a minority publication. Likewise, advertisements or notices of position openings for administrative positions may be placed in professional association publications, such as newsletters or other print or electronic media. Active recruitment for both faculty and administrative positions may be strengthened by the attendance of university representatives (possibly search and screen committee members) at conferences or organization meetings locally, regionally, nationally, and internationally.

To reach minority candidates, the institution could advertise in publications with a minority orientation (e.g., *Black Issues in Higher Education*), correspond with graduate schools that are known for their production of minority graduates, or send representatives to discipline-specific conferences and meetings where caucuses or interest groups (e.g., National Association for Women in Education) come together.

The timing of the advertisement may be more important for faculty positions than for others because faculty normally sign contracts for one or several academic years in the spring, and the fall term is traditionally the best time for a faculty member to start a new position. To some extent, this may also be the case for administrative positions, although administrators tend to have more flexibility, especially if they are not engaged in teaching. To hire for fall semester, as an example, the hiring administrator must "work backwards" and calculate how long the hiring process will take. Once this has been accomplished, the advertisement may be placed, allowing a few weeks for potential candidates to respond. For a fall hire, an ad placed during the winter term would certainly allow enough time for the faculty member to be identified and for that person to give notice to his or her present employer, if applicable. No matter what the timing of the placing of the advertisement is, it is crucial to establish a time line for the entire hiring process as soon as the decision to hire is made.

The advertisement should be composed by the hiring administrator and/or the search and screen committee and should include clear, concise information about the following topics: (1) the name and a short description of the institution and of the department, division, school, or unit in which the faculty or administrator will be employed; (2) enough of the job description so that the duties and responsibilities, academic background and/or experience required and preferred, and hierarchical relationships will clearly depict what is expected of the successful candidate; (3) the level and terms of the position (e.g., tenure-track or tenure-earning, senior-level management); (4) salary range (usually optional—see discussion under "Ethical Considerations"). The advertisement may also indicate whether the position is a new one, whether the search has been reopened, and the fact that the institution is an equal opportunity employer and will make special accommodations for disabled persons. Legal counsel should review and approve the advertisement format for appropriate language.

- **For some positions, consideration should be given to including a salary range in the advertisement or posting.**

When possible, clear and complete information should be provided to prevent potential candidates from being misled or from wasting time and effort and the institution from expending funds and employee hours in inviting and interviewing candidates when the salary being offered is out of the range those candidates are willing to consider. If the institution's salary offering is absolutely fixed with no room for negotiations, or if the salary and fringe benefits offered are not within the average range for a similar position in the same type of institution, it may be preferable to state the salary range in the advertisement, thereby eliciting a more realistic pool of candidates. To the candidate, "the sooner *is* the better" as far as knowledge of expectations goes, and the final round of interviews may be regrettably late to discuss such an important topic.

If the institution cannot find the right person, or if desirable candidates will not accept the position for the salary being offered, the hiring administrator may be faced with a decision to reopen the search. If the first search has uncovered highly qualified candidates who would not accede to come to the institution for the salary range opened, the institution may wish to consider including the salary range in the advertisement for the reopening of the position.

- **Opening the search process to minority candidates and constituting a diverse search and screen committee are administrative steps which help meet the legal requirements for nondiscriminatory hiring and support the institution's values.**

If usual search procedures do not normally yield a pool that contains minorities, the institution should examine its job-posting practices. The human resources department may be involved in developing or helping implement a plan or specific suggestions for reaching a broader pool of candidates. Recruitment efforts geared at attracting minority candidates must be proactive and planned. Some of these initiatives are mentioned in previous sections (see "Advertising considerations" earlier in this "Practical Suggestions" section).

- **The composition and role of the search and screen committee are important practical considerations.**

In addition to desired racial and gender balance on the search committee to avoid even the appearance of bias, the person or persons appointing individuals to the group may wish to include representatives of the various constituencies affected by the position. Search and screen committees might have representatives from the faculty, administration, student body, and trustees. Within each classification, representatives from a particular discipline, department, or area of interest might be sought, depending on the type of position being screened. Many institutions want those affected by the position to be represented on the search committee. For example, in searches for faculty positions, institutions may include administrators, students, and faculty from other departments along with the peer faculty from the hiring department who are certain to be included. For administrative positions, a more diverse grouping may be included. For an academic dean, for example, a committee may consist of a peer dean, the dean of student affairs, two or three faculty members, one or two department/division chairpersons, an administrator who will work cooperatively with the dean, and a secretary.[78] Depending on the level of the position, even trustees of the institution may be called upon to serve.

Important considerations are also the competency, integrity, professionalism, and availability of each of those named to the committee. The search committee and the manner in which the search process is conducted will invariably be perceived as representative of the personnel of the institution and the professionalism and quality of its operations. Hence, it is incumbent upon the institution to select conscientious, committed, and enthusiastic individuals who will conduct the search process in a professional manner and who will represent the institution in its best light. Members of the search committee may be appointed by an administrator or elected by groups identified as part of the committee (e.g., from among faculty, administrators, staff, students, board members, alumni, or community groups). The size of the committee may vary, depending mostly on the type and level of the position. Whereas the selection committee size for a faculty position may be small (3–5 members), the search committee for a presidential, vice presidential, or deanship position may be as large as 25 members. To keep confidentiality (if required or desired) and congeniality high, it is generally recommended to keep search committees as small as possible while still being representative of the desired constituencies.[79]

Other determinations needed are the level and amount of involvement the committee should have in the screening process, in the interview process, and in the final decision making. Search and screen committees often have an advisory role, making recommendations on a candidate or candidates to an administrator or group such as the board of trustees.

Once the administrator has decided the parameters of the involvement of the search committee, these should be made clear to prospective committee members. Some of the appropriate questions to answer in clarifying the committee's role are:

- Will the committee be involved in developing the job description of and/or the advertisement for the position?
- Will the committee be involved in the initial screening of candidates' applications and

materials to determine that minimum qualifications are met, or will the initial screening be done by others, such as the human resources department or the Office of Equal Opportunity?

- Is the committee's role in final decision making solely advisory?
- To whom should the final recommendations be directed?
- How many candidates may be on the final list of recommendations?
- Should the list be unranked or ranked?
- Should the committee submit the rationale for its decision(s)?
- If the committee is not successful in selecting suitable candidates, is a recommendation for readvertising the position possible?
- What are the budget parameters for the search?
- What is the time line desired for submission of the final recommendations?
- Will the deliberations of the committee be open to the public?
- How will the committee handle the press, inquiries from the general public, and inquiries from within the institution?
- Which is the appropriate stage to announce the names of finalists or semifinalists?
- Whose responsibility are reference checks?
- In addition to the committee, who should be included in the interviews?
- Who contacts the final candidate(s)?
- Who announces the results of the search after the successful candidate has accepted?

The charge to the committee by the hiring administrator or responsible party may be given to the search group verbally or in written form. Although the charge most often centers around the role of the committee, it should also include clarification and/or further details on the advertisement, the job description, the elements of the desired "fit" between the candidate and the position (which may not be included in the advertisement), and any other information that will help the committee find a successful match. For example, hiring administrators may wish to share their preference for candidates with a certain work or management style that will match (or complement) the superordinate's or subordinates', a preferred type of personality, or a proven commitment to the goals of the institution or unit. These attributes may or may not have been listed in the advertisement but, in the case of candidates with like qualifications, may become the basis of selection decisions.

- **The efficiency and quality of the hiring process may be enhanced by the creation of a manual for search and screen committees.**

Clear, written guidelines for search and screen committees can help them function more efficiently. These may be provided in a memorandum on the topic, or they may be included in a handbook or manual. The topics covered may range from the general to the specific and may include the following:

- Policies and procedures of the search process (e.g., nondiscrimination policies, philosophy of hiring practices, often provided by the institution's human resources office)
- Steps of the search process (e.g., composing the advertisement; review of résumés and/ or job applications; checking references; arranging for preliminary, phone, and face-to-face interviews; communications with applicants; the interview process; making the employment offer; negotiating employment terms)
- Charge to search committee
- Required paperwork throughout the process
- Suggestions for reviewing résumés and transcripts
- Basic legal and ethical issues (e.g., acceptable/unacceptable questions to ask of candidates and their references, confidentiality, role of affirmative action)
- Sample forms, sample interview questions, rating sheets, and the like
- Confidentiality policy (an oath of confidentiality may also be included if required/ desired)[80]

- **Background checks, when accomplished timely and with care, may save an institution time, effort, and funds.**

Searches for faculty and administrative positions in higher education have increasingly become national in scope. Consequently, the expense associated with bringing candidates in to campus or the employment location for personal interviews can be substantial. It is customary for an institution to pay for a candidate's travel and lodging. Depending on the position that is open, the institution may offer other courtesies, such as paying for an accompanying spouse or allowing an extended stay beyond the interview date so that the candidate may investigate real estate possibilities in the area. Multiplying the expenses of the numerous searches that colleges and universities perform annually can be a sobering experience. Therefore, in order to limit the field of candidates, and to pinpoint a better match between the candidate and the individual institution and department before extensive expenditures are made, telephone interviews with the references of the candidates on the "short list" or semifinalists (as well as preliminary interviews with the candidates themselves) are not only practical but essential.

Once an institution has considered the legal and ethical aspects of reference checks carefully, some practical matters need to be decided. Among them: (1) who will do the reference checks (e.g., search and screen committee member or members, human resources/personnel office, hiring administrator); (2) who will compose the questions to be asked; (3) whether all references will be checked; (4) whether people other than those listed as references by the candidate will be contacted; (5) whether the questions to references will be in writing, or verbal, or both; and (6) who will be privy to the results of the reference checks. The following are suggestions for reference checking that will help avoid possible future difficulties:

- Notify the candidate(s) who are being considered when reference checking will be performed. If the candidate has not listed any references or omitted superordinates from the candidate's current or past institution/employment, ask the candidate if there are any reasons why he or she does not want this contact to be made. The candidate may have valid reasons and should have an opportunity to express them.

- Honor a candidate's wishes to receive correspondence at his or her home instead of at the present employer's and/or not to contact the present employer as a reference unless the applicant is a finalist. If a candidate's wishes cannot be honored, the hiring institution should so notify the applicant as soon as possible after the receipt of the request.

- Provide a guide to acceptable and unacceptable questions to be asked of references.

- Write the questions to be asked of the reference even if the reference check is via telephone.

- Ask the same questions of all references; avoid sharing information already received from others.

- If you spot-check references, decide in advance what the process for spot-checking will be and be consistent in its application. Some of the options for spot-checking include checking only references from the candidate's current institution (or, if unemployed, last employing institution); checking professional references but not character references listed; checking two out of five references listed; and so on. Once the committee has identified final candidates, it may wish to contact them for the ·names of particular types of references not on their original list (subordinates/ superordinates, peer, character references, etc.).

- As a general rule, do not ask a reference a question you would not ask a candidate in an interview.[81] Relate the questions directly to job performance and avoid extraneous topics.

- Consider the importance of confidentiality in the process and plan accordingly. Some institutions may decide, for example, to restrict the copying of candidates' application materials.

- **A vital part of the process is conducting a lawful and effective interview.**

An institution should consider consulting an attorney to perform an audit of the institution's interviewing as well as its hiring process and relevant documents. Guidance on what types of questions to ask and to avoid is needed even for experienced interviewers. As a general rule, ask only what you need to know to enable you to make a hiring decision. It is usually safer to avoid questions that, although not discriminatory in and of themselves, may elicit answers that could later lead an applicant to claim that the interviewee(s) used such answers in a discriminatory manner. Questionable issues/queries may include:

- *Physical characteristics.* Height, weight, sex, age (unless a bona fide occupational qualification), or plans to have children or condition of pregnancy
- *Credit and legal history.* Wage garnishments, arrest records
- *Family relationships.* Father's surname, maiden name (unless necessary to verify educational or employment experience), marital status, spouse's name, names and ages of dependents
- *Background.* Birthplace; birthplace of parents; native tongue; own or rent residence; foreign addresses; national, religious, or racial affiliations of schools attended; lodge, church, or club memberships (professional memberships related to the position are fine); names of priest, rabbi, or minister; national origin; lineage; or ancestry, race, color

Sometimes candidates will voluntarily reveal some of the foregoing "questionable" information in their résumés, cover letter, or interview. That is, of course, acceptable. However, even though the applicant may volunteer questionable information, the search committee/interviewer(s) should not allude to it. As a precaution, interviewers should keep notes of the interview, creating a record of questions asked, answers given, and the reasons for the choices made. Such notes should be kept for the maximum time allowed for filing a legal action for discrimination in hire under federal law or state law or for other employment-related actions.

The following are suggestions for the conduct of an effective face-to-face interview:

- The interviewers should review the résumé and all applicable documents before the actual interview, as it is distracting to the candidate to appear before unprepared interviewers who are reviewing the candidate's résumé while they are asking questions. Advance review of the résumé and other documents may help the committee compose questions related to clarification of the résumé or other documentation or experience.
- Interviews, especially by a group, are stressful situations even to experienced interviewees. Try to put the candidate at ease by starting on time, by introducing the committee members and their respective positions to the candidate at the beginning of the interview, and by maintaining eye contact throughout. When time permits, a brief interlude of casual conversation before the introductions will serve as an icebreaker, allowing the interviewee to relax and establish rapport with the committee. After the introductions, describe the agenda of the interview and about how long it will take. A review of the job description should also include an opportunity for the candidate to state if he or she can perform the basic functions of the position, with or without accommodations. The rest of the interview should focus on background and experience clarification, the behavioral questions agreed upon by the committee, and probing questions when the interviewee's answer is not complete.

- Every interviewee should be provided with information about the institution and the position at the actual interview, preferably before the interview itself.
- Allow the candidate to add information and to ask questions of the committee.
- At some point in the interview, mention what the next step in the hiring process will be and the time line for the next step(s).
- Thank the candidate for his or her interest in the institution. Committee members are acting as ambassadors for the hiring institution.
- Each committee member should make his or her own notes on each candidate. When interviewing several candidates for a position, it is easy to forget an interviewee's answers or to confuse candidates and attribute an answer to the wrong candidate.
- The committee should ideally meet immediately following each candidate's interview, but they must definitely do so after all candidates have been interviewed. At this time, committee members may share their notes, fill out relevant forms, rank candidates, and take the next step in their decision-making process. The committee may wish to meet personally with the hiring authority in order to share their rankings and final decisions, or their recommendation may be forwarded in writing to the individual who will extend the job offer or who gave the committee its charge.

If the interview is being performed by telephone or other electronic means, the search and screen committee member(s) who is (are) on the line with the candidate should always introduce others who are in the room. Most of the guidelines for a face-to-face interview apply, except that interviewers should be aware of the disadvantage created by the candidate's lack of visual cues from the committee and the lack of eye contact, which creates rapport. Phone interviews should be of a preliminary nature, utilized to narrow the field of candidates or to gather preliminary information. A face-to-face interview with finalists is crucial.

- **In addition to the interview by the search committee, other activities such as a simulated teaching situation (planned as for real students), as a demonstration of teaching ability, may prevent a "bad hire."**

For a faculty position, a simulated teaching presentation may be a great predictor of future success with real students. Whenever possible, this type of presentation by the candidate should be scheduled and observed by the search committee, faculty in the hiring department, faculty from other disciplines, and administrators. Some universities ask that the candidate present a scholarly paper to the faculty in the candidate's discipline at the hiring university. Although the latter type of presentation may demonstrate the candidate's substantive knowledge, it may be inconclusive as a reliable measure of teaching ability. Additionally, a narrow-focus presentation to scholars in a specific discipline may not reveal the candidate's full intellectual interests.

If the idea of well-rounded scholars is attractive to the college or university, then the committee and other faculty may inquire about candidates' interests outside of their own disciplines, as well as query candidates about their academic values, philosophy, and ethics.[82]

Interviews with individuals outside the candidate's discipline (if a potential faculty member) or department (if a potential administrator) should be included either on a group basis, on a social basis, or as a formal or informal process. All-day interviews with both faculty and administrative positions allow the candidate to meet with a variety of groups or persons, as well as with people who may be peers in the same substantive area.

Interviews for administrative positions may also be full-day affairs or longer, depending on the position being filled, and several activities, such as role-playing or presentations, may be valuable. If confidentiality is a key issue, preliminary or even final interviews for some administrative positions can be held away from the campus.

- **Clear and timely communications with all candidates is an important part of the screening effort. A letter of offer may follow a verbal offer to the successful candidate.**

The professionalism of the institution is often judged by the communication, or lack thereof, between the hiring party and all candidates for a position. Some important guidelines follow.

- The institution's representative may acknowledge receipt of the candidate's application, taking that opportunity to request missing or additional information, informing candidates of any statutory open government laws or institutional policies related to the search, and providing candidates with a short summary of the screening process and its time line. Some internal policies of institutions (especially public institutions) require that prior to the interviewing process the institution (through its offices of human resources, equal opportunity, or other designated department) "certify" the applicant pool for appropriate diversity on the basis of race, national origin, and sex. Candidates may be requested to complete specific forms for that purpose, but the search and screen committee is usually not made privy to the individual responses.

- The institution should honor the requests of a candidate as to where and how to communicate with him or her; many candidates indicate a preference to receive mail, telephone, and facsimile communication at their residence rather than their workplace.

- Candidates who do not meet the minimum qualifications should be advised of this determination in writing as soon as possible.

- In the interest of time, candidates being offered a telephone and/or personal interview may be notified by telephone or electronic mail. This may be followed by written confirmation containing final details and a packet of information about the institution, school/department, and/or position.

- All unsuccessful candidates should be notified in writing. A personal telephone call to finalists, especially those who visited the campus, may be an appropriate gesture. When stating the reason why the applicant was not offered the position, a common and generally "safe" statement is that the position was offered to another individual "who was best suited for, or who best matched, the requirements of the position." The letter should convey the news in a brief, professional, simple, and upbeat manner, and the tone should be pleasant since the applicant's goodwill toward the institution is being tested. It is important to thank the candidate for his or her interest in the institution and in the position.

• The successful candidate may be contacted by telephone or other means to convey the good news and possibly to negotiate the terms of the offer, such as salary, fringe benefits, and moving expenses. It is advisable to follow any oral communication with a letter of offer outlining the agreed-upon terms. The letter of offer may precede the contract or letter of appointment, or a letter of offer itself may serve as evidence of an appointment. The written offer may be made contingent upon receipt of final documents, such as official transcripts, and/or the candidate's meeting legal requirements (such as an I-9 to live/work in the United States or medical/physical fitness for the position). A deadline for receipt of written acceptance by the candidate of all the terms of the offer should be set by the institution and communicated to the candidate.

• The concluding step of the hiring process is producing a clear contract.

If the contract for the employment of a new faculty member or administrator is specific and comprehensive, it is less likely that there will be a misunderstanding of the nature of the obligations of either party to the agreement and less likely for a controversy to arise.

Institutions should, as a preliminary step to developing a contract of employment, be clear about the nature of the appointment and what they expect from the faculty member or administrator. Legal counsel should be consulted in the development of a contract that is binding and that contains the provisions necessary for your institution. A list of items to consider for inclusion follows:

• Rank and title

• Tenure earning/credit toward tenure

• Term of employment/renewal of term

• Compensation/benefits/facilities provided

• Obligations

• Termination of employment

• Conditions, if any

• Reservation of rights to change policies and procedures incorporated into the contract

• Policies and procedures (these may be incorporated by reference and can include conflicts of interest, who owns patents and/or copyrights, grievances, employment policies)

• The time period for acceptance of the offer

• Provisions provided by legal counsel to clarify and define the agreement
• Special conditions

ILLUSTRATIVE CASE

Description

Private University was not subject to a mandatory affirmative action plan. However, the dean of the School of Arts and Sciences (Sylvia Christie) and the department chairperson of the English Department (Wilbur Beck) agreed that the department's search for a much-needed replacement to fill a recently vacated faculty position should attempt to attract qualified minority applicants. The student body of Private University was 13 percent African American, 10 percent Hispanic, and 5 percent other minorities, yet none of the ten faculty presently in the institution were members of a minority group. In fact, the entire faculty body of Private University was only 7 percent minority (3 percent African American, 4 percent Hispanic). The duties of the faculty position included teaching freshman composition courses, and the department chair was adamant that minority role models were sorely needed in his department. The dean of Arts and Sciences had once been the only woman in the faculty in the English Department at coeducational Private University, so she knew firsthand the importance of mentorship and role models.

The university advertised in several sources nationwide, which yielded 36 applications. The dean had appointed a search committee consisting of two faculty members from the English Department, one faculty member each from the departments of Social Sciences and Philosophy, and Diana Feinberg, a full-time administrator who was a grant writer for the university. The administrator on the search committee was the only woman and the only minority on the committee. The department chairperson met with the committee shortly after the members were appointed by the dean, to give the committee members the "Guidelines for Search and Screen Committees" booklet that the university's Human Resources Department had recently published and to discuss with the committee the needs of the English Department, especially in the area of freshman composition. Since there was a member of a minority group represented on the committee, and because of the absence of an affirmative action mandate, the English Department chairperson did not mention his preference for minority candidates.

The search committee selected eight of the applications as outstanding, based on the criteria they had established. At a third meeting of the committee, a vote was taken to narrow the field to a short list of five candidates. At a fourth meeting, telephone calls to references listed by the applicants were placed, with the entire committee in attendance. Questions to references were asked by the chairperson of the search committee, Denis Mulder, a Chaucerian specialist from the English Department. Of the five candidates, three were selected to come for personal interviews on campus: one African American woman, one white woman, and a white man. Interviews were set up within a period of two weeks, with a one-day schedule that included breakfast with the English Department, an interview with the search committee, and individual interviews with the chairperson of the English Department and the dean of Arts and Sciences. A tour of the campus and a visit to the Provost's office were also scheduled, although the Provost did not usually interview the candidates. After lunch with the dean, the candidates were asked to make a 20-minute presentation to the English Department, although the chair of the search committee did not specify the topic or situation. The white woman candidate gave a mediocre, lackluster presentation in a monotone voice. The other two candidates presented scholarly papers of interest to department faculty.

After the candidates' visits to campus, the search committee met to decide on one or two names to recommend to the dean. The white woman was eliminated. The African American woman had an excellent professional background, having taught at a prestigious private university. The white male had taught at two large state institutions, one of them a community college. Both had degrees from well-known graduate schools and had achieved an "A" average in their academic work. They were currently employed as assistant professors with tenure-earning status in their respective universities. The white male had published one textbook on linguistics and three articles in refereed journals. The African American woman had published five articles in various journals and edited a book of poetry. The woman had written four grants, of which two were funded; the man had not indicated any grant-writing experiences.

Private University, although encouraging research in its faculty, prided itself on being a "teaching institution." Using this rationale, two members of the committee, one of the members of the English Department and the faculty member in Social Sciences, voted for the African American female. They felt her experience and her grant-writing abilities would serve the university well. The rest of the committee was undecided as to whom would be the best candidate. They felt that the man had more experience teaching composition courses similar to those he would be teaching at Private University. The search committee decided to submit the two names, ranked, with the white male as first on the list, to the dean.

The dean called in the English Department chairperson upon receiving the recommendation of the committee. While in that meeting, the only female member of the search committee had called the dean, and said she needed to speak to him urgently. Taking the call, Diana Feinberg, the woman grant-writer on the search committee, confessed to the dean that she knew the African American candidate, as they had gone to graduate school together. She chose to withhold that information from the committee and felt that she could be objective. However, she now felt that in her attempt to be objective she had judged the woman applicant too harshly, trying to compensate for her friendship. Her vote for the woman would have placed that female candidate first on the list. Now she felt that she would be responsible if the woman candidate were not hired. The female candidate had not acknowledged the woman on the committee as an acquaintance at any time. The female committee member was upset that she allowed herself to stay on the committee after she saw that her friend was a candidate.

Feeling that the process had been tainted, the dean and the chairperson selected the white male to fill the position.

Analysis

• **Meeting the requirements of law.**

While the case illustration discusses the race and sex of the applicants and the need for diversity at Private University, there is no indication that the selections of the search committee or the final selection by the dean was made with race or sex or other prohibited considerations in mind.

Should race- or sex-conscious hiring decisions have been made under the circumstances described in the illustrative case? It is likely that the university was in compliance with the law when it made hiring decisions without regard to race or sex. The facts do not indicate that the university was ordered by a court to give racial or gender preferences in hiring. The case also indicates that the university was not required by law or regulation to have an affirmative action plan. The remaining question is whether voluntary affirmative action by Private University was permitted pursuant to Title VII. Although the law of affirmative action is not entirely clear and is changing, voluntary affirmative action plans under Title VII have been upheld when they were temporary, attempted to address a manifest imbalance between the numbers of minority workers available in the market and the numbers employed in the job category, and did not unnecessarily trammel the rights of the majority or create an absolute bar to majority workers. The facts of the case provide no information on a manifest imbalance between the market and the workforce. Unless such a situation exists and the plan to address it has the necessary characteristics, race- and sex-conscious hiring are probably not permissible.

Although there is no indication of racial or gender bias in the search committee, the committee was overwhelmingly composed of white males. Since a white male candidate was ultimately selected, there is the possibility of charges of discrimination. It would have been in the university's best interests to have a more diverse committee so that bias, if any, was balanced, and there would be no appearance of discrimination.

The facts do not reveal where the advertisement for the position was placed. Placement in publications that reach qualified minorities would be a further indication of providing equal opportunity. Placement in publications that are not widely used or seen by minorities may be deemed to cause discrimination by adverse impact rather than by direct intent.

• **Ethical considerations.**

There is a recognition by the dean and chair of the English Department that efforts should be made to attract qualified minorities, yet there is no evidence that this translated itself into appropriate action. The search committee was not constituted to reflect diversity, and there was no discussion of the need for diversity or the methods that might be employed to attract minority candidates.

In the matter of the qualifications for the position, there was general agreement on the qualifications needed, but there was a difference of opinion on value or importance of particular qualifications. Two members of the search committee chose the African-American female applicant because of her grant writing experience. Two other members of the committee were uncertain about their priorities, but favored the male applicant with directly applicable teaching experience, and one (the female member of the search committee) had other motives for her selection of the male applicant, which will be discussed below. The narrative implies that the search committee discussed these competing considerations and made a knowing selection of the male applicant on this basis.

Diana Feinberg, the female member of the search committee, indicated that she voted against the female applicant with the strong grant-writing background in a flawed attempt at objectivity. She felt she had been unduly harsh because the candidate was a friend from graduate school. The result was that the male candidate was first on the list sent to the dean.

On being advised of this situation, the dean felt that the process had been tainted. It had indeed. The impartiality and objectivity of the search member with prior, unrevealed knowledge of the candidate were compromised. She viewed the candidate she knew with a different standard than the one she applied to the other major contender for the position. Further, it provided her with information on which to base her decision that was not available to the other search committee members. Clearly, it was not an evenhanded process. The female search committee member should have immediately revealed her prior acquaintance with the candidate and recused herself. The committee could then have made a judgment about how or if her additional information might be fairly used in the selection process.

Putting the vote of the female committee member aside, the search committee was evenly divided on the ranking of the candidates submitted to the dean and chairperson for final selection. The dean and chairperson selected the male applicant, not on the ground that they believed him to be the better candidate but on the ground that the process had been tainted with regard to the female applicant. Although it is not specifically stated, it is likely that in addition to the tainting of the process by Feinberg's failure to reveal her past association with the candidate, the female candidate's failure to acknowledge this relationship was also deemed to have tainted the process and was central to the decision to choose the other candidate. Both had deceived the others and put their ethics and integrity in question.

If the process was tainted, was it appropriate to make *any* selection as a result of the process? One might argue that if the full story had been known, or the female search member not been part of the selection process, a different list of eight, five, and then three candidates may have been chosen. In fairness to the candidates, and to protect the integrity of the process, it probably would have been better to begin again, inviting all who participated, except the female finalist, to reapply.

It is not uncommon for candidates to ask that their identity and application be kept confidential and that current employers not be asked for references unless the applicant is under serious consideration. The knowledge that an employee is looking elsewhere can impact current working relationships negatively. In the case discussed, the search committee's reference check was held when the field was narrowed to five candidates. Being in the final five is certainly being in serious contention for the position. Could the reference check have been delayed until the field was narrowed to three? The answer lies in the balance between a desire to impact the current working situation of the fewest number of candidates, the importance of the information from references in further narrowing the field from five to three, and the expenditure of time and money needed to bring someone to campus whose references may reduce his or her chances of being hired.

• **Practical considerations.**

In the case before us, there was a clear need to fill the vacancy in the English Department. The needs of the position were discussed with the search committee, but no written job description appears to have been provided. It is also not clear that the search committee was told or reached consensus on the relative importance of the various tasks to be performed by the new hire. It would be in the institution's best interests to provide a job description and in so doing to define the essential tasks of the position (including the relative importance of each task). Such a job description could be of help in determining whether a disabled person is otherwise qualified to perform the essential functions of the position, with or without an accommodation. It can also be of help in deciding which candidate would best serve the institution because that candidate's background is more in line with the prioritized needs of the position. It is additionally helpful in advising the candidates about what will be expected of them at Private University.

We are not told where and when the university advertised the position. These decisions impact the number, diversity, and quality of the responses and should be considered carefully.

As previously mentioned, the diversity of the search committee is of importance in guarding against bias in the process. The composition of the search committee is also important in bringing in the points of view of those in the university who will be impacted by the new hire. The best person is more likely to be chosen if those who are aware of the need impact the process. The composition of this search committee appears to have been lacking in diversity.

Time was taken to acquaint the search committee with the needs of the English Department and the attributes of a well-conducted, professional search. The actions of the search committee (except those of the female member) reflect this education in conducting a search. The committee was able to move from a pool of 36 applicants to a short list of 2 for presentation to the dean and chairperson of the department without any problems in division of responsibility or communication about what was expected of them. The written handbook provided on the search process was an excellent practical aid in accomplishing this result.

NOTES

1. Title VII of the Civil Rights Act of 1964, as amended, 42 U.S.C. §§ 2000e et seq.
2. 42 U.S.C. 2000e-2(e).
3. *Pime v. Loyola University of Chicago*, 585 F. Supp. 435 (D. Ill. 1984).
4. 42 U.S.C. 2000e-2e(1).
5. 29 C.F.R. 1604.2(1).
6. *UAW v. Johnson Controls*, 499 U.S. 187 (1991).
7. *Dothard v. Rawlinson*, 433 U.S. 321 (1977).
8. *Collins v. Robinson*, 734 F.2d 1321 (8th Cir. 1984).
9. 29 C.F.R. 1601.1.
10. 29. C.F.R. 1601.13.
11. 29. C.F.R. §§ 1601.15, 1601.24, 1601.28.
12. 29. C.F.R. 1601.27.
13. Exempt religious institutions are those in which the institution has the status of a church and the faculty fit the definition of ministers. *EEOC v. Southwestern Baptist Theological Seminary*, 485 F. Supp. 255, aff'd in part, rev'd in part 651 F.2d 277, cert. denied, 456 U.S. 905 (1982).
14. 29 C.F.R. 1602.50.
15. *Zahorik v. Cornell University*, 729 F.2d 85 (2nd Cir. 1984).
16. *Dothard*, 433 U.S. at 321.
17. See *United States of America v. State of South Carolina*, 445 F. Supp. 1094 (D.C. 1977), aff'd, 434 U.S. 1026, 98 S.Ct. 756 (1978).
18. *Green v. Board of Regents, Texas Tech University*, 474 F.2d 594 (5th Cir. 1973).
19. *Brown v. Trustees of Boston University*, 891 F.2d 337 (1st Cir. 1989), cert. denied, 110 S.Ct. 3217 (1990).
20. *Kunda v. Muhlenberg College*, 621 F.2d 532 (3rd Cir. 1980).
21. Title VI of the Civil Rights Act of 1964, 42 U.S.C. 2000d.
22. *Personnel Administrator of Massachusetts v. Feeney*, 442 U.S. 256 (1979).
23. William A. Kaplin and Barbara A. Lee, *The Law of Higher Education: A Comprehensive Guide to Legal Implications of Administrative Decision Making*, 3rd ed. (San Francisco: Jossey-Bass, 1995).
24. 42 U.S.C. § 1981.
25. *Patterson v. McLean Credit Union*, 491 U.S. 164 (1989).

26. 20 U.S.C. § 1681 et seq.
27. 34 C.F.R. Part 106.
28. Civil Rights Restoration Act of 1987, 20 U.S.C. 1687.
29. *Grove City College v. Bell*, 465 U.S. 555 (1984).
30. See *Franklin v. Gwinnett County Public Schools*, 112 S.Ct. 1028, 1032 (1992).
31. 20 U.S.C. § 1681 et seq.
32. *Cannon v. Univ. of Chicago*, 441 U.S. 677 (1979).
33. *Cooper v. Gustavos Adolphus College*, 957 F. Supp. 191, 193 (U.S. D.Ct. 1997).
34. E.g., *Lowrey v. Texas A & M University*, 117 F.3d 242, 250–254 (5th Cir. 1997).
35. *Gwinett*, 112 S.Ct. 1028 (1992).
36. 42 U.S.C. § 294 et seq.
37. *Board of Education of City of New York v. Harris*, 444 U.S. 130 (1979).
38. 42 U.S.C. §§ 12111–12117.
39. 29 U.S.C. §§ 701 et seq.
40. 29 U.S.C. § 793.
41. The Civil Rights Restoration Act, 20 U.S.C. § 1687.
42. 29 C.F.R. § 1640.6(c).
43. 29 C.F.R. § 1625.12(d)(I).
44. 41 C.F.R. 60–2.1(a)–2.14.
45. *Local 28 of the Sheet Metal Workers' International Assn. v. EEOC*, 478 U.S. 421 (1986).
46. See *United Steelworkers v. Weber*, 443, U.S. 193 (1979).
47. *Johnson v. Transportation Agency*, 480 U.S. 616 (1987).
48. *Wygant v. Jackson Board of Education*, 476 U.S. 267 (1986).
49. 488 U.S. 469 (1989).
50. 480 U.S. 149 (1987).
51. *Hayes v. North State Law Enforcement Officer's Association*, 10 F.3d 207 (4th Cir. 1993).
52. *Mississippi University for Women v. Hogan*, 458 U.S. 718 (1982).
53. 515 U.S. 200 (1995).
54. 91 F.3d 1547 (3d Cir. 1996) (en banc).
55. See, e.g., *Hopwood v. State of Texas*, 78 F.3d 932, cert. denied, U.S. (1996). (The Fifth Circuit held that any program of admission that relied even in part on race as a criterion was a violation of law.)
56. "Settlement Prevents Supreme Court from Hearing Key Affirmative Action Case," *Chronicle of Higher Education*, December 5, 1997, A48.
57. Vietnam Era Veterans' Readjustment Assistance Act of 1974 (38 U.S.C. § 4212).
58. 38 U.S.C. 4301 et seq.
59. See *University of Pennsylvania v. EEOC*, 493 U.S. 182 (1990).
60. 583 So.2d 744 (1st Cir. 1991).
61. Id. at 752.
62. *Copeland v. Samford University*, 686 So.2d 190, 193 (Ala. 1996).
63. 240 N.Y. 328, 148 N.E. 539 (1925).
64. See, e.g., *Everhart v. Board of Education*, 108 Mich. App. 218, 310 N.W.2d 338 (1981).
65. *Schultz v. Roman Catholic Archdiocese*, 95 N.J. 530, 472 A.2d 531 (1984).
66. See, e.g., *Yost v. Texas Christian University*, 362 S.W.2d 338 (C. App. 1962).
67. *Wood v. Marston*, 442 So.2d 934 (1983).

68. *Subryan v. Regents of the University of Colorado*, 698 P.2d 1383 (Colo. Ct. App. 1984).

69. *Lewis v. Loyola University of Chicago*, 500 N.E.2d 47 (Ill. Ct. App. 1986).

70. *Brady v. Board of Trustees of Nebraska State College*, 242 N.W.2d 616 (Neb. 1976).

71. *Greene v. Howard University*, 412 F.2d 1128 (D.C. Cir. 1969).

72. *Billmyre v. Sacred Heart Hospital of the Sisters of Charity*, 331 A.2d 313 (Md. 1975).

73. James Thomas, "Ethics and Methods of Employment References," *ACA Bulletin* 80 (April 1992): 19–22.

74. Marcie Kingsley, "Honest Hiring: What Should We Tell Job Candidates About Personnel Problems?" *Journal of Library Administration* 14, no. 3 (1992): 55–63.

75. Judith Block McLaughlin, "Plugging Search Committee Leaks," *AGB Reports* 27, no. 3 (May–June 1985): 24–30.

76. Ibid., 24–25.

77. Donald Kennedy, *Academic Duty* (Cambridge, MA: Harvard University Press, 1997), 32.

78. John F. Cooper and John F. Garmon, *Personnel Selection: The Holistic Approach* (1990), ERIC ED 321 794.

79. Ibid.

80. A note of caution: If assurance of confidentiality of candidates is desired, it is often prudent to restrict the copying of candidates' application materials. For example, rather than duplicating all of the candidates' résumés for each member of the search committee to keep in his or her possession, the résumés and accompanying materials may be made available in a central office for the committee members' perusal on an as-needed basis.

81. Dennis R. Black and Matt Gilson, *Perspectives and Principles: A College Administrator's Guide to Staying Out of Court* (Madison, WI: Magna Publications, 1988), 72–73.

82. Steven M. Cahn, *Saints and Scamps: Ethics in Academia* (Lanham, MD: Rowman & Littlefield, 1994), 75–76.

Chapter 3

Compensation and Employment Issues

The compensation and other employment terms provided to faculty and administrators can impact their contentment and the quality of their performance, which can in turn affect the ability of the institution to fulfill its mission. Compensation and employment terms can also raise legal, ethical, and practical questions for the institution.

LEGAL PARAMETERS

- **Colleges and universities may not discriminate in compensation because of race, sex, religion, national origin, age, veteran status, disability, or other classification protected by federal, state, or local law.**

The strictures against discrimination in employment contained in Title VII, Title VI, Title IX, the Constitution, the Civil Rights Act of 1866, the Americans with Disabilities Act, Section 504, the Age Discrimination in Employment Act, 38 U.S.C. §§ 4212 and 4311, and Executive Order 11246, and state and local laws prohibiting discrimination which were discussed in Chapter 2, apply to compensation as well as to hiring.

- **Male and female employees hired to do the same work, requiring the same skill, effort, and responsibility under the same conditions, must be paid the same salary.**

While Titles VII and IX make it unlawful to discriminate on the basis of sex in employment, the Equal Pay Act[1] specifically makes it unlawful to pay a person of one sex less than a person of the opposite sex for the same work, requiring the same skill, effort, and responsibility under the same conditions. Statutory exceptions to the same-pay requirement are (1) a seniority system and (2) a merit system, that is, a system where earnings are determined by quality or quantity or a system where the differential is based on something other than sex. A good deal of controversy has revolved around whether differentials can be explained by sex-neutral factors such as market forces or rank or whether these factors are themselves the result of sex discrimination. Some factors that courts have found to account for differentials in pay without violating the law are (1) superior credentials and annual performance evaluations;[2] (2) merit, market forces, and matching salary offers of other institutions;[3] and (3) previous experience.[4]

When pay differentials were cast as merit based but relied on informal evaluations that were unsystematic and subjective, they were held to be a violation of the Equal Pay Act.[5] Well-thought-out evaluation procedures and careful records are helpful in defending against charges of a violation of the act.[6]

Although the Equal Pay Act is part of the Fair Labor Standards Act (FLSA) and has basically the same coverage as that act,[7] the responsibility for enforcement of the Equal Pay Act was transferred from the Department of Labor to the EEOC in 1979.[8] The EEOC has, however, retained the Department of Labor's procedures and requirements with regard to enforcement of the Equal Pay Act.[9]

- **Academic and many administrative employees are exempt from the Fair Labor Standards Act, but other employees, not exempt under the administrative, professional, or technical exemptions of the Fair Labor Standards Act, must be paid time and a half for overtime hours within the pay period it is earned.**

The FLSA requires that employees, unless exempted from the law, be paid overtime for hours worked in excess of 40 hours a week. The FLSA is applicable to colleges and universities. The FLSA exempts from its coverage, however, certain professional, technical, and administrative personnel. Consequently, most faculty and administrators will not be paid overtime. As exempt employees, they are expected to perform their assigned duties, however long it may take. Conversely, such exempt employees may not be docked pay for time off they may take during a workday as long as the job duties are accomplished.

Employees of public institutions are permitted to take compensatory time of an hour and a half for up to 160 hours of overtime instead of payment, as long as there is a clear understanding or agreement between the public employer and the employee that the time will be provided in lieu of payment, and the compensatory time is utilized in the manner prescribed by the FLSA.[10]

- **Conflicts of interest arising from the demands or the nature
of outside involvements or employment while employed by
the college or university may constitute a breach of contract,
or a violation of policy, by a faculty member or administrator.
In public institutions, conflicts of interest may also constitute
a violation of state law.**

A *conflict of interest* is a situation in which an individual has a relationship
(or has a family member who has a relationship) that could potentially affect
his or her independent, unbiased judgment in the conduct of his or her responsibilities for the institution.[11] Conflicts of interest can be subtle, as when permissible outside commitments (such as research collaborations or acting as a
consultant) diminish one's time for or commitment to the university.[12] In such
cases, the money received may reshape goals, split loyalty, lead to the use of
institutional resources for private gain, or create conflict between the obligations
owed to two entities. Conflicts of interest and commitment, real and perceived,
can be damaging to the institution. They may cause, among other possibilities,
litigation, embarrassment, and/or loss of confidence in the institution.

To protect against such conflicts and its associated problems, institutions have
developed policies that quantify, define, and prohibit activities that create real
and/or perceived conflicts.[13] A task force of the Association of American Universities, the American Council on Education, and the National Association of
State Universities and Land Grant Colleges developed a statement that encouraged institutions to establish and disseminate to faculty explicit policies on,
among other things, the extent of permissible outside consulting and the pre-
vention of double payment for the same duty.[14] Institutions may, by contract
and regulation, limit the amount of outside work of its faculty members.[15] State
laws may similarly contain ethics codes and rules that may prohibit employees
at public institutions and the members of the boards that oversee public institutions from engaging in behavior that creates a conflict with their public duty.
Federal laws applicable to federally funded research also prohibit various conflicts of interest.[16] Conflicts of interest that come before the courts are those that
result in a violation of policy, contractual commitment, and/or applicable law.
The following are some examples.

A professor's simultaneous full-time employment at two universities (preventing full-time application to scholarship and service) was deemed to constitute unprofessional behavior in violation of tenure regulations and warranted his
dismissal. The board of regents, in terminating the professor, found that by
secretly holding two positions he undermined a basic and necessary trust.[17]

A member of a public university's board of supervisors violated the state's
ethics code by entering into contracts with the university on behalf of the company he owned.[18] On the other hand, a law professor at a state institution was
not in violation of New Jersey's ethics code when he represented a client before
the Council on Affordable Housing. The court noted that faculty are not state

employees for all purposes and that there was no appearance of impropriety or trading on influence in this action.[19]

- **Collective bargaining in public institutions is a matter of state law. In private institutions, collective bargaining between faculty and the institution is regulated by the National Labor Relations Board and the National Labor Relations Act.**

Public postsecondary institutions are exempt from the jurisdiction of the National Labor Relations Board (NLRB) and are subject to state law.[20] A majority of states currently allow faculty to bargain collectively. The relevant state law may be specific to postsecondary educational institutions or may be aimed generally at public employees.[21] Faculty at private institutions, on the other hand, are subject to the jurisdiction of the NLRB.[22] However, private institutions that have a religious mission may be exempt from the reach of the NLRB.[23]

If a union has been recognized as the bargaining unit for the faculty, faculty members who are not members of the union may, nonetheless, be charged a fee for the services provided to the faculty by the union, unless the fee was not chargeable to the bargaining unit or, in the case of public institutions, it was for political activities about which the nonmember objected.[24]

- **Faculty who play a significant role in the governance of the institution may be deemed managerial for purposes of the National Labor Relations Act and consequently may not have the right to bargain collectively.**

Supervisory personnel are usually excluded from the bargaining unit. Thus, department chairs and others who hire and evaluate faculty may not be represented by the bargaining unit.[25] In *NLRB v. Yeshiva University*,[26] a divided Supreme Court held, based on the facts applicable to Yeshiva's faculty, that they were managerial and were not covered by the NLRA. In the majority opinion, the Court noted that at Yeshiva University the faculty "effectively determine its curriculum, grading system, admission and matriculation standards, academic calendars and course schedules."[27] The Court also pointed out non-academic powers of the faculty, which included recommendations on hiring, tenure, sabbaticals, termination, and promotion, as well as some decision making regarding teaching loads, student absence policies, tuition, enrollment levels, and even student admission, expulsion, and graduation.[28] Faculty, on the other hand, who do not have Yeshiva-like responsibilities have not been excluded from coverage by the NLRA.[29]

ETHICAL CONSIDERATIONS

Fairness, consistency, and respect for the individual are commonly held values in universities. Such values should express themselves in a compensation system that is gender neutral. However, it is difficult to distill gender bias out of market forces, consumerism, merit, seniority, and other modern-day factors that create pay differentials, especially among faculty members. The university must carefully examine its various compensation levels to ascertain if the system and its differentials are consistent with the institution's values and goals. Ideally, a dialogue should be established between the institution and those it compensates to aid in this examination.

• Is lock-step compensation desirable?

The complexities of a large number of institutions and the varied levels of autonomy within an institution's academic units tend to render one uniform compensation system difficult to achieve and even more difficult and controversial to maintain, except possibly in a strict collective bargaining environment.[30] Universities have typically used salary scales based on education and experience to compensate faculty rather than basing compensation on the amount of responsibility required of the employee and the skill with which it is done.[31] Such a method may offer the institution protection from charges of bias because everyone of the same education and experience is paid the same, but it may not motivate faculty to excellence or deliver value to the institution. Administrative and staff positions, on the other hand, are more likely to mirror the compensation strategies of the world outside the ivory tower and take responsibility, skills, need, and other factors into consideration when setting compensation. While this may have positive aspects, such as compensation reflecting value to the institution, it may also raise questions of discrimination when differences in compensation do not have a clearly perceived rationale.

In the last decade, the basis for faculty compensation has been expanded as many institutions seek to reward value provided to the institution. Compensation has been adjusted through complex equations based on faculty teaching load, market forces, number of students taught, teaching at off-site locations, number of different preparations in the same term, level of course or activity (undergraduate or graduate), additional skills necessary for the teaching assignment (such as simultaneous live instruction by compressed video, or synchronous or asynchronous online instruction), evaluation of performance, and others. As in business, this deviation from a simple set scale, full of subjective judgments, can raise questions of fairness and equal pay for equal work.

An institution should strive to make its compensation scheme reflect its values and priorities. In "lock-step" compensation, the values of consistency and equity are elevated. On the other hand, rewarding employees based on their performance addresses values such as academic excellence and value to the institution. It also provides for individual recognition.

• **What does the institution wish to reward? How can the institution reward performance?**

If an institution wishes to reward individuals on their performance, it must decide what aspects of performance it wishes to reward. Value audits, mentioned in Chapter 1, could be used to make this determination or, at least, pose the questions to consider. Once the specific aspects, skills, or performance the institution wishes to reward have been identified, it must decide on the process and measures to be employed in the reward system. This is no easy task.

One of the most debated issues in higher education today is the value of merit pay. Merit pay existed as early as the 1850s for elementary and high school teachers.[32] In the last 15 years it has become more prevalent for faculty, first in 4-year public/private colleges,[33] then in public higher education statewide systems (Texas[34] and Florida,[35] for example), and now in community colleges[36] and even outside the United States.[37]

Merit pay refers to monetary rewards given to faculty members or other employees to recognize outstanding, meritorious, or high-quality work performance, whereas *performance pay* is compensation for normal or average performance. Even though merit pay is neither a new concept nor a rarity, it is often not clear how salary increases ought to be utilized as individual rewards. What seems to be clear, however, is that increases in pay are perceived as measures of an individual's *value* to an institution.[38] In fact, the symbolic worth ascribed in the academic world to receiving merit increases may often exceed the actual dollar amount.[39]

Merit recognition, on the other hand, refers to nonmonetary rewards provided for outstanding performance, examples of which are certificates, verbal or written public recognition, plaques, special travel awards, laboratory or classroom equipment, and onetime monetary awards not added to an employee's base pay (bonuses). Some researchers claim that nonmonetary rewards are as important and effective in the improvement of faculty productivity as monetary rewards such as merit raises and bonuses.[40] In fact, a comprehensive study found that compensation level was rated not as first but rather as third in a list of most important determinants of faculty morale, regardless of institutional type.[41] Whereas four-year college and university systems tend to choose merit pay over merit recognition, community colleges and K–12 schools have utilized merit recognition programs, offering a wide variety of rewards.[42]

The definition of *meritorious performance* has been widely debated and is at the heart of the merit pay controversy. The literature reports many instances where faculty have not been able to agree on the definition of *merit, excellence,* or *quality*, much less on the criteria with which to measure it.[43]

Since the concept of merit pay is so value-laden, and values vary so widely on an individual basis and among the various constituencies of a learning community, it is not surprising that faculty, administrators, and the general public have a difficult time achieving consensus on what merit pay is supposed to reward. The awarding of merit pay or recognition for outstanding performance is certainly a subjective judgment, unless there are agreed-upon clear criteria with which to measure performance. What should those criteria be? Should the main criterion be *quantity* (e.g., number of students or courses taught, number of articles or books published, grants awarded) or *quality* (e.g, excellent peer evaluations of teaching, refereed publications only, teaching or research awards), or a combination of both? To add another dimension for pubic institutions, some state legislatures are increasingly proposing and approving measures that consider *outcomes* (e.g., student achievement in actual programs of study and/or standardized or certification/professional exams, rates of graduation, percentage of employability of graduates) rather than individual employee performance. The various plans that legislatures have proposed for all levels of public education (K–12, community colleges, four-year universities) call for rewarding faculty, programs, departments, or institutions as measured by *student learning* and subsequent ability to apply what they have learned, rather than just rewarding certain individuals for good teaching or research. In fact, in addition to the merit plans, some legislatures have advocated actually *funding* institutions, schools, or departments based on qualitative student outcomes rather than solely on a formula based on the numbers of students. This controversy rages on in states and at the national level. It can affect the entire compensation plan in a college · or university, since public institutions—and to a lesser but still significant degree, even private institutions—are dependent on federal and state funding. If there are cuts in a departmental or school budget, they most likely affect merit pools first, then cost-of-living adjustments and other across-the-board measures.

To assess the institutional values to consider the establishment of a merit system, the institution, school, and department should consider the following questions:

- What is most important to the institution?
- How does faculty recognition fit into the values and philosophy of the institution?
- What is the purpose of a faculty recognition program? Is it to reward excellence in teaching and therefore improve instruction, to stimulate the production of scholarly work or grantsmanship, or to raise the level of university or community service?
- Is the goal of the merit plan to attract better faculty or to motivate existing faculty?
- Do the institution and its employees value extrinsic (e.g., money or other tangible items) or intrinsic (e.g., peer or superordinate recognition) rewards?
- Does the institution wish to establish a link between improved performance and monetary rewards?
- What values of the institution would serve as institutional obstacles to the establishment of such a plan?

- Are the values/goals of the institution consistent with those of the school or department who is going to judge the meritorious performance?
- Are the values of the faculty being evaluated consistent with those of the administrators who may be the evaluators?
- Does the faculty perceive the system as clear, legitimate, and just?[44]
- Is the plan perceived as effective, balanced, and fair?[45]

Research on merit pay tells us that for a merit program to succeed, institutions must ascertain that the plan balances both the long- and short-term needs of the institution and that institutional needs are consistent with the needs and circumstances of each department. It is up to each institution to define its mission and select its priorities.[46] Again, the question must be asked, What constitutes excellence, and how is it measured? Is there a match between what the institutional culture believes is important and the behavior that it chooses to reward?

Some obstacles to the establishment of an effective merit program inherent in the value system of academic institutions have been identified in the literature. Some claim that the very structure of academia, with its multilevel hierarchy and differing criteria, works against the logic of the relationship between an institution's goals, meritorious performance, and merit pay. For example, in business and industry, incentive pay may be a motivating factor for a salesperson to increase the number of widgets he or she sells (since the clear goal is to sell widgets), but will the chemistry professor working at an institution with often conflicting goals see a clear link between doing his or her job well and criteria that will render him or her "meritorious"? In the academic world—where the great majority of institutions' published missions emphasize quality but merit criteria tend to focus on quantity—how can a faculty member judge when his or her performance is qualitatively superior?

Additionally, academia is a collegial environment, yet merit pay systems are competitive by nature, and the idealistic, rather than materialistic, nature of higher education purports not to value money as highly as in business and industry. Further, full disclosure of salary increases is necessary to reinforce the valued behavior in a merit pay system, yet the culture in higher education would in most cases reject the exposure that publishing salaries and salary increases would bring with it.[47] (This is of course not an issue in public universities, where salary increases are public information.)

The most frequently cited arguments *for* and *against* a merit pay plan are as follows:

For merit pay:

1. A good merit pay plan will attract and retain quality faculty.
2. The use of merit pay is very attractive to satisfy the need for accountability, which is demanded by governing boards, state legislatures, and accrediting bodies.

3. Corporations have for years paid for meritorious performance because of competitive pressures. The job market in higher education is becoming increasingly competitive.

4. A monetary reward for faculty meritorious performance provides an incentive for them to continue to produce at the same level.

5. Well-designed merit pay plans encourage excellence by materially reinforcing institutional values related to quality.

6. Administrators believe that if they have control over the reward system, they can influence behavior.

7. The philosophy of merit pay is appealing to basic American values that stress individualism, competition, achievement, and performance rewards. With merit, those who do not excel receive nothing, and those who perform receive their *fair* share.

8. Recognizing quality and productivity is an attractive construct.

Against merit pay:

1. It is difficult for all parties to agree on the purpose of or basis for merit.

2. Before merit can be awarded, institutions must ensure that all employees are compensated fairly and receive cost-of-living adjustments (COLAs).

3. Merit pay programs often do not achieve their goals. Funds earmarked for merit raises are usually so meager that the difference between performance pay and merit pay is not enough to influence behavior.

4. There is conflicting evidence as to whether there is a link between pay and performance.

5. Merit pay programs can cause rifts among faculty and between faculty and administration.

6. Some studies suggest that college and university faculty are internally motivated and are therefore unaffected by a merit system. Their productivity tends to remain the same whether or not they participate in a merit program.[48]

7. Unions usually oppose the establishment of merit pay systems.

8. Rating faculty can be arbitrary and subjective and may be a vehicle for discrimination against minorities. Favoritism and unreliability are two of the most cited problems perceived in faculty assessment.

9. There is a natural lack of quantifiable, tangible performance criteria when institutions are dealing with quality measures.

10. Administrators and/or faculty may avoid defining meritorious performance and clear criteria.

11. Rating employees differently based on established criteria takes a great deal of time, energy, thought, and effort, as compared to across-the-board raises, which are given to everyone regardless of the level of performance.

12. When criteria are not clearly established, administrators tend to develop their own, and the incidence of favoritism increases.

13. When given a choice, faculty generally do not support merit over COLAs tied to the inflation rate or across-the-board raises.[49]

14. In some institutions, merit pay is not tied to faculty evaluations.[50]

15. Recently hired junior faculty members who receive merit pay may be paid the same or more than their more senior colleagues. (This is part of the growing trend known as *pay or salary compression*.)[51]

16. There are political consequences to labeling COLA funds merit money. If legislatures or boards must cut, they often slash merit pools, which are considered luxuries.[52]

17. The majority of faculty and administrators, whose performance is adequate, may be demoralized when monetary rewards are given to just a few high-performing individuals. On the other hand, if merit is spread widely among employees, some may feel that a system that rewards everyone is really not a merit system because it encourages mediocrity.[53]

18. Dissatisfaction with current plans include the lack of inclusion of faculty in developing criteria and procedures for awarding merit; unclear, poorly defined, or questionable performance criteria; distrust of administrators who administer the plans; inconsistencies between merit pay and promotion-tenure criteria; and the concern that standardized student evaluations may not be an appropriate way to judge teaching performance.[54]

As can be gleaned from the foregoing, even though merit pay systems are becoming more common, there are still questions about whether they work in principle and in practice. Administrators rated tenure higher than merit pay in affecting faculty behavior,[55] and not surprisingly, so did faculty.[56] Although most faculty believed in the principle of pay based on performance,[57] they felt merit pay was divisive, and most would prefer the use of intrinsic rewards.[58] Cost-of-living adjustments were preferred over merit pay, but merit was preferred over discretionary raises.[59] Teaching was by far the most important value (and service the least important) for faculty when asked to rate teaching, research, and service. The major differences between public and private institutions were that public institutions tended to attach more weight to scholarly activities for tenured (and tenure-track) faculty, whereas private institutions rated teaching higher for tenure-track faculty than did public institutions.[60]

Considering the value-laden concepts involved in this issue, an institution that has a mandate to establish a merit system, or one that has determined that a merit pay program would be consistent with its values and goals, should proceed with extreme care if the program is to succeed.

• Could yielding to market forces in setting salaries result in unfair advantages for some groups?

Salaries, especially faculty salaries, are impacted by market forces. Customarily, institutions pay their faculty on a scale according to their rank (instructor, assistant professor, associate professor, full professor). For instance, a 1997–

1998 comprehensive report of average faculty salaries nationwide, conducted by the American Association of University Professors, showed that full professors at all institutions (except those in medical school) were paid an average of 60 percent more than assistant professors.[61]

Compensation plans in most institutions strive to maintain "an uneasy balance between following outside market forces and attempting to maintain some degree of comparability within a given rank."[62] To factor in market forces, many institutions also include a differential according to discipline to compensation based on rank and seniority. For example, business, engineering, and the "hard sciences" are more likely to be compensated at a higher rate than some discipline areas in arts and sciences such as history, philosophy, fine arts, or foreign languages. This differential between disciplines, within the same rank, can often be as high as $20,000 per year.[63] Most institutions often go to great lengths to pay their faculty competitively when compared with other institutions in the same category and type (e.g., two-year, four-year, comprehensive, private/religious). This seemingly neutral compensation practice may in fact mask a bias. Some highly compensated disciplines (e.g., engineering, business) do not attract or retain as many women and minorities as do other disciplines, and inequities may result when the salary averages for those disciplines are higher than those for disciplines that do "produce" women and minority graduates. Even a system based solely on rank and seniority, in which pay increases with years of service, may mean lower salaries for women and minorities who were not accepted in some disciplines until recently. Compensation often reflects prior societal or cultural discrimination.

Another phenomenon that causes increasing imbalances over time in an institution and within its academic departments is that of *salary compression*, which results when new employees are hired at a higher rate than those with more seniority in like positions and with like duties. In addition, outside offers of higher pay than an employee is currently earning for the same position affect an institution's attempts at consistency within its own pay scales when the institution, in order to retain its employee, attempts to match or surpass the outside offer. A related ethical issue is raised when employees court and entertain outside offers without intention of leaving their present institution but rather to manipulate or force their current employer solely to raise their compensation package.[64] A desire for fairness and equity would prompt an institution to analyze their compensation *and* hiring practices in light of these eventualities and the possibilities of creating or perpetuating discriminatory practices or negating the institution's values.

• **To what extent is increasing compensation through gifts and gratuities from vendors, students, and other entities an acceptable practice?**

Some positions in the university provide opportunities to increase compensation through gifts and gratuities from vendors, students, and other entities. Should these be viewed as a legitimate and acceptable basis for augmenting compensation, or should they be barred as opening the door to allegations of conflicts of interest? An institution should discuss the possibility of these offers and how they might impact decision making in order to develop guidelines for employees that are congruent with the values of the institution.

- **Are faculty who consult and perform other outside activities harming their institution by diminishing their commitment to their responsibilities? What is more important, an individual's needs to supplement his or her income or bolster a personal reputation or the institution's need to demand and expect a primary commitment to the position the individual fills?**

Faculty consulting and other outside endeavors are common activities widely engaged in by faculty and administrators throughout both public and independent institutions. However, policies regarding these issues vary from institution to institution or may be altogether nonexistent.

Faculty, and to a lesser degree, academic administrators, may request to engage in consulting and in other outside activities (e.g., serving on boards, teaching for other institutions) while under contract with their institution. Consulting outside the institution has been traditionally viewed as one of the major outside professional activities included in the *service* component of the familiar trio of faculty responsibilities and institutional functions, namely, teaching, research, and service.[65] Faculty consulting involves the application of a faculty member's professional and scholarly expertise outside his or her own academic institution, with or without remuneration. This definition, perhaps overly broad, is nevertheless one that most institutions use to define faculty activities that extend beyond a faculty member's contract with the institution.[66] Unless there is a clear policy against this type of activity, faculty are generally free to perform consulting and other outside activities, albeit with some time limitations set by some institutions. These limitations commonly involve a percentage of the employee's time commitment to his or her institution; many colleges and universities set a limit on outside consulting to the equivalent of one day per week.[67] Conflicts of interest or conflicts of commitment, however, may arise in the discharge of these activities.

Questions that institutions often consider prior to deciding if a policy is needed, or what the policy should contain, include the following: Would the institution and its mission suffer harm if faculty are given broad latitude to perform outside activities? Should the institution limit faculty members' right to supplement their income by consulting and/or outside activities, given the level of faculty salaries that it is offering? Should the institution limit faculty members' opportunities to serve the community outside the academic institution? If the institution wishes to limit faculty's outside activities, what should the parameters be? Should consulting in the faculty member's professional field be allowed but "moonlighting," or activities not directly related to the faculty member's profession, forbidden?

As to the first question (concerning the potential harm to the institution and those it serves caused by faculty who perform outside activities), some research indicates that faculty who perform outside activities are as active in their primary institution as faculty who do not. In fact, faculty who consult reportedly taught as many courses, devoted at least as many work hours to research and publishing, and kept as abreast of developments in their fields as those who did not.[68]

As to whether the institution should allow a faculty member to supplement his or her income by outside consulting, such a question assumes that faculty consult strictly for economic gain because faculty salaries are low and that the benefit of outside consulting flow only to the faculty member. This may not be the case; in fact, studies indicate that most faculty who consult do not have lower base academic salaries than their peers who choose not to engage in outside consulting.[69] Faculty appear to be motivated to consulting activities primarily by other factors, such as potential and perceived benefits to their professional reputation and careers or to their primary teaching and research and by social demands,[70] all of which may benefit the institution where the individual has his or her primary commitment.

The pros and cons of consulting may be summarized as follows:

1. Those opposing faculty engaging in outside activities contend that faculty consulting creates conflicts of interest and commitment and may lead to the abuse of academic freedom or to illegitimate use of institutional resources.

2. Those who claim that faculty consulting enhances the basic faculty responsibilities (teaching, research, and service) state that abuses are rare and that faculty consulting not only benefits the faculty member financially and reputationally but also benefits the faculty member's institution and society in general.[71]

Of the problems attendant to consulting, the improper use of university resources is a common source of concern. Faculty members may be utilizing their own institution's materials, equipment, and support staff without the institution sharing in the faculty members' financial gain.[72] The AAUP, in fact, considers such issues important enough to publish separate statements on conflicts of interest as well as on preventing conflicts of interest in government-sponsored research at universities.[73] (See Appendixes 4 and 5.)

Current technology and the world of electronic communications bring about other potential issues regarding conflicts of interest. As one example, consider the faculty member who in his web page on the university's server places a "hot-link" to his or her private consulting business. In fact, the faculty member is utilizing the university's resources to advertise and provide access to his or her own profit-making enterprise.

In extreme cases, conflicts of commitment result in a faculty member's changing his or her institution's instructional focus to match the individual's outside interest or scheduling the faculty member's responsibilities to his or her primary employer around the secondary outside activities, which thus assume primary status. Several extreme cases have came to light.[74] A recent and egregious case of conflict of interest and commitment cited in the legal parameters section in this chapter, *Zahavy v. University of Minnesota*,[75] demonstrates a clear clash of values between the institution and the faculty member. In this case, a tenured professor at the University of Minnesota appealed his dismissal for unprofessional conduct. The professor held two full-time tenured positions concurrently, one at the University of Minnesota and a second one at the University of North Carolina at Charlotte (UNCC), in violation of the University of Minnesota's policy against dual employment with another university. The university claimed that his dual employment caused a conflict of commitment by preventing him from discharging his duties of full-time teaching, research, and service, therefore misusing the university resources and time. The professor claimed that his teaching, scholarship, and service were not impacted and that his conduct did not impair his ability to discharge these duties successfully.

The university rules reflected its position that dual employment was harmful to the institution and to its students. The professor placed his financial gain from the dual employment above both universities' needs for a primary commitment and his obligation to abide by their respective rules. The court in this case determined that the university had been within its rights in dismissing the professor because he had misrepresented his employment status with another institution and had failed to maintain a relationship of trust with the administration and faculty of the university. His conduct impaired his professional fitness.

* **Should an institution set limits on faculty consulting and other outside activities?**

In the *Zahavy* case previously cited, the university's case against the professor was bolstered by its having and communicating a policy against dual employment. Faculty consulting, within reasonable limits, may, however, be acceptable and beneficial to the individual and the institution. What is reasonable, and who determines it? If limits are set, should they be measured based on a percentage of income or time, on the nature/purpose of the outside activity, or on a combination of some or all of these? A policy addressing limits on faculty consulting and other outside activities would define the institution's philosophy about the issue and would be an aid to both the institution and the individual in deciding the ethics of a particular situation. Lack of a policy provides no direction to the institution and individual faculty members in this common practice and may lead to abuse.

- **Can an employee's activities to further his or her financial interests harm the institution?**

In contrast to conflicts of commitment (which normally refer to individuals dedicating too much time/effort to activities outside their primary employment), conflicts of interest arise when employees pursue actions to bolster their own personal (including financial) interests when those actions may harm the institution.[76]

When an employee utilizes institutional resources for personal use or has an interest in an entity that does business with the institution, these circumstances should be avoided, or at the very least revealed to the appropriate officials. Such conflicts, if unknown to the institution, can be detrimental to its interest. Even the appearance of self-interest can be damaging to morale. The institution should be clear about its limits and requirements regarding conflicts of interest and communicate them to its employees.

- **Does institutional receipt of funds for research or services from government or industry present a possibility of conflict with its scholarly research?**

To obtain outside funding, researchers may compromise the proper conduct or direction of the research they are or will be conducting. Some may even compromise the accurate reporting of results in order to please the funding source. The search for truth, clearly compromised in such cases, can also be impacted by an unintended bias in favor of a grantor. Consequently, institutions should carefully examine research directions and funding sources to ensure that they are pursuing appropriate research goals in an objective manner.

In the 1980s and 1990s, numerous cases of fraud in research and other research misconduct have come to light, so that the American Association of University Professors has disseminated written guidelines intended to avoid conflicts of interest, especially in government-funded research.

Three categories of research misconduct have been identified: (1) authorship and the designation of academic credit; (2) illegitimate utilization of ideas or expressions of another; and (3) willful falsification of results or data.[77] Any or all of these have been uncovered through the vigilance of governments or other entities, causing a slow dilution of the public's trust.

PRACTICAL SUGGESTIONS

- **Assessing and monitoring pay equity must be an ongoing activity at every institution.**

An institution should establish a compensation program according to applicable laws and regulations and institutional values. Pay increases should also be based on clear and consistent criteria that are made known to employees. A consultant may be utilized to conduct a study or audits of the college's or university's compensation program, and counsel should be consulted to ascertain that all legal and regulatory requirements are being met.

Related institutional academic policies, such as the use of part-time (adjunct) faculty in lieu of hiring additional full-time faculty, tenure and promotion issues, pay differentials by rank and by discipline, "steps" awarded for length of service (seniority), early retirement programs/incentives, "reduction in force" policies, and other contract issues should be reviewed with the compensation program. These variables affect the general pool for employee compensation, which in turn affects the fiscal ability of the institution to implement a plan to remedy any inequities.

- **In deciding to yield to market considerations to determine hiring salaries, administrators must be aware that this practice will most likely result in employees with more seniority earning less for similar positions.**

As was mentioned in the ethical considerations portion, salary compression, which results when a new employee is hired at a higher pay than a current employee who is performing the same work, is a common phenomenon in higher education today. This happens because of market considerations, which force the institution to hire at "the going rate" to attract a professional. It can cause an imbalance in pay systems, often resulting in low morale. A systematic comparison of pay scales from similar institutions should be made before hiring new employees. To avoid salary compression and its negative consequences, the salary of current employees should be adjusted to market levels whenever possible. This would contribute to the health of the compensation program as it strives for equity and fairness, and it may help to avoid possible litigation under the equal pay act or other laws prohibiting discrimination.

- **When implementing a merit pay system, the institution must do so carefully to avoid common pitfalls.**

Some important guidelines in the establishment of merit pay programs are as follows:

- Rewards must be consistent with the institution's values.
- Disclosure of merit decisions is needed to verify the credibility of the system.
- As a general rule and in order to have impact upon behavior, merit pay should be at least two times the average increment. Merit pay becomes an incentive to improve performance only when salaries are already equal to the market.[78]
- An effective merit pay system should be managed at the university level to ensure fairness and to secure the necessary pool of funds. However, most merit pay systems

are operated at the school, department, or program level, whose administrators do not care to relinquish control.[79] (However, it should be noted that faculty are more likely to believe in departmental norms instead of those of the broader organization.)[80]

- Intrinsic rewards, such as recognition by peer or superordinates, can be implemented right along with merit pay. As the pay level goes up, intrinsic rewards become more effective.[81]

- When the amount of merit pay is small, lump-sum payments are preferred. Other monetary awards that are not added to the employee's base pay could be offered (such as graduate student assistance, travel money for a meeting or conferences, funds for library or materials acquisition, or course releases).[82]

- Faculty should have input in the selection of goals, objectives, and weighted criteria for measuring performance.

- Clear standards and definitions for quality, meritorious performance, and excellence (and adequate performance) should be disseminated in policy manuals regarding faculty compensation, merit pay, or merit recognition.

- Faculty should judge or help judge the performance of their peers.

- Chairpersons and other administrators should not share in the faculty merit pool.

- Rewards should be given to all who achieve stated goals, once a merit program has been initiated.

- Evaluative processes should be fair and administered consistently. They should be understood by all concerned. A "management by objectives" (MBO) approach could be utilized.[83]

- Qualitative evaluation plans may include a bilevel or even trilevel evaluation system in which you "rate" categories of merit (e.g., basic, superior, exceptional) and a "point" system in which different activities are assigned different points based on agreed-upon values; then the evaluation points are converted into dollars available.[84]

- Evaluation systems and merit pay criteria should be reviewed annually and be highly adaptive in that they should be able to reflect, on an ongoing basis any changes in university or departmental value or standards.[85]

Hunnicutt, Taylor, and Keefe,[86] Tracy and Muir,[87] Farmer,[88] and Rosenfeld and Long[89] are among the authors who describe effective merit systems that have been implemented in higher education institutions.

- **An institution should establish rules to govern the acceptance or rejection of gifts and gratuities from vendors, students, or other entities.**

In order to prevent even the appearance of impropriety, a college or university should promulgate personnel policies that detail what is appropriate and what is not appropriate regarding the acceptance of gifts and gratuities. Such rules should be disseminated to employees by the human resources department or other appropriate university unit with the advice of counsel. Many institutions establish internal rules that cover the acceptance of such gifts and gratuities. These often call for the employee not to accept a gift, to report the offer to appropriate superordinates, or to accept only seasonal gifts up to a certain value.

- **Policies on faculty outside activities should include a description of which outside activities are allowed (if any), the limitations as to purpose and extent governing consulting or other outside activities, and what procedures must be followed to obtain clearance from the institution to perform these activities.**

Policies on faculty consulting and outside activities vary in complexity, although policies in public institutions tend to be more detailed and prescriptive than those commonly found in private colleges and universities.[90] Most institutional policies include a statement of the faculty member's commitment to the institution, followed by a declaration of the nature of outside professional activities allowed within the faculty member's contract or appointment, if any are in fact permitted. It is common for the policy to assert that faculty outside activities should not interfere with the performance of the faculty member's responsibilities and commitment to the institution.

A review of several institutional policies revealed some similarities in items that were included. At a minimum, a policy on faculty outside activities should include:

- A statement of the professional commitment to the institution required by each full-time faculty member
- A statement that outside professional activities must not interfere with the performance of the faculty member's responsibility to the institution, the *primary* employer (conflict of commitment statement)
- A conflict of interest statement, with examples of activities or situations that could be considered potential conflicts of interest
- A statement on whether consulting (with or without remuneration), teaching/research for other institutions, membership on boards, or self-employment are allowed and what the institution's suggested parameters for maximum time commitment of faculty to these outside activities are
- A clear statement, with examples, about the use of institutional resources to support the faculty member's outside activities (may also include rules about the use of the institution's electronic mail, web pages, and other technology)
- Procedures for disclosure and resolution of conflicts of interest and whether annual disclosure is required

For both public and private institutions, most policy statements include a description of activities regulated through the policy, how those activities are to be limited or regulated, and what procedures, if any, need to be followed to secure permission from the institution before pursuing any outside activities.[91]

If AAUP's policies on conflicts of interest and/or commitment are to be used as guidelines for the institution, they should be referred to in the institution's policy, and a copy of such policies should be made available to those affected.

Some institutions have a separate policy for faculty, whereas others also include staff and administration in their conflict of interest policy[92] and address institutional issues. At least one university, for example, categorizes conflicts of interest into *individual* (referring to commitment to academic or institutional duties) and *institutional* (referring to a potential conflict between financial interests of the university and a faculty member's scholarly pursuits, especially the improper conduct of research or bias in reporting research results).[93]

ILLUSTRATIVE CASE

Description

Small Community College (SCC) employed two associate professors to teach in its budding communications program, which was part of the English Department. Associate Professor Y (white male) and Associate Professor X (white female) were hired at the same time, taught the same course load, were required to keep the same number of office hours, and served on two university committees each. The female faculty member's nine-month salary was $6,000 less than the male faculty member's. Associate Professor X asked for a raise to equalize their salaries. The chairperson, in refusing to adjust the female faculty member's salary, stated that Associate Professor Y's higher salary was justified in that his dissertation area (technology in the communications department) was "hot" and that he had earned his terminal degree in a more selective school than the female faculty member. Although both faculty members achieved the same level of scholarship in their respective doctoral programs (grade-point averages were the same), the male faculty member was continuously selected to attend community events to represent the department. The female faculty member was heavyset and did not seem to project the same type of image that the male faculty member did.

Associate Professor X appealed the chairperson's decision to the dean of Arts and Sciences, who took the issue under advisement and forwarded his recommendation not to adjust X's salary to the vice president for Academic Affairs, who makes the final decision on compensation matters. The female faculty member has threatened to take legal action against the college if an adjustment is not made to her salary.

The vice president for Academic Affairs, after consultation with university counsel, agreed to adjust the female faculty member's salary and suggested mediating the matter.

Analysis

• **Meeting the requirements of law.**

If Professors X and Y, who are persons of opposite sexes, are being paid differently for the same work, requiring the same skill, effort, and responsibility, then SCC may well be in violation of the Equal Pay Act. The first question is whether, in fact, they *did* have the same job, requiring the same skill effort and responsibility. The illustrative case reveals that the male faculty member was continuously asked to represent the department at community events. This additional effort and responsibility may be sufficient to support the conclusion that the jobs were different and may have required different skills. Were we to conclude, however, that the jobs were the same, the next level of analysis requires that we determine whether any of the statutory exemptions to the Equal Pay Act (seniority, merit, earnings based on quality or quantity, or other sex-neutral factors) could be applied in this situation. Clearly, seniority was not involved, and the issues of merit and earnings based on quality or quantity were not addressed, although the reference by the chairperson to "hot" when referring to the male professor's subject area could mean that more students selected this area of study. If this were the case, and such a factor as class size operated as a consistent factor in augmenting salaries, then this might serve as a justification for the difference in compensation. As for other sex-neutral factors, it should be noted that the chairperson of the department justified the differential on the grounds of superior credentials and the fact that the male professor's area of expertise was hot. Credentials might, under some circumstances, be judged sufficient to support a salary differential. In this case, however, it seems unlikely. The difference, a college degree from a more selective institution, seems minor, and it is unlikely that other faculty salaries are consistently differentiated on this basis. As for the male professor's area of expertise being hot, this might, as stated above, mean that he attracted more students. It could also mean that market forces made this area a more highly compensated one.

Whatever conclusion is reached about whether the Equal Pay Act was violated (and it is a close question), it would still be necessary to see whether sex discrimination was also present in the circumstances described. Although the facts suggest that the female faculty was not given community duties because she was heavyset and did not otherwise project the desired image of the university in the community, sex discrimination may have also been a factor. Further investigation of this point should be made. Discrimination, if present, on the basis of weight does not, however, constitute an actionable offense.

• Ethical considerations.

Not all discrimination is prohibited by law. An institution that values fairness might want to investigate this matter further to determine whether there was discrimination, even if it isn't actionable. In the circumstances described, the female instructor may have been barred from duties as a community liaison because of prejudices or because she lacked certain necessary presentation skills.

The institution, in evaluating the situation, would need to examine its values, the needs of the individual, and the needs of the institution.

• **Practical considerations.**

After considering this matter, it appears that the vice president of the institution concluded that action to equalize the compensation of the female professor or arrive at some acceptable compromise was in order. Such a decision could have been made because a close evaluation of the situation revealed that the female professor's position had some merit on legal or ethical grounds or because he wished to avoid the costs and publicity attendant to defending a lawsuit. The costs of a settlement may be more reasonable than the costs of litigation, and such a course of action should be evaluated, with counsel, in light of the strength of the case as well as other institutional concerns such as setting a precedent, incurring recurring costs, and demonstrating concern for institutional fairness.

Mediation can be an excellent tool in arriving at dispute resolution in situations where the parties are open to a settlement and direct negotiations are not effective or advisable. In litigation, the issues and resolutions must fit into legal prescriptions and terms, whereas in mediation, the parties craft their own resolution to the controversy with the aid of a neutral facilitator. In such a setting, real interests (rather than just causes of legal action) can be addressed and the basis for an ongoing employment relationship strengthened.

NOTES

1. 29 U.S.C. 206(d).
2. *Horner v. Mary Institute*, 613 F.2d 706 (8th Cir. 1980).
3. *Winkes v. Brown*, 747 F.2d 965 (9th Cir. 1982).
4. *Padway v. Palches*, 665 F.2d 965 (9th Cir. 1982).
5. *Marshall v. Georgia Southwestern College*, 489 F. Supp. 1322 (D.Ga. 1980).
6. See *Melanson v. Rantoul*, 536 F. Supp. 271 (1982).
7. 29 U.S.C. § 206(d). The Equal Pay Act is applicable to employees engaged in commerce, as commerce is defined under the FLSA. Unlike the rest of the FLSA, it applies to executive, administrative, and professional employees usually exempt from the FLSA, and it applies to local and state government employees unless they are specifically exempted. 29 C.F.R. § 1621.1.
8. 43 F.R. 19807.
9. 29 C.F.R. § 1620.1–1620.29.
10. 29 U.S.C. § 2070.
11. Richard T. Ingram, "A Board's Guide to Conflict-of-Interest and Disclosure Issues," *Trusteeship* (March–April 1993): 23–26.
12. William A. Kaplin and Barbara A. Lee, *The Law of Higher Education: A Comprehensive Guide to Legal Implications of Administrative Decision Making*, 3rd ed. (San Francisco: Jossey-Bass, 1995), 960.

13. Carol M. Boyer and Darrell R. Lewis, *And on the Seventh Day: Faculty Consulting and Supplemental Income*, ASHE-ERIC Higher Education Report No. 3 (Washington, DC: George Washington University, 1985), 49–51.

14. Steven Olswang and Barbara A. Lee, *Faculty Freedoms and Institutional Accountability: Interactions and Conflicts*, ASHE-ERIC Higher Education Research Report No. 5 (Washington, DC: George Washington University, 1984).

15. *Gross v. University of Tennessee*, 448 F. Supp. 245 (W.D. Tenn. 1978), aff'd, 620 F.2d 109 (6th Cir. 1980).

16. Kaplin and Lee, 961.

17. *Zahavy v. University of Minnesota*, 544 N.W.2d 32, 46 (Ct. App. 1996).

18. *In re Sheldon D. Beychok and Wolf Baking Company, Inc.*, 495 So.2d 1278, 1281 (La. 1986).

19. *In re Determination of Executive Commission on Ethical Standards Re: Appearance of Rutgers Attorneys*, 561 A.2d 542, 547 (N.J. 1989).

20. 29 U.S.C. § 152(2).

21. Kaplin and Lee, 171.

22. See Cornell University and Assoc. of Cornell Employers Libraries et al., 183 NLRB 41 (1970).

23. See *NLRB v. Catholic Bishop of Chicago*, 440 U.S. 490 (1979); *Universidad Central de Bayamon v. NLRB*, 793 F.2d 383 (1st Cir. 1986).

24. Kaplin and Lee, 178.

25. See 29 U.S.C. § 152.

26. 444 U.S. 672 (1980).

27. Id. at 676.

28. Id. at 677.

29. *Loretto Heights College v. NLRB*, 742 F.2d 1245 (10th Cir. 1984).

30. Kathryn M. Moore and Marilyn J. Amey, *Making Sense of the Dollars: The Costs and Uses of Faculty Compensation*, ASHE-ERIC Higher Education Report No. 5 (Washington, DC: George Washington University, School of Education and Human Development, 1993), 28.

31. Edward E. Lawler III, *From the Ground Up: Six Principles for Building the New Logic Corporation* (San Francisco: Jossey-Bass, 1996), 203.

32. Keith T. Miller, "Merit Pay from the Faculty's Perspective," *CUPA Journal* (Fall 1992): 8.

33. Ibid., 7, quoting D. E. Blum, "Concept of Merit Pay Professors Spreads as Competition Among Institutions," *Chronicle of Higher Education*, October 18, 1989, 1, 20.

34. Garland G. Hunnicutt, Rush Lesher Taylor, and Michael J. Keeffe, "An Exploratory Examination of Faculty Evaluation and Merit Compensation Systems in Texas Colleges and Universities," *CUPA Journal* (Spring 1991): 13.

35. Kristine L. Anderson, "Faculty Support for a Merit Pay System" (paper presented at the annual meeting of the Association for the Study of Higher Education, Minneapolis, Minn., 1992), ED 352 900.

36. Hans A. Andrews, "Expanding Merit Recognition Plans in Community Colleges," *Community College Review* 20, no. 5 (1993): 51–53, 56–57.

37. F. C. L. Allen, "Indicators of Academic Excellence: Is There a Link Between Merit and Reward?" *Australian Journal of Education* 34, no. 1 (1990): 87–98.

38. Donald Kennedy, *Academic Duty* (Cambridge, MA: Harvard University Press, 1997), 32–33.

39. Moore and Amey, 36.

40. Ibid., 34.

41. Ibid., 32.

42. Andrews, 51.

43. Lawrence B. Rosenfeld and Beverly Whitaker Long, "An Evaluation System for Measuring Faculty Performance," *ACA Bulletin* 79 (1992): 37.

44. Anderson, 1.

45. Dyanne M. Tracy and Sharon Pray Muir, "Overcoming Merit Pay Dissatisfaction: A Faculty-Developed, Bilevel, Criterion-Based Plan" (report presented at the annual meeting of the Association for the Study of Higher Education, Oakland University, Michigan, 1992), ED 352 701.

46. Miller, 8–9.

47. A. Lawrence Lauer, "Searching for Answers: Should Universities Create Merit Pay Systems?" *NACUBO Business Officer* (November 1991): 52–54.

48. Miller, 9.

49. Ibid., 11.

50. Andrews, 57.

51. Moore and Amey, 77–78.

52. Lauer, 53.

53. Hunnicutt, Taylor, and Keeffe, 14.

54. Tracy and Muir, 3, 10.

55. Gregory J. Marchant and Isadore Newman, "Faculty Evaluation and Reward Procedures: Views from Education Administrators," *Assessment and Evaluation in Higher Education* 19, no. 2 (1994): 150.

56. Miller, 10–11, 15.

57. Ibid., 11.

58. Donald W. Farmer, "Designing a Reward System to Promote the Career Development of Senior Faculty," *New Directions for Teaching and Learning*, no. 55 (1993): 49.

59. Anderson, 21–22.

60. Hunnicutt, Taylor, and Keeffe, 18.

61. "Facts About Higher Education in the U.S., Each of the 50 States, and D.C.," *Chronicle of Higher Education*, Almanac, August 28, 1998.

62. Kennedy, 33.

63. Ibid.

64. Ibid., 34.

65. Boyer and Lewis, 3.

66. Ibid., 3–5.

67. Kennedy, 243.

68. Ibid., 22–23.

69. Ibid., 42–43.

70. Ibid., iii.

71. Moore and Amey, 55.

72. Ibid.

73. American Association of University Professors, "On Preventing Conflicts of Interest in Government-Sponsored Research at Universities," *AAUP Policy Documents and Reports* (Washington, DC: American Association of University Professors, 1995), 116–

118; American Association of University Professors, "Statement on Conflicts of Interest," *AAUP Policy Documents and Reports* (Washington, DC: American Association of University Professors, 1995), 119–120.

74. Kennedy, 247.

75. 544 N.W.2d at 32.

76. Kennedy, 242.

77. Ibid., 211.

78. Lauer, 53.

79. Ibid.

80. Anderson, 5.

81. Ibid., 54.

82. Ibid.

83. Hunnicutt, Taylor, and Keeffe, 20.

84. Karl O. Magnusen, "Faculty Evaluation, Performance, and Pay: Application and Issues," *Journal of Higher Education* 58 (1987): 516–529.

85. Rosenfeld and Long, 39.

86. Hunnicutt, Taylor, and Keeffe.

87. Tracy and Muir.

88. Farmer.

89. Rosenfeld and Long.

90. Boyer and Lewis, 45.

91. Ibid., 45–53.

92. Tulane University Conflict of Interest Policy, at http://www.tulane.edu/coi-Policy.html.

93. Ibid., 2.

Chapter 4

Promotion and Tenure Issues

In academia, full-time faculty strive to achieve tenure if they are teaching in institutions that have a tenure system. Tenure usually means that absent specified cause, programmatic changes, or financial exigencies, the tenured faculty member will continue in the employ of the institution. The purpose of tenure, as reflected in the "1940 Statement of Principles on Academic Freedom and Tenure, with 1970 Interpretive Comments" of the American Association of University Professors and the Association of American Colleges, the policy adopted by the academic community, is to protect the right of college and university professors to pursue research, teaching, and publication without fear of termination for the content of their work.[1] In addition to providing this job security, tenure announces to the world that the faculty member has been judged by peers and superiors and found to possess valued competencies and characteristics. Conversely, the denial of tenure can be a powerful rejection that can impact the faculty member's academic career. From the institutional perspective, tenure usually means a work commitment to an individual for the duration of his or her work life. Understandably, few issues in higher education excite more interest and anxiety in faculty and pose a greater challenge to administrators.

Administrators must evaluate tenure and promotion questions objectively, knowing their crucial importance to the individual, against a backdrop of legal imperatives, academic and institutional traditions and standards, ethical judgments, and the practical considerations necessary to keep an institution functioning in an increasingly competitive environment that may be characterized by an oversupply of qualified academics in some disciplines as well as by escalating costs and declining profits.

LEGAL PARAMETERS

> • **The employment actions of public educational institutions are limited by the guarantees of the Constitution. Public institutions may not deny promotion or tenure in violation of constitutionally guaranteed First Amendment rights of freedom of speech, association, religion, and academic freedom. Freedom of speech rights for public employees are restricted to speech that is a matter of public concern and that does not conflict with the efficient delivery of services to the public. Neither public nor private institutions may deny tenure or promotion on grounds that breach guarantees of academic freedom contained in contracts between the institution and its faculty.**

Ordinarily, courts will not review the correctness of a tenure or promotion decision, deferring to the collective judgment of the institution.[2] This deference may be based on (1) respect for the institution's professional judgment and the court's comparative lack of expertise in the evaluation of the criteria for tenure or promotion[3] and (2) the economic and other long-term implications of the tenure or promotion decision for the institution, which make these decisions more difficult for the court to review than other employment matters.[4] With regard to a public institution, the court's deference can also be based on concern for the institution's academic freedom, that is, its right to determine who shall teach.[5] (See Chapter 6.) In the case of a public institution, however, the courts may intervene when the institution denies tenure or promotion to a faculty member because of discrimination in violation of the Constitution and/or Title VII (see the following section), when the institution denies a faculty member's constitutional due process rights (see the section in this chapter on liberty and property interests), or when the institution denies tenure or promotion because the faculty member has exercised First Amendment rights (see discussion that follows and Chapter 6).

In a public institution, a faculty member's protected First Amendment rights include freedom of speech, expression, association, and religion,[6] as well as academic freedom. It should be noted that *academic freedom* in this context refers to the rights of the individual faculty member, as opposed to those of the institution, and may, in fact, be in conflict with those of the institution.[7] Both individual and institutional academic freedom are aimed at protecting free inquiry, and both are a "special concern" of the First Amendment.[8]

Individual academic freedom has received legal definition through case controversies and is protected by the Constitution in public institutions through these precedents.[9] Cases regarding First Amendment protection for faculty members have arisen primarily in the context of termination or nonrenewal of contract but are applicable to the denial of tenure or promotion. These cases have changed in character over the years. In the 1950s and 1960s, such cases usually pitted the faculty member and the institution against the state's intrusion. Subsequent cases, which often involve other public employees, are more likely to pit the employee's rights and needs against those of the public institution.[10]

In the earlier line of cases, which grew out of the McCarthy era and its concerns, the courts generally did not support state-sponsored efforts to weed out "subversive" teachers from state educational institutions, whether tenured or untenured.[11] In *Keyishian v. Board of Regents*,[12] the Court found that the dismissal of faculty members who refused to sign a certificate saying they were not and never had been Communists was a violation of their freedom of association. In *Shelton v. Tucker*,[13] the Court, recognizing the special importance of the Bill of Rights and the Fourteenth Amendment for teachers, held that a state statute that required teachers to reveal all their organizational affiliations and contributions for the past five years was an unconstitutional infringement of constitutional rights.

In a more recent line of cases concerning the First Amendment rights of public employees, the Court has determined that the First Amendment's guarantee of free speech does not shield employees from negative personal decisions when their communications are deemed personal or come into conflict with the government's (or public institution's) efficient provision of services. The case of *Pickering v. Board of Education*,[14] which involved a termination rather than a tenure or promotion decision, asserts that while teachers have rights to comment on matters of public concern, this right may be outweighed by the state's interest in an efficient educational system. In *Pickering*, a teacher sent a letter critical of the school board to a local newspaper. The Supreme Court balanced the teacher's right to freedom of speech against the state's interest in maintaining an efficient educational system (one in which discipline and harmony have not been undermined) and, in this case, found in favor of the teacher. Among other things, the Court determined that the teacher had addressed a matter of public concern that had no detrimental effect on the operation of the school or his performance as an instructor. In subsequent cases, the Court clarified that a threshold factor in determining if a public or private communication by a faculty member is protected by the First Amendment is whether the communication is about an issue of public or private concern.[15] In a case where the Court held that a public employee's speech involved matters of personal concern regarding employment (e.g., a grievance or job-related condition), and not matters of public concern, it concluded that the speech had no First Amendment protection.[16] The parameters used to determine what would constitute a matter of public concern are unclear. Various courts have applied different standards to this determination.[17] When the speech at issue survives the threshold analysis and is deemed a matter of public concern, the institution may still take a legally permissible adverse personnel action if it can show (1) that the state's interest in efficiency is negatively affected by the speech or (2) that, absent the speech at issue, it would have taken the adverse action for other reasons (e.g., poor teaching, judgment, or scholarship).[18]

The definition of *academic freedom* in the "1940 Statement of Principles on Academic Freedom and Tenure, with 1970 Interpretive Comments" forms the standard for academia[19] and has frequently been incorporated into college and university policy and contracts. In this manner, it has become a contractual limit on the actions of both private and public institutions.[20] (See Appendix 6.) The legal and contractual parameters of academic freedom will be discussed in greater detail in Chapter 6.

- **Denial of tenure (as opposed to the termination of a tenured faculty member) in a public institution generally affords no due process rights. Faculty do not have a liberty or property interest in the grant of promotion or tenure.**

The Fourteenth Amendment to the Constitution protects individuals from the loss of property or liberty without due process of law. *Due process* includes adequate notice and a hearing before the loss is incurred. In 1972, the Supreme Court in the case of *Board of Regents v. Roth*,[21] which involved an assistant professor at a public university, established the rationale for due process claims when it held that the assistant professor had no due process right to a hearing or an explanation when his contract was not renewed because no property or liberty interest of his was violated by this action. The Court explained that a property interest was more than a "unilateral expectation" of continuing employment. It had to be an entitlement to continuing employment. Such an entitlement could be created by statute, regulations, contract (tenure), and/or mutual understanding. Thus, if the term of a contract expires, and there is no legal basis upon which to make a claim for continued employment or tenure, there is no right to a due process hearing.[22] Where, however, a professor relied on rules that said that the faculty member had tenure as long as his performance and attitude were good, the Court found that this professor did have sufficient entitlement to employment to trigger the right to a due process hearing when he was not rehired.[23]

According to the Court in *Roth*, a liberty interest requiring due process procedures would be triggered when an individual's standing in the community and associations might be damaged by the decision not to rehire that individual. A hearing would be necessary if the individual's name, reputation, honor, or integrity were at stake, or if the individual's freedom to take advantage of other employment was foreclosed. This was not the case in *Roth*.[24] In a later case, *Bishop v. Wood*,[25] the Court added that charges against the employee, privately communicated to that employee, could not be the basis for a claim that the employee's liberty interest was at issue. There had to be some public disclosure of the charges.[26]

- **Public and private institutions are prohibited by federal, state, and local law from discriminating on the basis of race, sex, religion, national origin, age, veteran status, or disability in matters of promotion and tenure. Public institutions are also prohibited from discrimination by the Constitution.**

For both public and private institutions, the prohibitions on discrimination in employment contained in the Constitution, Title VII, Title VI, Title IX, Section 1981 (Civil Rights Act of 1866), the Americans with Disabilities Act, Section 504, the Age Discrimination in Employment Act, 38 U.S.C. §§ 4212 and 4311, and Executive Order 11246, which are described in detail in Chapter 2, are applicable to the grant or denial of tenure and promotion. State and local laws prohibiting discrimination also apply to promotions and the granting of tenure in public and private institutions. Public institutions are also prohibited from intentionally discriminating in promotion and tenure decisions on the basis of race or gender by the Equal Protection Clause of the Fourteenth Amendment to the Constitution.[27]

- **There is no general privilege protecting the peer review process used to evaluate candidates for tenure and promotion from discovery where there are charges of discrimination.**

Tenure decisions are usually made as a result of review and evaluation of the tenure application at various levels within the institution. Recommendations for granting or denying tenure may be made by peers at the departmental level, continue with institution-wide faculty involvement, proceed to the dean's level, to the vice president for academic affairs, and finally be decided by the president of the institution, with the approval of the trustees.

A number of Supreme Court cases provide legal precedent for institutional academic freedom (i.e., institutional autonomy in decision making).[28] Courts have, therefore, been reluctant to interfere with such academic decisions.[29] Accordingly, many courts have protected the tenure process from discovery or limited such discovery.

In 1990, in the case of *University of Pennsylvania v. EEOC*,[30] the Supreme Court further defined the reach of institutional academic freedom and resolved existing conflicts in authority and opinion over the disclosure of peer review materials.[31] In this case, the EEOC sought to enforce a subpoena for tenure review materials pursuant to a charge of discrimination by an associate professor denied tenure. The Supreme Court unanimously recognized the doctrine of institutional academic freedom in instances where the government seeks content-based regulation or where the government seeks to infringe the university's right to decide who can teach. Since the Court determined that the EEOC subpoena did not direct the institution's activities or speech or directly infringe on its right to decide who would teach, the Court found that institutional academic freedom did not cover the peer review materials and held that there is no general qualified privilege based on academic freedom protecting this review process from discovery.[32]

In this case, the Court also recognized that society needs institutions of higher learning and that institutions of higher learning often need confidentiality to function effectively. The Court, nonetheless, rejected these points as a justification for creating a general privilege protecting tenure review from discovery, unless the plaintiff could show a specific need for the material. The Court reasoned that the specific-need requirement placed too heavy a burden on the plaintiff complaining of discrimination.[33] Deference to the institution in this matter could subvert Title VII's policy of providing full relief to the injured plaintiff.[34]

The absence of a qualified privilege does not necessarily mean unlimited access to peer review materials. In a 1988 case, the New Jersey Supreme Court refused a privilege for peer review materials but held that trial courts should issue protective orders to prevent unlimited access and overbroad discovery.[35] Other courts have had similar holdings.[36] Court-ordered redaction (the blacking out of names or other identifying information) has also been permitted by some courts[37] but was specifically not decided by the Supreme Court in the *University of Pennsylvania* case.[38] Although it is not entirely clear at this time, redaction may be a viable means of preserving anonymity in the peer review process.[39] Similarly unclear is the ability of the courts to use a balancing approach, such as the *Gray* test, which compared the plaintiff's need to know with the institution's need for confidentiality.[40] This is an option that the *University of Pennsylvania* case did not address.

Where state law provides access to peer review materials by the employee (right-to-know laws) or the public in general, regarding public institutions (sunshine laws), the reasoning and guidelines provided by the court in the Pennsylvania case are inapplicable.

• **Some courts order reinstatement, promotion, or tenure where discrimination has been found.**

The traditional reluctance of the courts to interfere in the academic decisions of colleges and universities[41] is in tension with the Title VII policy of making those discriminated against in employment whole (i.e., placing them in the position they would have been in, had there been no discrimination).[42] In cases where discrimination is found to have played a part in the treatment of a faculty member, money damages are favored by most courts, although this remedy may not fully meet the Title VII goal of making the plaintiff whole in a tenure case.[43] Despite traditional deference to the institution, however, a few courts have held that the award of tenure by the court is appropriate where the court determines that but for the discrimination the faculty member would have been tenured by the institution.[44]

- **Colleges and universities with tenure and promotion policies incorporated into statutes and supporting regulations or contracts of employment will be held to those procedures.**

Public universities may be legally bound by statutes and/or administrative regulations that govern their procedures in the award of a tenure. Similarly, both public and private universities are bound by those procedures that are part of their contracts of employment with faculty members. Failure to provide the required procedure could in such case be a breach of contract. The remedy for such a violation is probably not the award of tenure, which usually requires a subjective assessment. Where, however, the award of tenure was based on an objective criteria (e.g., merely putting in time), the remedy for not awarding the tenure as prescribed may be the award of tenure.

In cases where the contract of employment is silent or ambiguous on a particular point, the courts will look to the ordinary and customary procedures in the institution, or other institutions, to clarify and interpret the contract. In such cases, the courts may rely on the faculty handbook, even if not explicitly incorporated into the contract of employment,[45] or on the AAUP's "1940 Statement of Principles on Academic Freedom and Tenure, with 1970 Interpretive Comments" (see discussion in Chapter 6), which is incorporated into many faculty handbooks and is generally considered to be the norm in academic practice.[46]

Oral or written assurances by administrators have, in some cases, become contractually binding when the administrator was deemed to have the authority to bind the institution.[47] Generally, however, oral promises will not amend a written contract.[48]

- **Ordinarily, courts will not award de facto tenure where there are written tenure policies.**

De facto tenure is tenure awarded by a court based on the facts and circumstances (e.g., operative institutional regulations or verbal or written assurances to the faculty member) that create a legitimate expectation of continuing employment, even though no affirmative grant of tenure has been made by the institution. This may occur when tenure procedures are not clear and explicit or are not adhered to by the institution.[49] Where there is a formal tenure process in place, however, the courts will generally not order tenure on a de facto basis.[50]

- **Faculty members acting in bad faith or with malice in the tenure peer review process may not be protected from liability for defamation or other torts.**

Defamation claims against faculty members evaluating the tenure and promotion applications of their peers have increased in recent years.[51] A *defamation* is a false communication to a third party that injures an individual's reputation or good name.[52] Faculty members and administrators participating in the peer review process may be protected from liability for defamation by state common law that provides a qualified privilege for those with a common duty or purpose, such as peer review. This protection can be lost, however, if the communication in question goes beyond the interest of the group or is made to persons with no need to receive the information.[53]

ETHICAL CONSIDERATIONS

The tenure and promotion process includes self-judgment but, more important, judgment by others. The burden of a positive or negative decision in promotion, tenure, and continuation of employment sits squarely on the shoulders of peer reviewers, administrators, and trustees. These are weighty responsibilities in which the principles of fairness, honesty, consistency, and adherence to institutional standards play a critical role. In most institutions, the process of peer review is accomplished by matching the candidate's academic and professional credentials with the mission, vision, and needs of the college or university and the criteria and standards derived from these. When a negative tenure decision is made, it says that the needs of the institution are not served by an ongoing employment relationship with this individual. In institutions where tenure and/ or advancement must be achieved in order for the faculty member to be retained, a negative decision can be a critical blow to the individual's career and could have a great impact on the institution as well.[54]

• Is faculty tenure still a viable and desirable concept?

One of the greatest debates in education, especially in the last decade of declining enrollments and retrenchment, has been over faculty tenure. Advocates of tenure strongly assert that tenure protects a faculty member's academic freedom by providing a certain job security, and it provides an institution with a cadre of faculty with long-term commitments and loyalty to the institution.[55] Those who are against tenure, however, assert that it is an outdated concept that protects unproductive faculty and severely limits an institution's ability to respond to budgetary pressures as well as to internal and external concerns about faculty productivity and accountability. Estimates on the financial impact of one faculty member's tenure on an institution are estimated at $2 million for the 30 or even 40 years the individual may be associated with that institution.[56] Since federal law in 1994 has made mandatory retirement for higher education faculty illegal, those costs may escalate, and the potential for diminishing returns to the institution in terms of performance of an aging (albeit experienced) faculty are a serious consideration.[57]

A 1993 National Study of Postsecondary Faculty reported by the National Education Association found that 74 percent of full-time faculty nationally either have tenure or are eligible to receive tenure.[58] Clearly, tenure is very much alive and desired by faculty, although there is a growing trend in institutions to either abolish tenure or hire faculty members on nontenure tracks.[59] Concerns have been raised about tenured faculty becoming "deadwood," shirking their responsibilities, becoming stale, unproductive, and outdated, using students to produce their research and writing, and becoming more interested in the institution's politics than in continuing to improve their teaching abilities or producing publishable scholarship. Some claim that there are professors who would not be hired if they were seeking their own positions today. Others fear that tenure results in retaining mediocre or deficient tenured faculty who may keep bright, young minds who are enthusiastic about teaching and scholarship and who would improve an institution's academic excellence from gaining access to the increasingly fewer faculty positions in today's limited job market. On the other hand, advocates of tenure may point to the fact that incompetent or corrupt tenured faculty *are* being dismissed, as is evident in our courts, and that if incompetent tenured faculty still exist, they *should* be dismissed, and it is the institution's fault if they are not. Why endanger academic freedom and punish productive faculty members by keeping them from attaining or retaining tenure when dismissal of incompetent faculty is an avenue open to administrators?[60] Additionally, defenders of the tenure system challenge its critics by claiming that the myth that tenured faculty stop being productive is not supported by data. A recent national study reported that tenured faculty "publish more, teach more classes, and serve on more committees" than untenured faculty.[61] Each institution must decide whether it favors the traditional protection of academic freedom and individual employment achieved by tenure over practical considerations, including maintenance of a strong and fluid faculty.

- **Is the provision of job security for faculty an ethical responsibility of the institution?**

An argument advanced by some fervent advocates of tenure is that the institution has an ethical responsibility to provide job security for professors who have in turn given the institution their loyalty and hard work during the most productive years of their lives. They believe it is unethical to systematically replace these faculty with younger, less expensive instructors (because the newcomers may enter the institution at a lower rank than the senior faculty). Because entrance, promotion, and tenure criteria may have been less demanding when the senior members of the faculty first received promotion and tenure, some of these tenured faculty members would not be easily hired at other institutions. Should the institution nonetheless abolish or change its tenure system? Is it ethical for the institution to award merit raises only when a faculty member agrees to be on a non-tenure-earning, multiyear (e.g., five-year) contract, with a review before the next contract is offered?[62] Do the institution's needs and concerns take precedence over those of its employees?

In an effort to come to terms with increasingly confusing considerations regarding tenure, many colleges and universities have reverted to rolling or multiyear contracts, and some institutions have instituted modifications while keeping the tenure concept intact. These alternatives include offering both tenure and non–tenure track appointments; abolishing the "up-or-out" rule (i.e., the faculty member cannot continue at the institution beyond one terminal year if unsuccessful in obtaining tenure, usually within seven years of employment); establishing tenure quotas (due to tenure "density"—measured as a percentage of those with tenure in a particular institution, school, or department); or granting tenure only if a posttenure review system is agreed upon.[63] The question for each institution considering such steps is how the action contemplated preserves, protects, and enhances academic freedom, academic excellence, faculty members' job security, and the institution's viability and success. A discussion of ethics and values should be part of any decision that has the potential to affect the survival of both the institution and its faculty members. Tenure is clearly one of these important decisions.

- **Should tenure standards be clear and articulated, and should faculty receive periodic feedback regarding adherence to these standards?**

Not only do promotion and tenure policies, procedures, and practices vary across institutions and even within units or departments in the same institution, but there is also great variability in the specificity and wording of those policies and procedures. Although most colleges and universities have some degree of formality and clarity in their documents regarding tenure and promotion, some institutions either do not provide explicit written statements or do not consistently apply their own policies and procedures.[64] Institutional priorities should be clear if they are to produce equally clear and consistent policies and practices regarding promotion and tenure, and any changes in promotion and tenure standards should be made fairly and with input from those individuals who will be affected.[65]

Institutions should also strive for consistency in the application of tenure standards. Inconsistencies may arise when various persons are applying the rules or when changes are made in their application. Failure to clearly delineate and disseminate policies and procedures, or inconsistency in their application, could result in morale problems, in addition to litigation and negative financial consequences.

Further, annual feedback to the faculty member on how they are faring with respect to progress on attaining the standards needed for tenure and/or promotion would also meet the goal of fairness, as well as serve to protect the institution against the appearance of arbitrary or discriminatory tenure and promotion decisions or the possibility of having to award tenure or promotion to an unworthy candidate solely on the basis of faulty or unfair procedures or insufficient feed-back.

- **Should an institution monitor apportionment of work and resources so as not to unduly burden a faculty member's ability to meet minimum criteria for promotion or tenure?**

Oftentimes, the institution may intentionally or unintentionally burden a faculty member with teaching loads or committee (service) assignments that would effectively preclude the individual from meeting the required standards for promotion or tenure. A lack of institutional facilities and resources, such as laboratory equipment or travel funds for presenting papers at conferences, may also jeopardize a faculty member's chances for success. In some institutions, administrators encourage faculty to take on administrative assignments (such as department chairpersonships) without discussing with the individual what possible repercussions this would have in his or her quest for advancement. The needs of the administrator in that particular moment for the administrative skills of the faculty member or for help in committee work, accreditation self-studies, or other work, albeit important, may result in keeping the faculty member from meeting other minimum criteria for advancement or tenure. Junior faculty members may have the option of turning down these assignments, but they may feel that if they do, they will be viewed as uncooperative. Most important, they may hope or be led to believe that these assignments will mitigate any lack of compliance with other minimum criteria at the time of their review. Institutional policies and/or communications with the affected faculty member that address whether these assignments should or would serve to supplant minimum criteria may help to clarify alternatives and prevent the institution from being viewed as unfair at the conclusion of the evaluation period.

Certainly, at the time of hire or during the probationary period, department heads or deans should not make specific promises to faculty, such as teaching assistants or other resources to help them, unless they are certain that those resources will be available to them.[66] It can be demoralizing to promise help to a faculty member in meeting tenure expectations, not provide the help promised, and still expect the person to meet those expectations. Some institutions, in order to equalize opportunities among faculty during their probationary periods, may consider being supportive in cases of special needs, such as extending the tenure clock for faculty who have interrupted their careers for family responsibilities and providing flexible scheduling and on-campus child care facilities.[67] Time limits could also be extended for those who have been unduly burdened by assignments or if institutional resources, especially if promised, have not been available. These generous attempts at meeting faculty members' needs will need to be balanced against the need of an institution to be consistent in its treatment of faculty.

- **Can the subjective judgments required by tenure evaluations meet standards of fairness and consistency?**

The most controversial aspect of tenure, if granted at all by an institution, is the method of evaluation of the individual's proficiency, credentials, and experience. Of the three areas mentioned, "scholarship" (research and publications) seems to be the most ambiguous and difficult to measure.[68] This ambiguity and possible inconsistency in tenure and promotion review procedures have raised questions of fairness. Fairness is not served, for example, when senior faculty, who want to judge each case independently and have the maximum latitude for their evaluations, refuse to quantify or specify the standards that must be met (e.g., "publication of a minimum of two articles a year in refereed journals, or a book and two articles in nonrefereed professional journals," rather than "appropriate publications"). In other instances, fairness is not served when existing standards are not applied consistently, as when a well-liked junior faculty member's credentials and research and publication record are evaluated with much more leniency and granted a broader interpretation of existing standards than those of another faculty member who is not as popular.

- **Is noncollegial behavior an appropriate and just criterion by which to judge peers?**

Courts have generally upheld denials of promotion, tenure, or reappointment of faculty members when the institution asserts that an individual's temperament or research interests do not "fit" in with the rest of the faculty.[69] However, the use of "noncollegial behavior" as a criterion for denying advancement or tenure is problematic in that it may be used as a "red herring" for discrimination or denial of academic freedom.[70] Although the use of collegiality as a standard has been accepted in the courts, especially when it is listed as part of the performance criteria already spelled out in the faculty handbook or other vehicle of dissemination,[71] the ethical issue remains. Is "fitting in" with other colleagues integral to the mission of the institution? If a faculty member is competent but not well liked by colleagues, what value is most important, congeniality or academic excellence (or scholarship)? Faculty members who may "march to a different drummer" may be well liked by students and admired by the scholarly community for their ideologies but not accepted by their peers. Should the search for truth, academic freedom, or academic excellence be considered less important as values than collegiality or congeniality? On the other hand, when lack of collegiality poses serious problems affecting performance, is the institution not justified in considering this an important criterion by which to assess faculty? Ultimately, each institution must decide whether collegiality, with its potential for abuse and ambiguity, is of sufficient import to remain as a criterion for the award of tenure or promotion.

- **In cases where disclosure of peer review records is not mandated, how much confidentiality should be promised evaluators and how much information regarding reasons for denial should be given to the unsuccessful candidate?**

Unless compelled by a court, most institutions prevent disclosure of peer review information when an unsuccessful candidate has requested such information. This clearly places the interests of candor and protection of reviewers from exposure over the rights of the faculty candidate to confront his or her evaluators or to learn more about his or her deficiencies. The ethical dilemma here is the conflict between the needs of the unsuccessful candidate to examine the reasons for failure, weigh their validity, and learn from them and the needs of the institution to be able to assure reviewers of confidentiality in order to encourage candor in their evaluations of candidates.

Redaction of documents may be a way in which confidentiality can be preserved while still providing information and evidence that fairness, consistency, and justice were applied in the decision-making process. However, especially in small institutions, the candidate is likely to know who said or wrote what in the review committee (even when records are redacted), and therefore confidentiality may still be in jeopardy.

The institution should decide what values are important for them to preserve and protect during the review process and balance those against the needs of the faculty member who is seeking promotion or tenure.

- **Is placing quotas on the number of faculty who may be tenured ("tenure density") a fair and equitable procedure?**

Even when an institution takes extreme care to ensure that its tenure policies and the review process are legal and reflect appropriate institutional values (such as fairness, justice, equity, and academic excellence), practical and administrative realities (such as the budgetary impact of tenure) may prompt an institution to establish a quotas or quotas on the maximum number of faculty who may be tenured in a specific department, in a college/school, or within the institution itself. Ethical questions arise when faculty members have successfully jumped through all the hoops and worked hard to attain the standards required by the criteria for advancement or tenure, only to be told that even though they are meritorious and have met all requirements, the "elevator" is full. No one else can ascend to higher levels because the elevator may carry only so many people, even if the ones left behind are worthier than the ones already inside the car or already on the top floors. If, on the other hand, the institution makes its tenure density policy known in advance to those applying, does this eliminate the ethical dilemma? For many institutions it may, because they believe the institution's survival takes precedence over the needs of individual faculty members.

If the elevator carries too many people, it endangers the lives of all those already in it.

Other institutions wrestle with this approach because it can mean the loss of fine faculty members. Many institutions have an "up-or-out rule," which means that those not granted tenure must leave the institution if denied tenure. For those who performed well, tenure density can mean that despite their good showing, they will be denied a job. This could affect not only the morale of faculty members but also their performance and availability. Should an institution stretch itself financially to the detriment of the program and the students in order to meet individual faculty members' needs? Will this ultimately serve its needs best?

An important test of whether an institution's identified ethics and values are consistent with the institution's actions is the manner in which unsuccessful candidates for tenure and promotion are treated, even when their failure was caused by their falling below the desired minimum criteria. Where caring, compassion, tolerance, and individual dignity are values espoused by the institution, then it follows that the unsuccessful faculty member will be treated according to those values. This may mean that the institution will try to be helpful to the faculty member in his or her attempts at finding other employment, as suggested by the code of ethics of selected professional associations, further detailed in Chapter 5.

PRACTICAL SUGGESTIONS

There are fewer areas where clear policies are more important in order to meet legal requirements and exercise fairness and consistency than in reappointment, tenure, and promotion of faculty. The following practical suggestions are aimed at protecting both the institution and its faculty members.

- **Steps to minimize the possibility of litigation start with clear, written policies and procedures and consistency in their application.**

It is advisable for institutions to take the initiative in creating clear contracts and written policies and procedures regarding tenure and promotion that are consistent with each other and applied in a consistent manner. This can prevent misunderstandings or charges of favoritism or discrimination. It can also help to avoid an unintended result, should the matter be submitted to a court's jurisdiction. If a contract is ambiguous or there are gaps in the information it provides, courts look to handbooks, to policies, and if necessary, to academic custom and usage to determine the rights and obligations of both the institution and the faculty member.[72]

The following documents and information are recommended for institutions in order to minimize misunderstandings and legal action:

- *Faculty employment contract.* The terms of the contract should state whether the appointment is tenure earning, and it may also include mention of any prior years' service to be credited toward tenure and/or promotion. The contract may, if appropriate and consistent with the institution's intentions, also include a reference to other internal documents, such as a faculty handbook, or to external documents, such as the AAUP's "1940 Statement of Principles," where tenure and promotion rules may be found. A more extensive discussion of faculty contracts is found in Chapter 2.

- *Internal documents.* Faculty handbooks, policy memoranda, and other such documents should contain:

  1. Detailed guidelines for reappointment, tenure, and promotion to each faculty rank and the procedures to be followed (e.g., who will transmit the final decision to the candidate; by what means—verbal, written, or both; and what, if any, appeals process is available to the faculty member when a negative decision is made);

  2. The criteria for promotion and tenure that the institution, ideally with input from the faculty, has determined as important to its mission (e.g., teaching excellence, research and publications as evidence of scholarly work, research and training grants, presentations at national or regional conferences, institutional or community service);

  3. Means of evaluating performance (e.g., ratings on student, administrative, and/or peer evaluations that measure "teaching excellence"; weight accorded to types of books produced or articles published in refereed and/or nonrefereed journals; amount of research and the weight accorded to sponsored research such as grants or contracts; number of professional presentations; quantity and type of institutional or community service); [73]

  4. Procedural protections provided to faculty, such as grievance processes.

  Any changes to these documents, especially to policies, procedures, criteria, or standards, should be made after consultation with the faculty or representatives from the faculty (e.g., faculty senate or forum). Consultation with faculty, although often optional, is geared at creating a "buy-in" attitude to policies or procedures or at least at creating or maintaining an attitude of openness and participation, without which morale may suffer. These policies and procedures should also be widely disseminated before they become effective. Under some circumstances, the institution may decide to provide a "grandfather/grandmother" clause, which usually means that new policies and procedures would be applied to new hires but not to those faculty already at the institution.

- *External documents.* If external documents are relied upon (e.g., AAUP standards, accreditation guidelines), they may be referenced in the faculty contract or internal documents and made available to faculty members and administrators.

Institutions may avoid the judicial granting of de facto tenure or tenure by default upon a legal challenge of an unsuccessful candidate by having clear, written policies specifying the method of acquiring tenure in its internal documents and carefully adhering to its own policies. Internal documents should be consistent with each other and, to the extent possible, leave no gaps. Where gaps exist, the courts may look to academic custom and usage and external documents such as the AAUP standards,[74] even if they were not included by the institution in the tenure process.

It is important to note that in public or private institutions where faculty are under a collective bargaining agreement, such union contracts may include agreed-upon rules and criteria regarding tenure and promotion. Since collective bargaining is a complex legal area,[75] administrators as well as faculty members should seek special legal and administrative assistance in order to better understand the implications of the contract and their rights and obligations under that contract.[76] Collective bargaining agreements in public higher education are permitted in some form by state law in 35 states, and private and religious institutions may, under the appropriate circumstances, also be allowed to unionize based on National Labor Relations Board decisions.[77] Therefore, administrators and faculty members may be involved in a unionized environment during their professional lives that will affect how their tenure and promotion policies are formulated and implemented.

- **Once the policies have been determined and properly prepared, steps may be taken to disseminate the information fully and to provide faculty with regular and periodic feedback on performance.**

Courts will look positively upon institutions that not only keep faculty members informed of the institution's policies and procedures regarding promotion and tenure but also provide systematic feedback on their progress.[78] There are many avenues open to administrators by which to inform faculty members of their rights and obligations regarding tenure and promotion. Before faculty members are hired, they should be made aware of those policies and procedures that will affect their employment and their opportunities for advancement and job security. In addition, once employed, they should receive helpful information on how to meet the various requirements and standards for tenure and/or promotion and on how they are performing.

The following are some of the avenues that can be utilized for disseminating information and providing such help to tenure track faculty:

- *Faculty handbook.* In addition to tenure application procedures and standards, a handbook might also contain more general information, such as teaching methods encouraged by the institution and tips and strategies on how to deal with particular student populations.

- *Orientation program.* A onetime orientation session, or an orientation program of a longer duration, such as one academic year, could be implemented to orient and inform new faculty about the requirements for tenure and the tenure process.[79]

- *Mentoring program.* Mentoring is commonly used for minority junior faculty but is recommended for all new faculty;[80] senior faculty or administrators could be utilized effectively as mentors.[81]

- *Formal and informal networking.* Networking aids the faculty member in his or her introduction to others in the faculty and administration and prevents the confusion and anxiety that could set in for the novice, especially in the first year.[82]

- *Systematic feedback on performance.* Feedback on criteria and standards for promotion and tenure is usually given in a formal or informal meeting with a department chairperson at least once a year and should be preceded by self-assessment and review of pertinent documents, such as teaching evaluations by students and/or peers and/or superordinate, actual publications, research activities, university and/or community service activities.

- *"Survival guides" and books.* Topics of these guides usually include items such as time management, faculty/student relations, and university politics.

- *Workshops and seminars.* Whether offered by the institution itself or by others outside the university, these workshops and seminars commonly focus on teaching methods, on how to publish or how to write grants, and on how to be an effective committee member.

The role of administrators in this ongoing review process cannot be overemphasized. Although a department chairperson may lack knowledge and/or authority, they are definitely instrumental in the socialization, mentoring, and review of junior faculty. The department or division chairperson is often the key person in making certain that funds are available to tenure track faculty for portfolio-building activities, such as attending conferences and meetings, and for research or project activities. Acutely aware of the tenure and promotion process, the chairperson may serve well as a junior faculty member's mentor.[83] In smaller or less complex institutions, a dean may serve this purpose as well, besides being supportive and approachable. In addition to meeting the faculty member's needs for information, assistance, encouragement, and support, this systematic faculty orientation and socialization will protect an institution from the perception that faculty were set up to fail.

- **Clear procedures and documentation of subjective and objective measures of performance are of utmost importance in the evaluation process for promotion and tenure.**

Most faculty jobs are complex and involve a multitude of roles in addition to teaching or research. They can also require involvement in departmental and institutional committees, community service, student advising, and even administrative tasks. For this reason, several people may be involved in the assessment. It is unlikely that one person will be qualified to assess all facets of the faculty member's performance and do so objectively. Multiple measures of performance are also advisable to lessen the possibility of discrimination or the perception of disparate treatment, as are multiple assessors.[84] Multiple assessors may include a review committee made up of the faculty member's peers (usually senior faculty, with the possible addition of an administrator), experts in the discipline of the faculty member from outside the institution, and most likely as a second or third level of review, top administrators such as a dean, and the chief academic officer or provost. The chief academic officer may also monitor the process of granting tenure and promotion throughout the institution and can thereby ensure that the policies and procedures are consistently implemented by the various academic departments, protecting the institution as well as the faculty candidates.[85]

Multiple performance measures may include student evaluations of teaching and/or advising; peer assessments of research, teaching, or publications; assessments of review committees, department heads, and other administrators; and critiques of evaluators from outside the institution ("external" reviewers).[86] The latter usually serve as consultants, and their evaluations are utilized to supplement rather than supplant those of the internal review committee and university administrators. These consultants or experts in the field are normally used to evaluate research and publications rather than teaching. In selecting external reviewers, it is important to match the candidate's and reviewers' areas of expertise, provide them with pertinent policies, procedures, and forms, and make certain that the verbal or written communication to the reviewers does not betray any prejudice or preference for a particular decision.[87] Careful records should be kept in case the matter results in a legal action.

Although administrators' roles in tenure and promotion decisions vary according to the nature and complexity of the institution, their most important role is to ensure that the institution and the individual are both protected. Typically, administrators, often with input from the faculty and following previously set procedures, will select the composition of the review committees and external reviewers, if any. They may also monitor the proceedings to ensure that they are carried out according to established procedures and, lastly, will notify candidates and process any grievances according to policy. Those charged with selecting the members of the internal review committees should look for the following characteristics in making their selections: (1) expertise in the faculty member's field and therefore ability to judge professional and academic credentials; (2) rank senior or at least equal to candidate; (3) familiarity with the day-to-day performance of candidate; (4) knowledge of the institution's mission, policies, and procedures.[88] In addition to institutional policies and procedures, administrators may help committee members understand their role and make their important and often sensitive role easier by providing as much guidance as possible. Some institutions and associations have developed their own guide to serving on promotion and tenure committees, which may include how to document and assess the different facets of faculty productivity.[89]

- Peer evaluators and administrators must be schooled and oriented as to their responsibilities vis-à-vis the institution's

**mission and must understand that they may be accountable
for their decision making during the peer review process.**

Administrators must keep current with legal trends regarding disclosure of
peer review materials in order to advise reviewers as to their rights to confidentiality. It is possible that peer review records will not be kept confidential in
case of claims where constitutional or civil rights are at issue, and peer evaluators should be so informed prior to their serving on the review committee or
as an external reviewer. Once a request for disclosure has been made, it is
advisable that institutions review their internal documents prior to complying
with such a request. Collective bargaining agreements or other internal polices
of the institution may contain certain obligations with respect to the disclosure
and retention of personnel records, including those regarding peer review. Although peer reviewers should be told that there may be a possibility of disclosure
of peer review materials—redacted or unredacted—upon a legal challenge, or,
in some cases, for certain internal purposes, such as grievances, it is imperative
to stress the importance of their general confidentiality. An unsuccessful tenure
candidate, for example, may not have a claim for damages based on defamation
if negative information is not made public. Peer reviewers should refrain from
commenting on the work of the committee unless authorized by a university
official.

- **Clear grievance procedures and opportunities for dispute
  resolution may avert potential lawsuits. Private institutions
  would benefit from demonstrating that they provide basic
  rights to faculty members, including a grievance process.**

It is advisable for institutions to have some internal processes for settling
complaints and disputes. The processes may vary, and some may be prescribed
by law or by a collective bargaining agreement. Dispute resolution may include
informal consultation, grievance procedures, mediation, arbitration, and formal
hearings.[90] Grievance procedures are, however, the most common and are seen
as means of ensuring fair treatment and avoiding litigation. A *grievance* is generally defined as a complaint based on a circumstance or action that is viewed
as just cause for protest. Grievance procedures, therefore, describe a system for
handling these complaints or disputes. Such a system may be simple, such as a
grievance committee that has the power to settle disputes, or more complex,
such as mediation or other dispute resolution processes.

Effective faculty grievance procedures are well disseminated, accessible, and
easy to use. They provide faculty and administration with an opportunity to
present their respective positions and evidence, and they should be structured
to yield decisions that are objective, consistent, and free from external and internal politics. Exhausting available internal grievance procedures may be necessary, under state law, before further external action or litigation may be

undertaken.[91] As with any processes that may be reviewed at a later date in a court of law, clear records are recommended, and if the institution is utilizing external precedents, such as AAUP rules, such rules should be made available in their entirety to all parties in the grievance process.

- **If an institution wishes to establish a tenure density criterion in reappointment, promotion, and tenure decisions, the rules should be logical, reasonable, and detailed, in order to stand up to a possible challenge in the courts.**

An institution may decide that it wishes to limit the numbers or percentages of faculty who may achieve tenure or advancement in rank. Some institutions have found that the effects of granting tenure or promotion to all those who prove they are qualified by the institution's own rules may be too devastating financially, both in the short run and certainly to their long-range fiscal plans. Declining enrollments and resulting retrenchment have made colleges and universities concerned about commitments that may extend several decades. Concurrently, and in deference to academic freedom and expertise, courts have generally not interfered with institutions in their determinations of the criteria and standards utilized in tenure and promotion decisions. This includes a policy or rules on tenure density, if these are logical, reasonable, and detailed.

Some tenure density rules establish a quota on how many faculty members may achieve tenure in a particular department or school and/or as a percentage of the entire faculty of the institution. Tenure density rules should state precisely at what point saturation is to be reached and what happens to faculty members who qualify for tenure or advancement through a peer review process or automatic tenure but do so at the time in which the institution has reached the saturation point. These procedures should include what criteria (e.g., seniority, rank) are to be used by a committee or administrators in case several faculty members are successful candidates within the same year but due to the tenure density rule are not all granted what they seek. If there is an "up-or-out" rule, provision must be made for terminating the faculty member, usually with a minimum of a year's notice, as recommended by the AAUP.[92] Alternatively, the rules should state if an extension is possible in the likely event that in subsequent years a tenured faculty member's retirement may "open up a slot" for the junior faculty member who was successful in his or her probationary period and was recommended for tenure (a "holding pattern"). In summary, tenure density rules must be as specific and clear as reduction in force rules, since they have the same effect for the institution and its faculty members.

ILLUSTRATIVE CASE

Description

Public University had clear and specific tenure and promotion policies and procedures that were published and disseminated in its Faculty Handbook and incorporated into each faculty contract by reference. Although no specific tenure quotas by department were established as criteria, there was mention in the handbook of a tenure "saturation" percentage of 75 percent of the total faculty in a school or college at the university. The criterion for tenure density had never been implemented, since the percentage of tenured faculty in each of the six schools was under 75 percent in fact, in the School of Education, only 62 percent of the faculty had tenure.

Roger Ordoñez, a 35-year-old Hispanic male, was hired as an assistant professor in the Education Department. He quickly became respected by his colleagues due to his popularity with his students and his hard work in school and university committees. By the end of his third year at Public University he had published two articles, one of which was coauthored and appeared in a refereed journal. About that time, Public University was beginning to prepare for reaccreditation by its regional accreditation association. The dean of the School of Education asked Dr. Ordoñez to head the school's self-study, a step required in the reaccreditation process. Although this request was very complimentary, Dr. Ordoñez had concerns that the time he would spend researching and writing the self-study would take away from his efforts to publish one book or five articles, a requirement for tenure, before having to submit his tenure application in his sixth year. If he did not obtain tenure and promotion, he would be dismissed from the university. Although he feared he would be considered less than a team player if he refused the chairpersonship of the self-study offered by the dean, he took his concerns to his department chairperson. He asked specifically what would happen if, as a result of the time commitment of the self-study and subsequent accreditation visit over the next two years, he failed to publish a book or at least three more articles, which would meet the minimum publication requirement. He hesitantly inquired if his teaching load could be reduced. The department chairperson told him that he should really take the self-study opportunity because the fact that the dean trusted him to accomplish that very important task reflected well on his abilities and leadership. The chairperson said that he was certain that when Dr. Ordoñez came up for tenure, the committee would take the self-study assignment into consideration. He counseled Dr. Ordoñez not to ask for a reduced teaching load because he received such high evaluations from students. After thinking it over, Dr. Ordoñez accepted the self-study chairpersonship for the School of Education. He became so involved in this task that he was only able to publish one additional article before the sixth year of his probationary period had ended. The self-study was well written, the school did very well in the accreditation visit, and the dean was pleased and sent Dr. Ordoñez a congratulatory letter.

During the sixth year of Dr. Ordoñez's employment with Public University, the provost merged the School of Education with the College of Arts and Sciences. The department chairperson of the Education Department left the university without writing a letter of support for Dr. Ordoñez, who applied for promotion and tenure that year, in accordance with the policies and procedures of the university. However, due to the merger and an increase in tenured faculty in the College of Arts and Sciences over the previous two years, the percentage of tenured faculty members in the now-combined School of Arts and Sciences (which included the former School of Education) rose to 76 percent owing to heavily tenured Arts and Sciences departments.

The peer review committee, consisting of faculty members from the now Department of Education and the new chairperson, upon review of Dr. Ordoñez's credentials, recommended that he be promoted to associate professor (a requirement for approval of tenure). However, the committee failed to recommend that tenure be granted, citing the tenure density rule. The committee did not mention any other reasons for its denial of tenure in its letter to the dean, but the notes of the committee meetings did reflect discussions that although Dr. Ordoñez excelled in teaching and service to the institution, his publication record did not meet the minimum standards stated in the Faculty Handbook. There was further mention in the committee as to his hard work in the reaccreditation process, his many committee assignments, his congeniality, and his total dedication to the students and to his colleagues. Someone on the committee stated that, although not required to do so, Dr. Ordoñez had office hours every day of the week and was available to students at least 40 hours each week. The dean of the School of Arts and Sciences denied tenure to Dr. Ordoñez and sent the recommendation to the provost, who also denied tenure. Finally, the president of the university, also denying tenure, sent a Notice of Nonreappointment with twelve months' notice to Dr. Ordoñez, in accordance with the university's policies on nonreappointment, which followed AAUP recommendations on dismissal of faculty members employed for more than two years.

Dr. Ordoñez filed a grievance, stating that the tenure density quota in the new School of Arts and Sciences prevented him from gaining tenure, whereas if the School of Education had not merged with the School of Arts and Sciences, the percentage of tenured faculty would have allowed him to achieve tenure. He further stated that his department chairperson (no longer at the university) had counseled him to accept the chairpersonship of the school's self-study and that the chairperson had stated that his service to the institution would be taken into consideration. Dr. Ordoñez stated that in the past other faculty members who had applied for tenure and had been given special assignments had been able to substitute some of the publication requirements for the special assignments. Further, he claimed that if the committee had not deemed him worthy of tenure, they would not have recommended promotion to associate professor. Finally, Dr. Ordoñez stated that Public University had an affirmative action policy quoted in the Faculty Handbook, which was incorporated by reference into his faculty contract. He therefore asserted he must be considered as a minority for purposes of tenure and that the university had a contractual obligation to advance minority applicants.

Analysis

Roger Ordoñez was a victim of bad timing. When he started at Public University, tenure density was not a concern. When he was "up for tenure" it was fatal to his application. Certainly from Dr. Ordoñez's perspective, he was treated unfairly. He performed well, he accepted a difficult assignment, he relied on the assurances of his chairperson and his dean, and after six years of effort and excellent teaching, he was denied tenure and given notice of termination because too many others had been tenured before him.

- **Meeting the requirements of law.**

The first question to be examined in this case is whether the university was legally permitted to set a tenure saturation level and not allow tenure awards that would exceed that level. Based on institutional academic freedom and the traditional deference the courts have given to academe, we can assume that absent some other legally prohibited reason for the decision not to give Dr. Ordoñez tenure, the answer is that it could deny him tenure on this ground. There are no legal requirements that obligate Public University to award tenure to a particular candidate. The courts have supported the university's right to determine who shall teach at its institution and how many of its teachers will be tenured, unless these decisions are based on legally prohibited bases. For example, in denying tenure, Public University could not violate constitutional requirements (First Amendment, equal treatment, and due process) and the terms of applicable statutes and regulations.

The university was also bound by the terms of its contract with Dr. Ordoñez and the policies and procedures incorporated into the contract or mandated by law. There is no indication in the case description that tenure was denied for a legally prohibited reason.

In this case, Public University had a tenure saturation policy described in its Faculty Handbook and incorporated in this policy by reference into its faculty contracts for employment. Both Dr. Ordoñez and the university were bound by this policy. To have awarded tenure when the saturation exceeded the designated level would have been in violation of a policy that had been developed, promulgated, and incorporated into the regulations that guided the university's conduct.

Perhaps Dr. Ordoñez was suggesting that because he started his tenure process in a separate School of Education, his application should be considered only in relation to the numbers of tenured faculty in Education, despite the merger. In other words, he should be "grandfathered" in this respect. Certainly, if his contract with the institution stated by its language, or by the policies it incorporated by reference, that he would be granted tenure unless the School of Education faculty had a tenure density of 75 percent, he might have an arguable position. The position would be weaker if this was implied rather than stated. Some courts have demonstrated that they support the right of an institution to make changes that can impact individual faculty negatively unless the institution is contractually bound not to do so. There is no indication in the facts presented that Dr. Ordoñez had the contractual protection described.

Dr. Ordoñez's affirmative action claim is inappropriate in this context. Affirmative action, if applicable (see Chapter 2 on hire), would only come into consideration if the university were considering two or more qualified persons for one available tenured space. In that event, remedying past discrimination might justify considering Dr. Ordoñez's minority classification in choosing between the candidates.

• **Ethical and practical considerations.**

Tenure density policies are controversial. Many believe that they are unfair to individual faculty members as well as to the institution. An outstanding, hardworking member of the academic community can lose his or her position and be lost to the institution because the numbers are not in his or her favor at the time of application. On the other hand, Public University and others have decided that while this may be a hardship for the individual as well as an element of loss for the institution, it is on the whole a protection of the viability of the institution. Concerns about obligations to the work life of numerous individuals, all of whom may not be necessary to the operation of the school, at a time of escalating costs, may have led Public University to opt for the fiscal control that a tenure density policy allows.

In his grievance, Dr. Ordoñez did not argue that the tenure density policy was incorrect or illegal. Instead, he asserted that the merger between the Schools of Education and Arts and Sciences prevented his gaining tenure. He implies that the merger was unfair. The implication might be that his needs should have influenced the actions of the university, and the merger should not have occurred. Such a position would probably not find strong support. The policy of tenure density itself indicates that this university determined that institutional needs take precedence over individual needs. Assuming the reasons for the merger were not the denial of tenure to Dr. Ordoñez and others in the School of Education, but were based on practical and academic considerations, a balance between Dr. Ordoñez's loss and the university's needs would weigh in favor of the university.

Dr. Ordoñez also states in his grievance that he was counseled to accept the chairmanship of the self-study and that this should have substituted for the publication requirement that he was unable to meet because of the demands of this assignment. He clearly performed well, and, he pointed out, his colleagues deemed him worthy of tenure, as evidenced by the promotion they approved. The facts indicate that while Dr. Ordoñez's failure to meet the publication requirement was discussed along with other aspects of his performance, including his excellent work on the self-study and as a teacher, it was the tenure density policy that resulted in the denial of tenure. Under the circumstances of the operative density policy, tenure could not have been awarded even if the publication requirement was clearly and fully met.

One wonders, however, why Public University and Dr. Ordoñez went through the entire tenure evaluation process if the density did not permit the award of tenure, no matter what the evaluation. Such a futile exercise can mislead and increase the possibility of strong feelings and legal action. Perhaps Public University should consider adopting alternatives to a denial of tenure and termination of employment for faculty who are deemed worthy of tenure but are denied on the grounds of saturation alone. Maybe a special designation could be created that indicates that the award would have been made but for tenure density statistics, or perhaps an opportunity to take the first available tenure slot, should it occur within a designated period of time, could be offered.

Under the circumstances presented, denial of tenure to Dr. Ordoñez, though unfair to him individually, was legally, ethically, and practically appropriate for Public University, although the tenure evaluation procedure followed, with its inevitable negative conclusion, may have been unfair and unnecessary and exacerbated Dr. Ordoñez's feelings of mistreatment.

NOTES

1. American Association of University Professors, "1940 Statement of Principles on Academic Freedom and Tenure, with 1970 Interpretive Comments," *AAUP Policy Documents and Reports* (Washington, DC: American Association of University Professors, 1995), 3–7.

2. Clisby Louise Hall Barrow, "Academic Freedom and the University Title VII Suit After *University of Pennsylvania v. EEOC* and *Brown v. Trustees of Boston University*," 43 *Vanderbilt Law Review* 1571, 1573, n.3 (October 1990).

3. *Faro v. New York University*, 502 F.2d 1229, 1231 (2d Cir. 1974).

4. Barrow, 1574 n.12.

5. See, e.g., *Sweezy v. New Hampshire*, 354 U.S. 234, 249 (1957); Susan L. Pacholski, "Title VII in the University: The Difference Academic Freedom Makes," 59 *University of Chicago Law Review* 1317, 1318 (1992).

6. U.S. Constit. amend. I.

7. Terence Leas and Charles J. Russo, "*Waters v. Churchill*: Autonomy for the Academy or Freedom for the Individual?" 93 *Ed. Law Rep.* 1099 (1994).

8. *The Regents of the University of Michigan v. Ewing*, 474 U.S. 214, 226 (1985), citing *Keyishian v. Board of Regents*, 385 U.S. 589, 603 (1967).

9. See 385 U.S. 589.

10. William A. Kaplin and Barbara A. Lee, *The Law of Higher Education: A Comprehensive Guide to Legal Implications of Administrative Decision Making*, 3rd ed. (San Francisco: Jossey-Bass, 1995), 301.

11. Richard H. Hiers, "Academic Freedom in Public Colleges and Universities: O Say, Does That Star-Spangled First Amendment Banner Yet Wave?" 40 *Wayne L. Rev.* 1, 5–10 (Fall 1993).

12. 385 U.S. 589.

13. 364 U.S. 479 (1960).

14. 391 U.S. 563 (1968).

15. See *Connick v. Meyers*, 461 U.S. 138 (1983).

16. *Givhan v. Western Line Consolidated School District*, 439 U.S. 410, (1979).

17. Hiers, 25–35.

18. *Mt. Healthy Board of Education v. Doyle*, 429 U.S. 274 (1977).

19. Barrow, 1581.

20. Kaplin and Lee, 300.

21. 408 U.S. 564 (1972).

22. See id.

23. *Perry v. Sindermann*, 408 U.S. 593 (1972).

24. 408 U.S. 573.

25. 426 U.S. 341 (1976).

26. *Bishop v. Wood*, 426 U.S. 341 (1976).

27. See Chapter 2.

28. See, e.g., *Ewing*, 474 U.S. 214; *Widmar v. Vincent*, 454 U.S. 263 (1981); 354 U.S. 234.

29. See nn. 2–4.

30. 493 U.S. 182 (1990).

31. Barrow, 1585.

32. *University of Pennsylvania v. EEOC*, 493 U.S. 182 (1990).

33. Id. at 192–194.

34. Pacholski, 1317.

35. *Dixon v. Rutgers*, 541 A.2d 1046. (1988).

36. See, e.g., *EEOC v. University of Notre Dame du Lac*, 715 F.2d 331 (7th Cir. 1983).

37. *EEOC v. Franklin & Marshall College*, 775 F.2d 110 (7th Cir. 1985).

38. 493 U.S. at 202 n.9.

39. Barrow, 1596.

40. *Gray v. Board of Higher Education*, 692 F.2d 901 (2nd Cir. 1982).

41. See, e.g., 474 U.S. at 225.

42. *Albemarle Paper Co. v. Moody*, 422 U.S. 405, 418–419 (1975).

43. Barrow, 1600–1602.

44. *Brown v. Trustees of Boston University*, 891 F.2d 337 (1st Cir. 1989), cert. denied, 110 S.Ct. 3217 (1990); *Kunda v. Muhlenberg College*, 621 F.2d 532 (3rd Cir. 1980); *Pyo v. Stockton State College*, 603 F. Supp. at 1278 (D.N.J. 1975).

45. *Greene v. Howard University*, 412 F.2d 1128 (D.C. Cir. 1969).

46. Steven Olswang and Barbara A. Lee, *Faculty Freedoms and Institutional Accountability: Interactions and Conflicts*, ASHE-ERIC Higher Education Report No. 5 (Washington, DC: George Washington University, 1984), 9.

47. *Lewis v. Loyola University of Chicago*, 500 N.E.2d 47 (Ill. Ct. App. 1986).

48. *Baker v. Lafayette College*, 504 A.2d 247 (Pa. Sup. Ct. 1986).

49. *Jones v. University of Central Oklahoma*, 13 F.3d 361 (10th Cir. 1993).

50. *Omlor v. Cleveland State University*, 543 N.E.2d 1238 (Ohio 1989).

51. Kaplin and Lee, 130.

52. *Black's Law Dictionary*, 6th ed. (St. Paul, MN: West, 1990), 417.

53. William L. Prosser and W. Page Keeton, *Prosser and Keeton on the Law of Torts*, 5th ed., ed. W. Page Keeton (St. Paul, MN: West, 1984), 828–829.

54. Frank Daly and Barbara K. Townsend, "Faculty Perceptions of the Department Chair's Role in Facilitating Tenure Acquisition" (paper presented at the annual meeting of the Association for the Study of Higher Education, Minneapolis, MN, October 29–November 3, 1992), ED 352 912, 1.

55. Terry L. Leap, *Tenure, Discrimination, and the Courts*, 2nd ed. (Ithaca, NY: ILR Press, 1995), 62.

56. George R. LaNoue, "Ethical Issues in Faculty Evaluation," in *Ethics and Higher Education*, ed. William W. May (New York: American Council on Education, Macmillan, 1990), 145.

57. Donald Kennedy, *Academic Duty* (Cambridge, MA: Harvard University Press, 1997), 134.

58. John Lee, "Tenure," *Update: NEA Higher Education Research Center* 1, no. 3 (1995): 1–6.

59. Leap, 64.

60. Burton M. Leiser, "Threats to Academic Freedom and Tenure," 15 *Pace Law Review* (1994): 15–67.

61. Lee, 5–6.

62. Kennedy, 137.

63. "U. of Mass. Trustees Reject Tenure for Three Professors," *Chronicle of Higher Education*, September 8, 1995, A27.

64. Benjamin Baez and John A. Centra, *Tenure, Promotion, and Reappointment: Legal and Administrative Implication*, ASHE-ERIC Higher Education Report No. 1 (Washington, DC: George Washington University, School of Education and Human Development, 1995), 3.

65. William G. Tierney and Robert A. Rhoads, *Faculty Socialization as a Cultural Process: A Mirror of Institutional Commitment*, ASHE-ERIC Higher Education Report No. 93–6 (Washington, DC: George Washington University, School of Education and Human Development, 1994), 49.

66. Leap, 198.

67. Ibid., 201.

68. LaNoue, 146.

69. R. M. Hendrickson and B. A. Lee, *Academic Employment and Retrenchment: Judicial Review and Administrative Action*, ASHE-ERIC Higher Education Report No. 8 (Washington, DC: Association for the Study of Higher Education, 1983), ED 240 972, 133.

70. Michael A. Olivas, *The Law and Higher Education: Cases and Materials on Colleges in Court*, 2nd ed. (Durham, NC: Carolina Academic Press, 1997), 318.

71. John W. Mullaney and Elizabeth M. Timberlake, "University Tenure and the Legal System: Procedures, Conflicts, and Resolutions," *Journal of Social Work Education* 30, no. 2 (Spring–Summer 1994): 176.

72. Baez and Centra, 19.

73. Leap, 193–194.

74. Baez and Centra, 26.

75. Gwen B. Williams and Perry A. Zirkel, "Academic Penetration in Faculty Collective Bargaining Contracts in Higher Education," *Research in Higher Education* 28, no. 1 (1988): 76–95.

76. Ibid., 15, 32, 34–39.

77. Ibid., 33.

78. Tierney and Rhoads, 44–45.

79. Ibid., 46.

80. Leap, 196.

81. Tierney and Rhoads, 53–61.

82. Ibid., 35–47.

83. Fran Daly and Barbara K. Townsend, "Faculty Perceptions of the Department Chair's Role in Facilitating Tenure Acquisition" (ASHE annual meeting paper, Minneapolis, MN (October 1992), ED 352 912, 7–16.

84. Leap, 204.

85. Mullaney and Timberlake, 179.

86. Leap, 204.

87. Mullaney and Timberlake, 178.

88. Ibid., 178–179.

89. Robert M. Diamond, *Serving on Promotion and Tenure Committees: A Faculty Guide* (Boston, MA: Anker, 1994).

90. Mullaney and Timberlake, 179.

91. Leap, 205–207.

92. Baez and Centra, 31.

Chapter 5

Terminations, Nonrenewals, and Reductions in Force

The termination or nonrenewal of a faculty member is one of the most difficult situations facing an academic administrator. Often there are personal as well as working relationships at stake and negative personal consequences for the employee and his or her family that make the action difficult for both employee and administrator. A termination is also of great interest to other employees who, in concern for their own futures as well as that of the terminated employee, may monitor the dismissal to see that all protection and procedures have been scrupulously provided. Consequently, a termination or nonrenewal can potentially have a significant impact on the legal health of the institution and on the morale of the entire institutional community.

Faculty under contract (tenured and nontenured) may usually be terminated only for a reason designated in the contract of employment, applicable collective bargaining agreement, or in the case of public institutions, applicable laws and rules. On the other hand, whether or not the institution retains a faculty member whose contract has expired is usually within the discretion of the institution, as long as the nonrenewal does not violate law or policy.

LEGAL PARAMETERS

- **Public and private institutions are prohibited from taking discriminatory employment actions.**

The prohibitions against discrimination in employment previously discussed with reference to hire (Chapter 2) and to the denial of tenure or promotion (Chapter 4) are also applicable to the termination of employment of faculty. The Constitution prohibits public institutions from discriminating because of race, sex, and gender. Under federal law, no institution may make termination decisions because of an individual's race, sex, religion, national origin, age, veteran status, or disability. State law may add to this list prohibitions based on other classifications such as marital status and sexual preference.

There are two different legal theories pursuant to which the institution terminating a faculty member may be held liable for discrimination: treating one or more members of a legally protected group differently than others (disparate treatment) or adopting a policy or procedure that unduly burdens one or more of the protected classifications (disparate impact).[1] In the university setting, disparate treatment is more commonly encountered. Tests and seniority as a basis for termination, which are often the focus of disparate impact claims, are not usually relevant to university or college employment.[2]

Although courts have been reluctant to become involved in academic employment matters because of concerns about the courts' ability to assess academic credentials and the courts' recognition of institutional academic freedom,[3] current judicial trends show an erosion of this deference when Title VII antidiscrimination protection is at issue.[4] Title VII is the principal federal statute protecting against discrimination in employment based on race, sex, religion, national origin, and retaliation for making a charge of discrimination. It is explained more fully in Chapter 2.

- **Terminations at public institutions must meet the constitutional requirements of the First and Fourteenth Amendments.**

The substantive due process protection provided by the Fourteenth Amendment guarantees that the reasons for terminating a tenured faculty member at a public institution are not over broad, arbitrary, and capricious or otherwise impair a constitutional right. For example, termination may not rest on unequal treatment or on the faculty member's exercise of First Amendment rights, including academic freedom. Free speech rights do not, however, protect faculty and administrators from termination when the speech in question is found to concern personal matters rather than issues of public concern[5] or if the speech regards public matters but conflicts with the institution's interest in providing an orderly and efficient education.[6] (See the discussions concerning the First Amendment in Chapters 4 and 6.)

Whenever a faculty member's liberty interest (usually reputation) or property interest (usually entitlement to continued employment) is impacted, as may be the case in the termination of a tenured faculty member or a faculty member working under an effective contract that is not due to expire, the faculty member is entitled to procedural due process.[7] The Supreme Court, in the case of *Cleve-*

land Board of Education v. Loudermill, stated that due process requires, at a minimum, notice of the charges and an opportunity to present one's side of the matter before the termination takes place. This hearing need not be elaborate. Its requisites vary depending on the nature of the interests involved and whether additional process is available in subsequent proceedings.[8] A Minnesota appeals court has held that due process proceedings in the case of a terminated tenured teacher must provide (1) notice in sufficient detail to permit the faculty member to refute the charges; (2) names of those whose charges constitute the basis for the termination and the facts upon which they rely; (3) reasonable time to prepare and opportunity to present a defense; and (4) and an impartial tribunal.[9] An Ohio appeals court held that due process in such circumstances requires (1) notice of the reasons for the termination before the final action; (2) adequate notice of a hearing; (3) a hearing at which the teacher may submit evidence to refute the charges; and (4) a final statement of the grounds for termination, if it should occur.[10] The final statement or decision has been found inadequate to satisfy due process when it did not provide a clear statement of the reasons for dismissal and the evidence that supported the conclusions drawn.[11] In *Matthews v. Eldridge*,[12] the Supreme Court held that procedural due process must be tailored to the situation considering the interest at risk, the chances of erroneous deprivation of the interest because of the procedure and the value of additional procedures, the nature of the government's interest, and the fiscal and administrative burden involved in additional procedures.[13] Based on the reasoning in *Matthews*, the court in *Frumkin v. Board of Trustees of Kent State*,[14] in considering the pretermination hearing for a tenured associate professor with an unsatisfactory performance record who was discharged when the federal funding for his position was cut, supported the institution's denial of a full adversarial trial in the pretermination hearing. The court held that under the circumstances involving Dr. Frumkin (it believed he had ample opportunity to present his case), due process did not require that Dr. Frumkin's counsel examine and cross-examine witnesses.[15]

Courts have distinguished between the process due when a termination is for cause and one that is based on financial exigency. In the case of financial exigency, a posttermination hearing was deemed adequate if it allowed a faculty member to challenge the sufficiency of the evidence for the layoff and the institution's adherence to the applicable criteria. A faculty member is entitled to an opportunity to allege that the true reason for the termination is constitutionally impermissible or arbitrary.[16] The specific criteria used to determine who will be terminated for a financial exigency or programmatic change and the order in which they are applied are not mandated by the Fourteenth Amendment to the Constitution, as long as they are reasonable.[17] Schools may consider factors other than tenure status or seniority in determining who should be terminated (e.g., enrollment, course and program evaluation, research, etc.).[18] However, uniform application of the criteria may be necessary to avoid charges of discrimination or arbitrary and capricious action.

In terminations for cause, due process requires that the institution's statement of required and/or prohibited behavior of faculty members may not be so vague that it fails to give faculty members adequate notice of what is expected.[19] Courts have, however, supported general statements of standards of behavior without specifics,[20] especially where it could be assumed that a reasonable person would know, based on the general statement, that the behavior in question would be prohibited.[21] Courts have also allowed institutions some latitude in interpreting the reach of their stated terms or standards.[22]

- **Termination procedures must conform to applicable statutes and regulations, collective bargaining agreements, and/or contracts of employment.**

In addition to meeting constitutional demands, public institutions must adhere to the requirements of applicable law, rules, and contracts with regard to the process and procedures afforded to the faculty member upon termination.[23] All institutions, public and private, must comply with the provisions of operative collective bargaining agreements and employment contracts. Failure to do so can result in a breach of contract action that may entitle the faculty member to relief.[24] However, minor deviations from such obligatory procedures that do not affect substantial interests would probably not be actionable.[25] Where there is a statute or regulation applicable to faculty in a public institution, its requirements may prevail over conflicting contractual terms.[26]

While some courts have held institutions to their promulgated policies whether or not they have been explicitly incorporated into contracts of employment (see following section), others have held that language in employment handbooks which is not incorporated in the employment contract is not binding.[27]

- **Tenured faculty may be terminated for reasons enumerated in statute, collective bargaining agreement, employment contract, institutional or governmental policies, and applicable regulations, or for reasons commonly regarded by the academic community as incorporated into the concept of tenure.**

Public and private institutions must adhere to contractual provisions (including those in collective bargaining agreements) and, in the case of public institutions, applicable laws and regulations for the reasons that may justify the termination of a tenured faculty member or one working under an effective contract. The reasons may be set out in the contract or in the institution's policies and bylaws, which are frequently incorporated by reference into the employment contract. Some institutions also incorporate the AAUP position (i.e., terminations may be made only "for adequate cause, except in the case of retirement for age, or under extraordinary circumstances because of financial exigencies")[28] directly or indirectly by adopting it as a policy. Courts have also incorporated the university's regulations into its contracts for employment even when the contracts themselves did not expressly provide for this incorporation.[29] In a case where financial exigency was not specified in a faculty member's contract as a reason for termination, or provided for in the college's bylaws, the court nonetheless held that the academic community recognized that tenure implicitly incorporated the ability of the institution to terminate tenured faculty for financial reasons, and thus a bona fide financial exigency could justify the termination of tenured faculty. The court pointed out that the purpose of tenure was to protect faculty from termination based on the content of teaching or research or for opinions voiced by a faculty member outside the classroom. A termination based on financial exigency being unrelated to these issues does not threaten the values protected by tenure.[30]

Similarly, federal courts and the AAUP in its "1940 Statement of Principles" recognize that a public institution has an implied contractual right to terminate a faculty member whose position is eliminated as part of a good-faith change in academic programming.[31]

The reasons that are commonly utilized to justify the termination of tenured faculty fall into two categories: One arising from financial or programmatic needs and the other related to the behavior and/or performance of the faculty member ("adequate cause"). In many institutions *adequate cause* is not specifically defined.[32] In others, the specific behaviors that constitute adequate cause may vary. Adequate cause has commonly included incompetency, insubordination, immorality, and neglect of duty. The AAUP has cited both incompetence and moral turpitude as possible grounds for dismissal. The Commission on Academic Tenure in Higher Education, established in part by the AAUP, recommended that adequate cause be restricted to incompetence or dishonesty in teaching and research, substantial and manifest neglect of duty, and personal conduct that substantially impairs the fulfillment of institutional responsibilities.[33] Where the contractual term, statute, or regulation does not specifically cite the behavior deemed to be adequate cause, courts may look to the AAUP and other institutions to determine custom and usage[34] or apply common sense in interpreting the reach of the criteria for termination. Courts have supported terminations for incompetence when they have been supported by the necessary evidence.[35] Courts have also supported adequate cause terminations for dishonesty,[36] sexual harassment,[37] and neglect of duty and insubordination.[38] Dismissals for insubordination are controversial. A charge of insubordination can be a subterfuge for retaliation based on speech. Even when intentional denial of speech or academic freedom is not the case, there can be a conflict between speech rights and the institution's legitimate need to provide its educational service without disruption (see the discussion concerning constitutional requirements).

- **The burden of proof of the existence of a bona fide financial exigency is on the institution. "Reductions in force"**

necessitated by financial exigencies and/or programmatic changes should be based on good-faith judgments of what is in the best interest of the institution and should be applied uniformly.

Courts have supported the termination of tenured faculty for a bona fide financial exigency even when there is no express grant of authority to the institution to terminate tenure faculty on this basis.[39] The burden of showing that a bona fide financial exigency exists is on the institution.[40] When financial exigency is defined in the contract governing the employment relationship with the faculty member being terminated, the institution must show that the requirements of the definition have been met.[41] In *AAUP v. Bloomfield College*, where 13 tenured faculty members were terminated, the institution failed to prove the existence of "extraordinary circumstances because of financial exigency" as required by its contract of employment, and the court therefore found that the employment contract had been breached and ordered the reinstatement of the terminated faculty.[42] A financial exigency is based on the availability of operating funds and not on capital assets.[43] It may be restricted to the particular department in which the faculty member is employed and need not be institutionwide.[44]

In a public institution, the criteria used to determine which faculty member or members will be terminated in the event of a financial exigency or programmatic change must conform to constitutional requirements (i.e., they cannot be discriminatory, deny free speech, be arbitrary or capricious—(see the section regarding public institutions) and must further conform to any applicable statute, rule, or contract. Where a financial exigency or programmatic change results in a termination, a private institution must refer to its governing employment contract and policies in determining the standards and procedures it will use in selecting those who will be terminated.[45] The court in *Krotkoff v. Goucher College* noted the AAUP position that "termination of continuous appointments because of financial exigency should be demonstrably bona fide" and asserted that the understanding of "bona fide" in this context by the academic community is that the institution use fair and reasonable standards to determine which faculty will be terminated.[46]

ETHICAL CONSIDERATIONS

Most faculty and administrators would agree that terminations for cause do not pose an ethical conflict as long as required standards of behavior and performance are clearly defined and communicated, employees are made aware of unmet expectations, and the legal requirements related to contracts, applicable law, and due process are met. On the other hand, reductions in force resulting from financial exigencies and programmatic changes, and not from poor performance, may raise numerous ethical questions and are often fraught with accusations of lack of fairness and loyalty. A reduction in force causes morale problems even when legally defensible. Institutional culture is very much at stake during such retrenchment. It is important to develop consensus on the criteria to be applied in determining who will be terminated before embarking on a downsizing venture. Personnel actions that are based on issues and principles determined through dialogue and participation by all concerned will more likely be fair and be perceived as such.

- **Is it ethical to tolerate gross misconduct or incompetency in an employee when termination for cause is an avenue open to administration?**

There is widespread acceptance in academia for the concept of termination of faculty and administrators for just cause, although cause may be defined differently among institutions. In fact, the American Association of University Professors, in its "1940 Statement of Principles on Academic Freedom and Tenure,"[47] sanctions termination for cause as long as provisions for a fair process are present. Yet there are many cases of misconduct and incompetency among faculty and administration that are ignored. Tenured professors are rarely the target of terminations for cause. The reasons most often cited for this are the reluctance of colleagues and many administrators to (1) label faculty by such an action unless there is strong proof of totally reprehensible or incompetent behavior that renders the faculty member unfit to teach or carry out his or her other duties and (2) spend the time and incur the emotional and financial costs necessary to terminate a tenured faculty member. In addition, proving incompetency or misconduct can be a tricky endeavor. The exact nature of the incompetent or inappropriate behavior must be well documented, and clear records are essential if the disciplining or dismissal is to stand up to a possible challenge by the employee. Further, there are usually requirements that the employee be advised of his or her failings and given an opportunity for remediation. Many administrators fail to keep any written records of the negative behavior or the ensuing warning or reprimand. As a result, faculty who miss their classes without notice, come to class unprepared, fail to meet office hours and keep appointments, dodge committee work, do not return students' papers or submit grades in a timely manner, or misuse class time may be ignored or, at best, lightly reprimanded. Unless there is a posttenure review, inadequate scholarship or poor teaching may also go unnoticed or unremediated. Sexual misconduct and fraud, on the other hand, are frequently acted upon because failure to do so can result in legal action against the institution. Academia seems to draw an invisible line between the obvious and the more subtle, albeit equally destructive, behaviors that have a negative impact on students and on the profession in general. Challenges and legal action based on incompetency are few compared to those arising from obvious misconduct, yet the effects of poor teaching and academic neglect may be multiplied by the number of students and colleagues with whom an incompetent faculty member comes in contact. Those in charge need to weigh the damage to students and to the mission of the university of not acting when it is known that a university employee is not discharging his or her duties in a competent manner.[48]

• Should personal bias/preferences be an acceptable basis for termination?

Court cases and anecdotal evidence indicate that all too often employees are dismissed or nonrenewed because of discrimination, personal bias, or preferences of an administrator, under the guise of cause or institutional needs. Such action is not only unfair to the individual terminated but also fails to reflect the institution's values or serve its best interests. In making and/or reviewing termination decisions, an administrator should analyze the reasons for the dismissal or nonrenewal to make certain the institution's values and needs are governing the action. For example, the institutional consensus may be that competency and excellence in performance should be the primary criteria for selection and retention. Is it ethical on such a campus, then, to terminate someone who is competent but not well liked and retain someone less competent but popular? Could the reverse be ethical if collegiality is determined to be the institution's most valued criteria? Clearly, an action based not on institutional values or needs but on the preferences of an administrator would be questionable at any institution.

The American Association of University Administrators, in their "Professional Standards," makes a strong statement regarding an administrator's responsibility to "treat subordinates fairly and equitably, and to avoid arbitrary or capricious actions, especially in situations relating to performance evaluations, promotions, demotions and/or the termination of employment."[49] (See Appendix 3 for the entire text.) In the same document, the AAUA also asserts the right of administrators to be treated in a similar manner by their superordinates.[50]

• Are reductions in force a fair and appropriate response to financial exigencies?

Reductions in force pose a dilemma that involves fairness to the institution and to the employee. Oftentimes in a reduction in force, competent, loyal employees not only lose their positions and livelihood but receive a severe moral blow from which it may be difficult to recover. Nonetheless, financial exigency may require this drastic action to ensure the survival of the institution and of the remaining employees.

To the extent possible, the institution should attempt financial cuts and changes in its operations without implementing a reduction in force and without affecting the quality of the services of the institution. Unfortunately, administrators are faced with impossible odds in achieving this goal. Cutting expenses usually does not yield sufficient results, because salary and benefits constitute the lion's share of institutional expenses—approximately two thirds—and, therefore, serious cost-cutting measures usually include the reduction of labor costs in the form of salary and benefits.[51] Some of the alternative options that institutions have implemented (salary freezes, office reorganization, early retirement plans, faculty buyout programs, reassignments, flextime, voluntary separation/layoffs, outsourcing of services), even when combined, often fall short of the bottom-line goal. Therefore, even heroic measures may not be enough to prevent administrators from facing necessary but painful cuts in faculty, staff, and administration. Ultimately, when the survival, health, and welfare of the institution are at stake, the values and ethics in academe support a decision to reduce the workforce. It is the administrator's task to ensure that the choices as to who is to be terminated and how the terminations are carried out are made with attention to ethical principles and respect for institutional values, including preserving the dignity of the individuals who must be terminated.

- **How do you implement a reduction in force (RIF) in an ethical manner?**

Once the decision has been made to reduce personnel, the goal of ethical staff reduction is to utilize approaches that ''conform to the institutional culture and allow the organization to retain its quality and vitality.''[52]

In determining a fair and just procedure for implementing a reduction in force, administrators are faced with difficult decisions, for which, most likely, they have not had any training. Few courses and seminars are available in managing reduction and downsizing, yet the skills for managing reduction are more complex, and more difficult, than the skills required in managing growth or stability.[53]

Some of the questions that must be addressed include how the targeted terminations are apportioned. For example, will cuts be made in a centralized or decentralized fashion? Will they be made across the board or according to a predetermined set of priorities? Studies seem to indicate that decentralized cuts are most effective because top administration, especially in large institutions, are not familiar enough with all units and their work to be able to downsize individual departments effectively. Some advocate that decentralized decision making led by deans, directors, and department heads ensures a higher level of support and comfort among the entire workforce.[54]

Terminated employees are understandably concerned about the future and perplexed because the concept of a family (where one is taken care of indefinitely and is not betrayed)[55] ceases to exist. It is helpful when the institution, in a humane and usually optional gesture, actively provides help and support to employees being released. In fact, the ''Professional Standards'' of the AAUA includes a clause that states that administrators have the responsibility (within the limits of their positions) to ''provide professional and technical support to subordinates whose employment is terminated for reasons other than for cause."[56] Similarly, the AAUA states that administrators have the right to receive the same professional and technical support from the institution in seeking new employment.[57] These statements are not incompatible with the concepts of family and fidelity and help to meet the ethical standard of fairness.

- **In downsizing the workforce, how does an administrator determine who stays and who goes fairly?**

Seniority, the most legally defensible basis for downsizing, may not serve the institution's best interests. Critics of across-the-board reduction in force by seniority claim that this traditional layoff plan upsets gains in diversity, because it means that the last hired will be the first to go. Since gains in recruiting and hiring women and minorities, in many institutions, have been made only recently, an institution would disproportionately lose the advances they have made to become diverse and multicultural. Layoffs by seniority may also fail to serve the goal of the institution of retaining high-quality staff because performance and longevity may not be necessarily related or may even be in an inverse relationship. If diversity is an important value in the institution, administrators may wish to explore other methods to preserve their gains in this institutional objective.

If the institution's values and needs would not be served by across-the-board reductions, another less common method, the *function-oriented approach*, may have merit, depending on the situation and demographics of the institution. This approach calls for administration to analyze what functions must be performed, who among the employees is essential to those tasks, and then creatively reorder responsibilities to accomplish them more efficiently. The values prevalent in this approach are, therefore, related to efficiency and productivity. Advocates of this method, such as Wesleyan College and Middlebury College, both of which implemented reductions in force early in the 1990s, also feel that the function-oriented approach is more effective than other ways to implement cuts, including seeking volunteers to leave.[58] When you seek volunteers, you often lose the people the institution wants to keep. This may create a need to hire new staff to perform necessary duties without relieving the institution of the need to cut other positions.[59]

A third method for selecting those to terminate would be to use a bottom-line analysis to help evaluate positions. For example, those departments or persons who produce more get to stay.[60] In addition, there are a number of other criteria to consider that could be important for the survival and health of the institution, such as program quality, student demand, market conditions, and suitability of programs to the institution's mission. This approach responds to the demands for entrepreneurship and financial priorities as values. Institutions may be wise to think through different scenarios of varied approaches to determine which method is best suited to the institution and reflects its values.

PRACTICAL SUGGESTIONS

- **Policies regarding terminations, nonreappointments/ nonrenewals, and reductions in force must be written in a clear and detailed manner.**

Policies are more likely to be effective if they are developed through participation by faculty and staff as well as by administrators and when they reflect the culture of the institution.

Regardless of the level of participation from the constituencies affected, when writing policies and procedures regarding terminations, nonreappointments, and reductions in force, institutions would be better informed and therefore better protected if administrators would consult with appropriate experts, such as university counsel, accountants, affirmative action and/or human resource specialists, and union representatives. These individuals would review drafts and make recommendations before the final versions are approved and disseminated. The policies and procedures should be written so that they can be clearly understood by all who would be affected and with enough detail to avoid ambiguity in terms and substance.

Policies and procedures for termination for cause should be as specific as deemed advisable by legal counsel. In both public and private institutions, the policies can determine whether a behavior or circumstance can legally justify a dismissal. The phrase "any good cause" may not be interpreted by the courts, upon a challenge by an employee, as a specific enough reason to include the facts regarding the terminated employee.[61] Financial exigency and program discontinuance have been recognized by the courts and by academe as sufficient reasons to terminate employees, and policies should reflect these eventualities. Specific behaviors that justify termination for cause, such as incompetence, insubordination, moral turpitude, and others, can also be mentioned in policies as definitions of "good cause" and have been widely accepted in academic circles as well as in the courts.

If there is mention of reduction in force by financial exigency, the institution must decide if the term is to include the financial state of the institution as a whole or of a particular unit. Sometimes financial issues lead to the discontinuance of a major or activity or to the closing of a facility such as a satellite campus. Some policies specify on what grounds tenured and untenured faculty may be dismissed due to the elimination of a department or a program.[62]

It is advisable for an institution to distinguish between financial exigency and program discontinuance unrelated to financial exigency when drafting or amending contracts for nontenured and tenuretrack faculty, when interpreting existing tenure contracts, or when writing or revising applicable policies and procedures to be included in other documents. Although public institutions should first and foremost ascertain that state law has been followed in the drafting or revision of the policies and procedures, many public and private institutions may choose to adopt the AAUP's recommended regulations on these matters, as long as these do not conflict with applicable law and administrative regulations. The AAUP standards can be incorporated by reference into faculty contracts, faculty handbooks, or other appropriate documents. It is important for institutions to realize that silence on a particular policy or procedure could later on be filled in or interpreted by the courts, upon a challenge by a faculty member, by following AAUP "industry" requirements on the issues.[63]

For public institutions, policies and procedures regarding financial exigency or program closure or discontinuance may be defined not only in the individual faculty member's contract, and/or in the collective bargaining contract, but also in the state constitution or state statutes or in the administrative rules and regulations that implement said statutes.[64] These documents should be consistent with one another.

- **Terminations for cause during the term of an employee's contract call for policies and procedures providing due process.**

When terminating an employee for cause during the term of his or her contract, public institutions are required, and private institutions are strongly encouraged, to provide due process procedures for the protection of both parties (see "Legal Parameters" section of this chapter). Policies regarding dismissal and due process procedures should be clearly stated and disseminated. They can be part of the faculty contract, an appendix, or written somewhere else, such as in a faculty handbook. Policies and procedures written in separate documents such as a faculty handbook may be made a part of the faculty contract or letter of appointment by including a reference to the handbook or other document where the policies and procedures are to be found.

Actual due process or "fair" procedures may vary depending on whether the institution is public or private. A public institution may be bound by state law to adopt policies and procedures regarding dismissal and due process that are written and approved outside the institution. It is the institution's responsibility to carry them out and to prevent the adoption or implementation of any institutional rule that may conflict with those set by a higher authority. Here again, it may be helpful to the private institution to base its policies and procedures for due process on the AAUP guidelines.

- **Faculty and some administrators may have a right to a notice period in cases of nonrenewal or termination. Buyout of the notice period may be a consideration.**

When the decision is made to terminate a tenured faculty member, or not to renew the contract of a faculty member who is untenured or of an administrator with a term contract, and the non-renewal or non-reappointment is not for cause, a notice period is customary and ethically desirable. The length of the notice period will vary according to applicable laws and institutional regulations and policies. If a notice period is normally granted, the length of the notice and other details should be part of institutional documents, and/or stated in the faculty or administrative contract, if not already stipulated in a collective bargaining agreement. The length of the notice period may be contingent upon years of service or other criteria. For untenured faculty who are non-renewed without cause, the industry standard is a year's notice. Notice period for administrators varies widely from institution to institution, and with the level of the position. Most institutions do give written notice to employees, and many use thirty days as a notice period.[65]

Administrators may decide to buy out (pay) an individual's notice period, so that his or her employment would terminate sooner, by paying the individual the salary and benefits he or she would have earned during the notice period. This decision may be made if there is not sufficient work for the individual, or if there are other concerns. However, caution is advised because the faculty member may view a buyout as discriminatory or an attempt to quiet his or her dissent. It is a good idea to review the facts with counsel before action is taken and to explore the availability of securing a release of liability as part of the buyout action.

An alternative to a buyout of a notice period may be reassignment of the duties of the individual vis-à-vis the needs of the institution and/or unit. The availability of this action depends on whether the controlling contracts and policies of the institution permit the reassignment. Where possible, reassignment of duties can also eliminate or postpone the need for filling the position that is being vacated.

- **Cost-cutting options include salary freezes, reorganizations, early retirement plans, faculty buyout programs, reassignments, flextime, voluntary separation/furloughs, layoffs, and outsourcing.**

When it becomes apparent that cost-cutting measures are necessary, the administration should calculate how much to reduce and make provisions to reduce expenses permanently. In order to accomplish the task in a thorough manner, zero-based budgeting may be advisable. This type of budgeting asks managers to justify expenditures in every line item of the budget. Zero-based budgeting, although not necessarily recommended as a normal budget process, provides administrators with an understanding of the unit's mandatory commitments and forces unit managers to justify and prioritize expenditures in every line item of the budget.[66]

Immediate measures to reduce expenditures while a major cost-cutting plan is on the drawing board include:

- Delaying salary increments (freezing salaries) for a specified period
- Limiting new faculty, administrative, and staff hiring, with a provision for and process to determine essential positions
- Limiting temporary employment and supplementary (including overtime) hours
- Reducing the use of outside contractors, or deciding to outsource (contract services performed by the institution, such as food service or security), to an outside entity, depending on cost analysis of which is more cost-efficient, while retaining quality of services
- Limiting capital expenditures
- Cutting staff benefits and student aid
- Increasing numbers of students and/or raising tuition
- Expanding continuing education and summer programs.[67]

This is only a partial list, and some of the items may be drastic, undesirable, or impractical, affecting the institution's effectiveness without yielding the desired permanent reductions that a larger reduction in force might accomplish.

Some institutions may be more creative than others, and early retirement plans, faculty buyout programs, reassignments, and the use of flextime (fluctuating schedules), voluntary separations, and layoffs have been instituted by an increasing number of colleges and universities.

- **Once the decision to downsize has been made, there are important implementation strategies that should not be ignored.**

The vision and the mission of the institution should drive any downsizing plan. Change, especially retrenchment/downsizing, is very painful for many people throughout the institution. Therefore, a downsizing plan may be more effective if it is arrived at by consensus or after consultation with those whose operations will be affected. That means that unit managers should be involved, since they have the best knowledge of priorities in their units, and there must be a "buy-in" of the plan for a smooth implementation. Some institutions use task forces to plan; others employ outside experts. In any case, a downsizing plan could take up to a year to implement, and some may take two to three years to fully put in place.[68]

In determining unit cuts, administrators would do well to analyze for each unit the centrality of the program to the mission of the institution, the quality of the program or major, the demand for the program's services, its costs (relative to comparable programs within the institution and at other institutions), the potential redistribution of resources, negative effects of cutbacks, the protection of rights of tenured faculty, and adherence to policies regarding untenured faculty, administrators, and staff.[69]

Whether cuts are made across the board or by priorities, major guidelines for reductions are:

- Cuts should not transfer responsibility to other units without being accompanied by funds to discharge those responsibilities.

- Reductions in staffing should be related to reductions in work.

- Objectives and expectations must be revisited to prevent frustration and low morale in a unit that has changed in size or scope.[70]

- Support staff must be kept at a level necessary to maintain the effectiveness of a unit.[71]

A sign of the times is that a number of institutions have already experienced downsizing and resizing, especially in the last decade. The methods and steps an institution may want to take on the road to effecting reductions should suit the circumstances of each institution. However, administrators from institutions who have experienced downsizing have suggested that institutions may wish to avoid totally centralized decision making, continuation of unaffordable benefits, short-term closures, short-term widespread layoffs, layoffs by seniority, reduction in hours, and reduction in salaries.[72]

- **Administration should maintain prompt and candid two-way communication with all constituencies from the moment a fiscal problem has been identified.**

Institutions who have had successful downsizing experiences assert that communication about fiscal problems and possible cuts should start early, at the first sign of trouble. Constituencies in the institution will be more cooperative if they have a sense of involvement, communication, and honesty from the administration. Two-way communication can be accomplished through many channels and is important to diffuse and diminish anxieties.[73] Employees who will be terminated in a reduction in force, and their colleagues, should hear the news in a timely and appropriate manner. If an outplacement or consultant firm is employed, the institution should preserve control so that the collegiality individuals expect in academia is not violated. Administrators who will dispense the bad news might benefit from training on how to deal with various situations that may arise.[74]

- **Reduction in force implementation must include planning the best way to break the news to those who are to be dismissed and to those who remain.**

How to break the news to those being terminated will require some planning. First and foremost, public institutions must follow any applicable laws, rules, or guidelines for giving notice. In private institutions and for those public institutions that may have latitude as to how to convey the news, experts advise to do so privately, in a neutral location, although the literature is divided as to what day of the week and what time of day are better. Administrators should allow time for the employees to vent their feelings.[75] Those conveying the news should be straightforward, should be familiar with the policies so they can answer any questions, and should schedule enough time to explain all the issues; but they should also be brief enough not to belabor a discussion over a decision that has already been made.[76] Those who remain employed by the institution should also be briefed as to the planned action and how the decisions were made. When no further cuts are planned, this information should be communicated to those remaining to alleviate any concerns they may have about their own positions. It is also advisable to issue a clear press release announcing the reduction, the general reason for the steps taken, and the number of jobs that have been eliminated. This may help to forestall rumors and misinformation in the community.

- **Institutions can provide practical, humane support for those whose positions are being eliminated.**

Many institutions have provided practical, humane support for those who are losing their jobs. This support ranges from counseling to help in retraining and searching for new positions. Support groups have also been found to be effective, and continuation of benefits for a specified period of time is certainly a way in which institutions can help alleviate pressure and anxiety.[77]

Whatever support activities are offered, however, do not come without attendant costs. Administrators must make certain that costs are included in the budget for the support given to those losing their jobs and that individuals with responsibilities for implementing support procedures are identified and trained.

ILLUSTRATIVE CASE

Description

Dr. Everett Carter was hired as an assistant dean of the Health Sciences Division of Parks Community College, 1 of 20 public community college institutions in the state. Funding for community colleges had decreased steadily for three years, due to a drop in enrollments and public support for education. In an effort to avoid a reduction in force, the college had instituted measures to try to meet the budget shortfalls. These measures included freezing administrators' salaries for two years, and faculty salaries for one year, reducing travel budgets, and contracting out (outsourcing) security, computing services, payroll services, and food services. However, after two years, when no progress had been made in preventing budget deficits, the central administration moved to make programmatic decisions that would result in cuts in faculty, administration, and staff.

Claiming financial exigency, the college decided to eliminate three of its six health-related majors. The three majors that were to be eliminated had lost enrollments due to declining demands in the marketplace. The few students who were enrolled in the majors were to be serviced by a combination of full-time instructors in the remaining majors and part-time instructors specializing in the three majors being eliminated. Dr. Carter, one of three assistant deans in the Health Sciences division, taught one course per term in one of the majors being eliminated and helped with the administration of all of the majors in the division. Two untenured full-time faculty teaching in the majors to be cut were given termination letters that stated the elimination of the majors as the cause for termination. Both faculty members were given, according to the policies set in the Faculty Handbook, notice for one academic year and were offered payment of one academic year's salary in lieu of "living out" their notice. One faculty member took the payments in lieu of notice, and the other decided to continue to teach throughout the notice year. Dr. Carter was given a letter of termination stating financial exigency as the cause of his dismissal. The Faculty Handbook and Employee Handbook of the college were silent on the matter of financial exigency as a cause for dismissal. Programmatic changes were mentioned as a possible cause, along with incompetency, immorality, and insubordination. Administrators were bound by the policies and procedures found in the Employee Handbook, and the relevant policy on termination stated that administrators were to receive a 90-day notice.

Dr. Carter was given a 90-day notice in his termination letter, with no offer for payment in lieu of notice. The dean of the Health Sciences division presented the letter to Dr. Carter in the division office and offered to hire him part-time to teach in the core areas of the division for the remainder of the academic year. Dr. Carter, quite distressed at his dismissal after five years of employment as an assistant dean at the college, where he had received excellent evaluations, declined the offer of part-time teaching and asked for a grievance hearing on his termination. Everett Carter claimed that the other two assistant deans, a female and a minority male, had been in the division for at least one year less than he and that their evaluations were not as exemplary as his. As far as he had been told, there had been no consideration by the top administration of terminating the other two assistant deans. The college agreed to a hearing, and Dr. Carter was allowed to bring counsel or other representative, although the attorney or other representative could not speak or cross-examine witnesses. Since there were no collective bargaining agreements for faculty or administration in the college, Dr. Carter decided to bring an attorney to the hearing. After Dr. Carter presented his case with the assistance of his attorney, the committee took the matter into advisement and later informed Dr. Carter that it was upholding the decision to terminate his position.

Analysis

- **Meeting the requirements of law.**

Parks Community College had a shortfall in its operating funds, and after futile attempts to resolve the monetary deficiency through cost-cutting measures, it had begun to cut programs and staff. Do these circumstances constitute a bona fide financial exigency under the law? While the courts have not always agreed on the precise definition of financial exigency that would permit the termination of contract employees, there is some consensus that there must be an insufficiency of operating funds to cover expenses and that this insufficiency cannot be remedied by less drastic means. Although we are not given a full picture of Parks' finances, it appears from the case presented that the institution was experiencing a financial exigency.

Does this exigency permit the nonrenewal of untenured faculty? Untenured faculty have no property interest in their employment beyond the termination date of the contract under which they are teaching and consequently no right to a due process hearing. Parks' Faculty Handbook, which may or may not have been incorporated into employment contracts, provided for a year's notice of termination. Consequently, if Parks allowed the terminated faculty to complete their current contract year and provided the one year of notice (or one year's pay in lieu of notice, which did not violate any contractual obligation), Parks would have conformed to its regulations and contract and would have been in conformance to the legal requirements on this issue. If, on the other hand, Parks had terminated these faculty members during the effective term of their contract year, then it would have had to terminate them for a reason permitted by law (statute and Constitution) or contract and provide a due process hearing. In this instance, the Faculty Handbook, which may or may not be explicitly incorporated into the contract, stated that programmatic changes justified termination. Some courts have held that the terms of the handbook are part of the contract even when they were not explicitly incorporated. Even if this were not the case in the jurisdiction that included Parks, the termination may have been supported because it was based on a bona fide financial exigency that led to the programmatic changes. Some courts and the AAUP have stated that a financial exigency, even if not specifically provided for in contract, is appropriate grounds for termination of faculty under contract.

Does a programmatic change based on a financial exigency permit the termination of Dr. Carter, an administrator, during the effective term of his contract? The facts provided assert that Dr. Carter, whose contract was in effect, was bound by handbook provisions, incorporated into his contract, which allowed for dismissal for the reasons stated in the handbook during the term of the contract, upon 90 days' notice. One of the stated reasons was programmatic changes. As stated above, some courts have also upheld a termination based on financial exigency. In this instance, however, the programmatic change resulting from the financial problems at Parks required that only one of three administrators at Carter's level be terminated. Under the Fourteenth Amendment to the Constitution, the selection of Dr. Carter for termination could not have been arbitrary and capricious, nor could it have been accomplished without providing

Dr. Carter with a due process hearing. Also prohibited would have been a termination for the exercise of his First Amendment freedoms. Finally, under Title VII of the Civil Rights Act of 1964, the Age Discrimination in Employment Act, and the Americans with Disabilities Act, or other applicable laws prohibiting discrimination in employment, the reason for the selection of Dr. Carter for termination instead of one of the other two administrators could not have been based on his race, gender, nationality, age, disability, or other protected classification. The facts do not tell us why Dr. Carter was selected, but the implication is that race and gender did play a part. Carter was the senior administrator, and he had the best record of performance. Clearly the basis for the selection was not seniority or skill. Even if there were another plausible basis for the selection, Parks may face legal action because the apparent reason may be discriminatory. A public employer such as Parks could make employment decisions based on race and sex only in compelling circumstances that meet the standards of Title VII and of the Equal Protection Clause of the Constitution.

The issue here is not the financial exigency or the programmatic change but the basis of the selection of Dr. Carter for termination. The hearing provided should give Dr. Carter an opportunity to challenge the standards of selection and their application to him. We do not have sufficient facts to evaluate the adequacy of the hearing. However, the law would probably support the institution's decision to allow Dr. Carter the presence and advice of counsel but not permit counsel to speak or cross-examine witness.

- **Ethical considerations.**

Parks tried other means before reducing its workforce, demonstrating its concern for its employees. The facts convey an effort by Parks to give Dr. Carter a part-time position, although they were under no obligation to do so. This demonstrates at the least that there was a concern for his welfare. Since we do not know the reasoning process that led to the selection of Dr. Carter for termination, we cannot evaluate this choice against the institution's values, mission, and needs. If the decision were an attempt to retain diversity among the administrative staff, it may have reflected values of the institution but, in this case, may not have met legal standard. One might also question the manner in which Dr. Carter was advised of his termination. The facts do not indicate that he was advised of the reasons for his selection to be terminated. The institution may well have treated him in this less-than-forthright manner because of concerns about the legal issues raised by choosing him for termination. If this is the case, one might question the ethics of these actions.

- **Practical considerations.**

Budget and practical fiscal considerations were the motivating force behind the actions taken. In this situation, the practical concerns were paramount and could not be ignored, lest they threaten the survival of the institution.

NOTES

1. See Chapter 2, "Hiring Issues."

2. George R. Kramer, "Title VII on Campus: Judicial Review of University Employment Decisions," 82 *Columbia Law Review* 1206, 1211, 1213 (October 1982).

3. *Dorsett v. Board of Trustees for State Colleges and Universities*, 940 F.2d 121, 124 (5th Cir. 1991).

4. See Chapter 4, "Promotion and Tenure Issues."

5. *Givhan v. Western Line Consolidated School District*, 439 U.S. 410 (1979).

6. *Pickering v. Board of Education*, 391 U.S. 563 (1968).

7. *Board of Regents v. Roth*, 408 U.S. 564 (1972); *Perry v. Sindermann*, 408 U.S. 593, 598 (1972).

8. 470 U.S. 532, 543 (1985).

9. *King v. University of Minnesota*, 744 F.2d 224, 228 (8th Cir. 1985).

10. *Potemra v. Ping*, 462 F. Supp. 328, 332 (E.D. Ohio 1978).

11. *Clarke v. West Virginia Board of Regents*, 279 S.E.2d 169, 177 (W.Va. 1981).

12. 424 U.S. 319 (1976).

13. Id. at 333–335.

14. 626 F.2d 19 (6th Cir. 1980).

15. Id. at 20–21.

16. *Johnson v. Board of Regents of the University of Wisconsin*, 377 F. Supp. 227, 239 (Dist. Ct. W.D. Wisconsin 1974), aff'd, 510 F.2d 975 (7th Cir. 1975).

17. *Brenna v. Southern Colorado State College*, 589 F.2d 475 (10th Cir. 1978).

18. See *Milbouer v. Keppler*, 644 F. Supp. 201, 204 (D. Idaho 1986).

19. William A. Kaplin and Barbara A. Lee, *The Law of Higher Education: A Comprehensive Guide to Legal Implications of Administrative Decision Making*, 3rd ed. (San Francisco: Jossey-Bass, 1995), 272.

20. *Arnett v. Kennedy*, 416 U.S. 134, 157 (1974).

21. *San Filippo v. Bongiovanni*, 961 F.2d 1125, 1137 (3rd Cir. 1992).

22. *Korf v. Ball State University*, 726 F.2d 1222 (7th Cir. 1984).

23. See *Subryan v. Regents of the University of Colorado*, 698 P.2d 1383 (Colo. Ct. App. 1984).

24. See *Sternsrud v. Mayville State College*, 368 N.W.2d 519 (N.D. 1985).

25. *Piacitelli v. Southern Utah State College*, 636 P.2d 1063, 1066 (Utah 1981).

26. *Subryan*, 698 P.2d 1383.

27. *Marson v. Northwestern State University*, 607 So.2d 1093 (La. Ct. App. Nov. 4, 1992).

28. American Association of University Professors, "1940 Statement of Principles on Academic Freedom and Tenure, with 1970 Interpretive Comments," *AAUP Policy Documents and Reports* (Washington, DC: American Association of University Professors, 1995), 4.

29. Timothy B. Lovain, "Grounds for Dismissing Tenured Postsecondary Faculty for Cause," *Journal of College and University Law* 10 (1983): 419–421; *Pundt v. Millikin University*, 496 N.E.2d 291 (Ill. Ct. App. 1986).

30. See *Krotkoff v. Goucher College*, 585 F.2d 675, 678–680 (4th Cir. 1978).

31. *Jimenez v. Almodovar*, 650 F.2d 363, 367–368 (1st Cir. 1981).

32. Lovain, 422.

33. Ibid.

34. See, e.g., *Krotkoff*, f85 F.2d at 678–679.

35. *Chung v. Park*, 377 F. Supp. 524, 529 (M.D. Pa. 1974).

36. *Jawa v. Fayetteville State University*, 426 F. Supp. 218 (E.D.N.C. 1976).

37. *Lehman v. Board of Trustees of Whitman College*, 576 P.2d 397 (Wash. 1978).

38. *Garret v. Mathews*, 625 F.2d 658 (5th Cir. 1980).

39. *Krotkoff*, 585 F.2d at 675.

40. *AAUP v. Bloomfield College*, 322 A.2d 846 (N.J. Super. Ct. 1974), aff'd, 346 A.2d 615 (App. Div. 1975).

41. *Pace v. Hymas*, 726 P.2d 693 (Idaho 1986).

42. 322 A.2d. 846.

43. 585 F.2d at 675.

44. *Scheuer v. Creighton University*, 260 N.W.2d 595 (Nebraska 1977).

45. *Krotkoff*, 585 F.2d at 682.

46. Id. at 682.

47. American Association of University Professors, 3–7.

48. Steven M. Cahn, *Saints and Scamps: Ethics in Academia* (Lanham, MD: Rowman & Littlefield, 1994), 91–93.

49. American Association of University Administrators, "Mission Statement and Professional Standards" (Tuscaloosa, AL: American Association of University Administrators, 1994).

50. Ibid.

51. Barbara S. Butterfield and Susan Wolfe, *You Can Get There from Here: The Road to Downsizing in Higher Education* (Washington, DC: College and University Personnel Association, 1994), 9.

52. Ibid., 43.

53. Ibid., 45.

54. Ibid., 46.

55. Catherine L. O'Shea, "Necessary Losses: Easing the Pain of Reductions in Force," *Currents* (Washington, DC: Council for the Advancement and Support of Education, September 1991), 62.

56. American Association of University Administrators.

57. Ibid.

58. O'Shea, 59.

59. Ibid., 58–59.

60. Ibid., 59–60.

61. Kaplin and Lee, 358.

62. Mary Beth Karr, "Financial Exigency as Just Cause for Dismissal of Tenured Faculty in Higher Education: What Are the Legal Issues?" (paper presented at the annual meeting of the Midwestern Educational Research Association, Chicago, IL, October 7, 1991).

63. Kaplin and Lee, 359.

64. Ibid.

65. Butterfield and Wolfe, 54.

66. Ibid., 10.

67. Ibid., 2, 4.

68. Ibid., 1–3.

69. Ibid., 4–5.

70. Ibid., 6.

71. O'Shea, 59.
72. Butterfield and Wolfe, 47–48.
73. O'Shea, 60.
74. Ibid., 59–60.
75. Ibid., 61.
76. Butterfield and Wolfe, 57–60.
77. Ibid., 55, 60–61.

Chapter 6

Academic Freedom

Academic freedom, a multidimensional concept applicable to both the faculty and the institution, is frequently invoked by both and is viewed by the academic community as part of its foundation. It is, nonetheless, a concept whose meaning and boundaries have been a matter of some dispute[1] and whose protected freedoms may be in conflict with one another.[2]

Academic freedom for the faculty and for the institution have roots back to the Middle Ages.[3] The popular understanding of academic freedom, however, is now based on the "1940 Statement of Principles on Academic Freedom and Tenure" developed by the AAUP and its administrative counterpart, the Association of American Colleges (AAC).[4] The "1940 Statement" has been widely endorsed by the academic community and incorporated into faculty contracts and policies in both public and private institutions.[5] The "1940 Statement" defines academic freedom from the faculty perspective as the faculty's freedom to research and publish, to teach, and to communicate extramurally.[6] In the 1940s, academic freedom (for faculty and for the institution) also began developing a legal definition, applicable to public institutions. This definition, based on the constitutional protection of the First Amendment,[7] along with the public institution's contractual obligations and applicable statutes and regulations, regulates the scope of academic freedom. In private institutions, on the other hand, the scope of academic freedom is based on applicable statutes and on the contractual obligations of the institution and on custom and usage in the academic environment.[8]

The cases before the courts involving academic freedom have changed in their focus over the last 50 years. During the 1940s and 1950s, the McCarthy era, the issues were based on First Amendment claims and found the institution and its faculty aligned against the government, which sought control of the content of speech and association in its concern about subversion.[9] In the more recent cases, faculty (and students) and the institution seek the support of the courts for their academic freedom claims against one another.[10]

LEGAL PARAMETERS

- **Academic freedom for individuals and educational institutions, although not specifically mentioned in the Constitution, has been called a special concern of the First Amendment.**

Academic freedom was first linked to the First Amendment by Justice Douglas in his dissent in *Adler v. Board of Education.*[11] In that case, schoolteachers, claiming a violation of their First Amendment rights, challenged New York State's Feinberg law. This law made persons ineligible for public school employment if they were members of an organization declared by the board of regents to advocate the illegal overthrow of the government. The Court upheld the Feinberg law, reasoning that the school system could make such reasonable requirements of its teachers, who were free to go elsewhere if the school system's requirements conflicted with their beliefs.[12] Justice Douglas, on the other hand, voiced the opinion that the law made the teachers second-class citizens because it denied them freedom of thought and expression. He said that everyone is entitled to these freedoms, and none need it more than teachers. He stated that there could be no academic freedom in an environment where teachers are under surveillance and feared for their jobs. Under such circumstances there could be no exercise of the free intellect.[13]

Six years later, in *Sweezy v. New Hampshire,*[14] the Court held that the First and Fourteenth Amendments applied when Sweezy, a faculty member, declined to answer the state attorney general's questions concerning his acquaintance with the Progressive Party and the content of a lecture he had given at the university. Sweezy's academic freedom and freedom of political expression had been invaded. Chief Justice Warren, writing for the Court, said, "To impose any straight jacket upon the intellectual leaders in our colleges and universities would imperil the future of the Nation."[15] Justice Frankfurter, in his concurring opinion, recognized the threat posed to the First Amendment by such governmental inquiry. He believed that government must abstain from intrusion into intellectual freedom except in exigent and compelling circumstances. In support of the institution's right to academic freedom as well as that of the petitioner, Frankfurter went on to assert the four essential freedoms of the university: "[T]o determine for itself . . . who may teach, what may be taught, how it shall be taught, and who may be admitted to study."[16]

In 1967, in *Keyishian v. Board of Regents*,[17] the Court held that the Feinberg laws considered in the *Adler* case were void for vagueness in that one could not know where the line existed between an abstract statement of doctrine and an intention to indoctrinate or incite to action.[18] Justice Brennan, writing for the majority, referred to the classroom as a marketplace of ideas and declared that any attempt to "cast a pall of orthodoxy over the classroom" would not be tolerated."[19] He called academic freedom a special concern of the First Amendment.[20] The Court held that even for the legitimate government purpose of protecting the education system from subversion, freedom of expression could not be suppressed if another more narrow means of achieving this protection were available.[21]

The teacher's rights to freedom of association and freedom of expression were further established by the Court in other actions that similarly challenged the constitutionality of state statutes that sought to chill free association or extract a loyalty oath.[22] In *Shelton v. Tucker* the Court declared, "The vigilant protection of constitutional freedoms is nowhere more vital than in the community of American schools."[23]

Other cases heard in the 1950s and 1960s noted the institution's right to academic freedom without distinguishing between the faculty and the administration or determining which group within the institution constituted the institution. In 1978, institutional academic freedom was recognized in the *Regents of California v. Bakke*.[24] Although the Court held that the goal of diversity was an insufficient justification for the university's admissions policy, Justice Powell reiterated that academic freedom was a special concern of the First Amendment and permitted the university to make its own judgments about education and the selection of its student body. Justice Powell cited the four freedoms of the institutions that Justice Frankfurter first described in *Sweezy*.[25] Further support for the institution's right to academic freedom can be found in *Widmar v. Vincent*,[26] where Justice Powell asserted the right of the institution to determine how best to allocate its scarce resources or determine on academic grounds who shall teach, what may be taught, how it should be taught, and who may be admitted to study.[27] Institutional academic freedom also received support from a unanimous Court in *The Regents of the University of Michigan v. Ewing*,[28] where a student claimed denial of due process in his expulsion from the medical school. Justice Stevens, writing for the Court, said, "Academic freedom thrives not only on the independent and uninhibited exchange of ideas among teachers and students . . . but also, and somewhat inconsistently, on autonomous decision-making by the academy itself."[29] The Court upheld the faculty's decision to expel Ewing.[30]

While recognizing the relationship between academic freedom and the First Amendment, the Supreme Court has not clearly differentiated between academic freedom as applied to individuals and academic freedom as applied to institutions. The circumstances under which each is considered by the cases cited above have been different and have not pitted the individual and the institution against one another. Subsequent cases do, however, address the issue of the point at which the individual faculty member's freedom of expression conflicts with the institution's rights.[31]

- **Faculty members' academic freedom in the classroom is limited by the academic freedom of the institution to determine what shall be taught and how it shall be taught.**

The courts have given the institution the right to determine the content and methodology they believe appropriate for their mission and purpose.[32] The classroom is the arena where institutional authority is at its greatest.[33]

Courts have supported the institution's right to expect faculty to use appropriate teaching methods[34] and to meet their requirements with regard to course content and grading.[35] Academic freedom does not permit speech that is at variance with the established curriculum, that is destructive to the proper functioning of the institution,[36] or that interjects religion into the curriculum.[37] There are, however, some limitations on the institution's freedom in the classroom. For example, a California court held that a college could not cancel a drama class on the ground that the chosen performance contained vulgar language,[38] and the Sixth Circuit held that a professor could not be required to change a grade that it deemed to be a symbolic communication entitled to First Amendment protection.[39]

- **The academic freedom of institutions to determine who may teach is limited by the constitutional, statutory, and contractual rights of individuals.**

Institutional academic freedom to decide who may teach does not permit a breach of a contract of employment between the institution and the faculty member or the violation of statutory or constitutional protection applicable to faculty.[40] See Chapters 2, 3, and 5 for a discussion of the statutory and constitutional protections limiting the institution's actions. Contractual protections vary from institution to institution.

The generally accepted standard for the protection of academic freedom of faculty is contained in the "1940 Statement of Principles on Academic Freedom and Tenure"[41] (see the discussion concerning the AAUP standards in the "Ethical Considerations" portion of this chapter). The AAUP standards are incorporated by reference into many faculty contracts of employment. Even where these standards are not explicitly incorporated into contracts, the courts may look to them as the "industry standard" and hold the institution to its requirements (see Chapters 4 and 5).

- **The freedom of faculty members to propound unpopular ("politically incorrect") ideas is protected, but obscene speech and profanity in the classroom with no educational purpose is not protected.**

The courts support the right of expression of faculty whether or not the views expressed are believed offensive to religious, political, or other beliefs.[42] The views of Professor Michael Levin regarding the intellectual inferiority of black people were found to be offensive by students, other faculty, and administrators at the City College of New York. The federal court, however, supported Dr. Levin's claim that the disruption of Dr. Levin's classes, which the university failed to quell, and the actions taken by the university, including the setting up of a shadow class, were an attack upon his tenure and impermissible because they were in response to Levin's free expression of ideas. The court supported his right to pursue scholarship wherever it led as long as it was not outweighed by a legitimate educational interest.[43]

In another case at the City College of New York, the controversial views of Professor Leonard Jeffries about the superiority of "sun people" (dark-skinned) and his allegedly anti-Semitic remarks expressed off campus caused the college to replace him as chairperson of the Black Studies Department. The district court found that the college had violated Jeffries's First Amendment rights by this action based on the content of his speech about matters of public concern that did not interfere with the functioning of his classroom. Unless the comments had negative effect on his employment, the odious nature of Jeffries's off-campus comments did not justify retaliatory action. The First Amendment protects even morally reprehensible views. The court observed, however, that the Constitution did not prevent the college from disciplining a professor who engaged in a systematic pattern of racist, anti-Semitic, or other such remarks in class because such abusive behavior chills the free exchange of ideas. The court also pointed out that the college did not have to subject its students to absurd theories in the classroom.[44]

In the case of *Silva v. University of New Hampshire*,[45] students complained about Professor J. Donald Silva's sexual references. He likened the relationship of a writer and his subject to a sexual relationship. He also explained in detail how a writer's focus is like sex, and in another classroom discussion, he used a simile involving belly dancing. The university, without offering Silva a hearing, determined that he was guilty of sexual harassment and took action against him for creating a hostile and offensive environment in violation of the university's sexual harassment policy. Dr. Silva brought an action in federal court. Although Professor Silva did not have unlimited license to say or do anything he wished, the court found that his speech was not sexual in nature. It held that the context in which he made his comments and his valid educational objectives had to be taken into account. The court also stated that the charge against Silva for "outrageousness" was subjective and did not take into account the nation's great interest in protecting academic freedom.

In a more recent case, the Ninth Circuit held that the application of the college's sexual harassment policy to a faculty member's long-standing teaching methods, without prior notice, was a violation of the professor's First Amendment rights.[46]

Obscene expression, however, is not protected by the Constitution,[47] and consequently academic freedom would not shield a faculty member's obscene classroom speech. Even profanity by a faculty member, without academic purpose or justification, was deemed by one court to be "a deliberate, superfluous attack on a 'captive audience' with no academic purpose or justification."[48] The guidelines for determining what obscenity is are not clear-cut.[49] The courts currently apply the following guidelines provided by the Supreme Court in *Miller v. California*:[50] (1) whether the average person applying contemporary community standards would find that the work as a whole appeals to the prurient interests; (2) whether the work describes in a patently offensive way sexual conduct, as defined by applicable state law; and (3) whether the work, taken as a whole, lacks serious literary, artistic, political, or scientific value.[51]

- **The display of artistic expression of faculty or students that does not seek to make a political or social statement and that is sexually explicit can be regulated as to location by the institution to protect others from being the unwilling recipients of offensive material.**

Where sexually explicit paintings were displayed in an area regularly used by the public, including children, who would be a captive audience, the First Circuit Court of Appeals supported the right of the university to remove the paintings.[52] Similarly, the Seventh Circuit held that the removal of art works on windows to a less public location was not a violation of a faculty member's First Amendment rights where the material was of a sexual nature, was offensive to members of the university community, and was visible to those who did not elect to enter a gallery to see them.

- **Outside the classroom, faculty members are limited in their free speech concerning institutional matters if the subject is not a matter of public concern or if the speech is in conflict with the public employer's provision of services to the public.**

In cases concerning the rights of public employees, the Court has determined that the First Amendment's guarantee of free speech does not shield such employees from negative personal decisions when their communications are deemed personal or come into conflict with the government's (or public institution's) efficient provision of services. The case of *Pickering v. Board of Ed-*

ucation,[53] which involved a termination, a teacher sent a letter critical of the school board to a local newspaper. The Supreme Court balanced the teacher's right to freedom of speech against the state's interest in maintaining an efficient educational system (one in which discipline and harmony have not been undermined) and, in this case, found in favor of the teacher. Among other things, the Court determined that the teacher had addressed a matter of public concern that had no detrimental effect on the operation of the school or his performance as an instructor. In *Connick v. Meyers*,[54] Meyers, who opposed her transfer of responsibility, had attempted to refute the contention that her fellow staff members did not share her concerns by circulating a questionnaire dealing with, among other things, transfer policy, office morale, and the need for a grievance committee. She was fired for this action, and she sued, claiming a violation of her First Amendment rights. The Supreme Court reversed the lower courts and held that her First Amendment rights had not been violated. The Court said that when an employee does not speak as a citizen on matters of public concern, and instead speaks as an employee on matters of personal interest, the federal court is not the appropriate forum to review the employer's action in response.[55] Speech regarding job grievances or other job issues has been held to be a private concern and have no First Amendment protection.[56] In *Rankin v. McPherson*,[57] the Court clarified that determining if a communication by a faculty member is about an issue of public or private concern is a threshold factor in deciding whether the speech is protected. In *Givhan v. Western Line Consolidated School District*,[58] the Supreme Court held that communications delivered in private as well as in public could have First Amendment protection. Courts have, however, been inclined to classify speech delivered in private and not voiced to the general public as being of private concern.[59]

Once a court determines that the speech at issue is public, it will then engage in a balancing test, based on the *Pickering* case discussed above, to determine whether or not the state's interest (those of the institution) outweigh the faculty member's claim to First Amendment protection.[60] Even if the state's interest does not outweigh that of the individual, the institution may still take a legally permissible adverse personnel action if it can show that, absent the speech at issue, it would have taken the adverse action for other reasons (e.g., poor teaching, judgment, or scholarship).[61] (See the discussion concerning the First Amendment in Chapter 4.)

- **Academic freedom does not protect research from court-ordered disclosure.**

More often than not, academic freedom does not shield research from disclosure pursuant to a subpoena. Courts have balanced the plaintiff's need for the information at issue against the burden to the researcher and the public's interest in protecting the confidentiality of academic research.[62]

• **Faculty in private institutions do not have constitutional protection and must rely on contracts with the institution to protect academic freedom.**

Institutions that have a contractual obligation to academic freedom (whether through provisions developed by the institution or through the incorporation of the AAUP's "1940 Statement of Principles on Academic Freedom and Tenure") must adhere to those requirements. Courts may also hold institutions to the academic freedom policies or practices, even if they have not been specifically incorporated into the contracts of employment.[63] Theoretically, faculty are also contractually bound by these provisions and any limitations they may contain relating to faculty conduct,[64] but practically speaking, the protections have been utilized to protect faculty rather than to restrain them.

ETHICAL CONSIDERATIONS

Education as a profession is still engaged in defining academic freedom, judging its importance, and determining "whether or when it should yield to other, competing values."[65] If, however, we agree that a central value of higher education institutions is the search for truth, then we may agree that academic freedom is essential for its discovery. Truth seeking and discovery are facilitated when professors and their institutions remain free to pursue scholarship, wherever it may lead. The academy has found it difficult, however, to define the *boundaries* of academic freedom and to determine when, if at all, internal and external controls are justifiable. These tasks are complicated by the fact that academic freedom, or the perceived lack thereof, is intricately linked to institutional climate and morale and because administrators, professors, and students often have differing and conflicting perspectives on its boundaries and application.[66]

• **Should individual academic freedom take priority over institutional academic freedom?**

There is general agreement that academic freedom is "positive, valuable, fair, good, contemporary, strong, active, democratic, dynamic, complex, liberal, and broad."[67] However, one battle that still rages has each academic constituency insisting that either individual academic freedom or institutional academic freedom should take priority. The issue is complex and involves the balance between professors' rights to freedom of thought and expression (professorial autonomy) and the right of the institution to control how it meets its commitments and duties to its clients and stakeholders (institutional autonomy).[68] Nonetheless, examining the claims of professors versus those of the institution/administration in terms of institutional values may shed light on these two competing, albeit meritorious, points of view.

The American Association of University Professors makes a strong statement regarding individual academic freedom when it defines the rights of professors as "freedom to pursue research and publication in concert with other academic duties, freedom in the classroom to discuss his or her subject, and the right to speak on nonacademic issues just as an ordinary citizen."[69] Many faculty claim that free speech should take precedence over any institutional control, even in private institutions, where there is no constitutional protection for individual faculty members. Any attempt to control or limit faculty's individual rights is seen by faculty as a breach of academic freedom.

However, faculty also have some responsibility to the institution and to all of its constituencies. The AAUP, in its original as well as in its later interpretative statements, acknowledges some of these responsibilities.[70] For example, when speaking extramurally, as is their right, faculty members also have the responsibility to "uphold the reputation of their profession and institution."[71] While exercising their right to speak, they must nevertheless be accurate, careful, and sensitive to and tolerant of others and their views and acknowledge that they are speaking individually and not on behalf of their institution.[72] And, in the classroom, although faculty have the freedom to teach, it is a freedom that the AAUP and others reserve to discuss *relevant* subject matter in the classroom, even if it is controversial; therefore, instructors have the attendant responsibility to remain on the subject and consciously and consistently avoid "intruding material" that has no relation to the subject they are teaching.[73]

As to the interests claimed by institutions, they do have authority, seen as an "institutional" right to academic freedom formally recognized by courts. It includes the rights of colleges and universities to select appropriate curriculum to be taught by the faculty, to set certain teaching standards, and to ensure that faculty are meeting those standards.[74] The privileges afforded faculty by academic freedom should also be balanced with a healthy attitude toward academic duty.[75] Just as faculty members need to be free from unnecessary restraints imposed by the institution and from the external world, institutions need to be free from judicial review for exercising their responsibility to their constituencies, their community, and society in general.[76]

It is the inherent tension between these two accepted values—institutional academic freedom and individual academic freedom—that is always at the heart of the ethical dilemma of which should take precedence or where the boundaries should be drawn. An example of this dilemma is the setting of curriculum and teaching methods. If the institution, acting reasonably and in accord with its mission and procedures, chooses a curriculum (usually with faculty involvement), should an individual faculty member who is an acknowledged expert in his or her field set his or her own curriculum, teaching standards, or teaching methods, claiming individual academic freedom? What is more important, the duty of the institution to its constituencies to safeguard their stated mission or the individual faculty member's freedom to determine these matters? If the line between academic freedom and control is unclear at best, who draws the boundaries? How is the issue resolved when both types of academic freedom have their own merit? Which should take precedence?

The answer to the question of which should take precedence may be different in each case, although this suggests continued inconsistencies and debate. Undeniably, there exists a mosaic of competing interests and values, each meritorious: the academic freedom of individual faculty, institutional (administrative) academic freedom, student academic freedom, and the needs of society at large. Academic administrators can only attempt to understand the various points of view and attempt to be fair and congruent with institutional values in resolving these disputes.

• Should freedom of expression and artistic freedom be boundless?

Should censorship ever override free speech? Can academic and artistic freedom be compromised and still survive? Should the interests of the state be weighed against an individual's freedom of expression? These are relevant and important questions that have arisen in the past decades. They are of even greater concern today because of the advent of technology and, specifically, the Internet, which has provided academia increased opportunities for expression and a broader reach.[77]

Although academic freedom, which includes freedom of expression, is accepted as an important value, it is only one value among many.[78] What occurs when academic freedom, or freedom of expression, conflicts with other important values in our society, such as equality and human dignity? How do we choose a course of action among competing values, all of which are compelling?

Dworkin, in stating several arguments for solving these questions, sets forth two theories. One is that a value may have limits. For example, we may value the sanctity of life, yet we might also believe that when the quality of life is negative, it limits its value. In that case, euthanasia may be preferable to saving life at all costs.[79] Dworkin's second argument involves a compromise of a value because it is "overridden by a competing value."[80] As an example of the latter argument, he advances the need for choosing censorship when there is a matter of national security in the balance or when "hate speech" results in negating human dignity, equality, or justice and may actually violate our right to physical security.[81]

There is a continuum of belief on values, from total acceptance of a value without limits to acceptance with many exceptions. This is also true for the values of freedom of expression and artistic freedom. Those who advocate for freedom of expression and boundless artistic freedom claim that individual freedoms such as freedom of speech are natural or civil rights, and as such, they should not be curtailed in any form in the name of institutional academic freedom or policy. Truth is truth, no matter the price, they assert, and it should never be compromised, stifled, or diminished for the sake of political correctness, no matter what the forum.

Many institutions, conversely, claim that freedom of expression by employees is not absolute. For example, the courts have repeatedly recognized the needs of the institution in finding the balance between freedom of expression of an academic speaking out on institutional issues, on the one hand, and the institution's needs to protect its mission, services, and working relationships, on the other.[82] In fact, as discussed in the section on legal parameters in this chapter, numerous court cases have established the limits to constitutionally protected speech to matters of public concern and denied such protection in cases where a faculty member speaks out on personal matters, such as institutional or unit operations (e.g., departmental administration, curriculum, promotion and tenure of colleagues, the right of the institution to reorganize or implement reduction in force measures, accreditation, and personal complaints regarding salaries, promotion, tenure, and related internal matters).[83] Notwithstanding these limits to protected speech that have been recognized legally, most courts and academics abhor any erosion of freedom of expression on academic matters, where academic freedom exists not just for those who teach but also for society as a whole. To this day, society (the nonacademic community) has remained largely faithful to their trust that universities are the places where new truths will be discovered and applications for old knowledge found. As some point out: "Discoveries are made, at least in part, because inquiring minds have an opportunity to challenge one another, to debate their methods and their conclusions, and to question their findings."[84] This challenge, debate, and further investigation cannot occur when professors who espouse controversial or even seemingly heretical ideas are silenced or ignored. Scientific and scholarly progress cannot be made if so-called heretical views are not brought to light to be subjected to the scrutiny of others through "observation, research, and whatever objective, scientific method is appropriate to the subject matter at hand."[85] The belief, for example, that the earth is flat could not have been proven false if these views had not been exposed to research and scrutiny. And, ultimately, most will agree that universities and professors should be engaged in the task of providing students tools with which to arrive at the truth and in teaching them the importance of critical and independent thought.

Artistic expression is another highly debated issue when the value of artistic freedom and the institution's right to limit it clash. Those who advocate for total freedom of expression feel that ideas, including those expressed artistically, should not be repressed or limited because they may be offensive to certain political, religious, or personal views. Indeed, courts have generally supported this view, except when a captive audience is exposed to artistic works that may be sexual in nature. In such cases, the courts have supported the modification of the setting and/or the location where the art will be displayed. The idea here is that the freedom to express oneself must also recognize another person's freedom *not* to listen, and when both are in conflict, community standards and other factors enter into the decision as to which will prevail.

The AAUP has prepared and disseminated a statement on academic freedom and artistic expression, which should aid faculty and academic administrators in clarifying this issue.[86] (See Appendix 8.) It does not, however, resolve the basic tension between those who accept limits and those who do not. The statement was originally adopted in the 1990 Wolf Trap Conference on Academic Freedom and Artistic Expression, sponsored by the AAUP and other entities, and was officially endorsed by the AAUP, also in 1990.

- **Is political correctness more important than academic freedom?**

Political correctness (PC) is as nebulous a term as *obscenity* because both are value-laden and because values in our society are so diverse. *Politically correct speech* generally refers to that which does not go against accepted societal norms regarding race, gender, political, or sexual orientation. Values associated with political correctness are respect, human dignity, equality, justice, and diversity.[87] Although these are cherished values, critics of the emphasis on political correctness in academia over free expression decry PC as an assault on the very foundation of academia. They assert that higher education must remain a marketplace of ideas that promotes free exchange as integral to truth seeking, even though these ideas may be distasteful in some political or social contexts. Clearly, critics caution, emphasis on political correctness will stifle the expression of ideas out of fear of retribution. The dilemma is how to welcome differing ideas without offending others, therefore satisfying both imperatives.[88] In many cases, this may not be possible. It is particularly difficult because today's technology broadens the definition of "community" far beyond that of the institution. For instance, university and college courses and other offerings, through the Internet and World Wide Web, may now become available to a national and even international audience whose sensitivities, values, and morals may be markedly different than those of the host institution. The definitions of political correctness and obscenity, so tied to societal and community norms, would therefore also be stretched far beyond institutional boundaries, with possible negative consequences for the institution.

Recently, hate speech has come to the attention of the public. Like political correctness (its antithesis), the content of hate speech is usually associated with race, gender, ethnicity, religion, and sexual orientation; but, unlike political correctness, it does not seek respect for differences. In fact, hate speech can incite intolerance, violence, and unrest.[89] To prevent incidents, a number of institutions have established or are considering hate speech codes. Advocates of such codes claim that a clear definition by the institution of speech that is considered offensive, and what punishment is to be doled out to those who knowingly engage in such negative expression, will be a deterrent. Critics of hate speech codes, however, argue that the codes teeter dangerously close to censuring speech that is solely offensive or unpopular and is therefore protected versus speech that is unprotected and defined more strictly as "fighting words that present a clear and present danger of violence."[90] The courts have been wary of speech codes because of overbroadness. They reflect our society's belief in the importance of free expression unless the speech is pornographic or a real danger to others.[91]

- **When may religious values, dogma, and mission in religious institutions supersede academic freedom?**

The AAUP no longer endorses a special departure from academic freedom for religious institutions.[92] As a result, many religious institutions do not adopt the AAUP standards because those institutions believe that their purpose or mission to transmit a particular religious position is a stronger value than that of academic freedom. Since independent institutions, including private religious colleges and universities, are not bound by First Amendment protections, the institution may elevate the importance of their mission above that of individual academic freedom in and out of the classroom. As stated earlier, the courts have tended to emphasize institutional academic freedom, recognizing, especially for private religious institutions, "the institution's right to establish and maintain a distinctive academic identity."[93]

Students and employees are not required to attend or work in these institutions; however, by their acquiescence to study or work there, they are implicitly accepting the institution's mission and standards. In the interest of fairness, clear policies should be created and disseminated so that faculty, students, and staff know what is expected before they commit to work or study at the institution. Private religious institutions may engage in indoctrination and in the propagation of a particular doctrine and could (as long as they violated no laws, faculty contracts, or their own policies and procedures) dismiss faculty members who deviate from their accepted doctrines. For private/independent colleges and universities that have adopted the AAUP guidelines by contract or through policies and practices, on the other hand, the difference between the protection of academic freedom given their faculties and that given faculties in public institutions is not great.[94]

- **Should the source of funding for research determine what research should be done?**

The AAUP "1940 Statement" mentions freedom in research and in the publication of results, and the 1990 AAUP "Statement on Professional Ethics" states that professors must never compromise their freedom of inquiry or engage in activities that would result in conflicts of interest.[95] Indeed, research and publication are the two functions in which institutions are less likely to wield their authority.[96] The researcher, usually a faculty member, has a responsibility to conduct these functions ethically. Since the quest for truth is accepted as the central value and purpose of research, then freedom in research becomes necessary to assure that higher education institutions continue to be sources of truth and "traditional spheres of free expression."[97] Nevertheless, a conflict of interest may easily arise between the needs and purposes of the research as seen by the researcher and the source of funding. Adherence to primacy of the search for truth should prevent an academic from yielding to these pressures.

• Should the public know what research is being done?

Does the public have a right to know what research is being performed in higher education institutions even before the results of such research are known? If the value of openness is found to be important, then confidentiality in research may be limited by the right of the public to know how funds are being spent, especially in public institutions.[98] When there is a need to choose between academic freedom and academic openness, institutions usually choose openness, claiming that it serves to protect the institution rather than the individual researcher.[99] However, those on the other side of the argument support the freedom of researchers to engage in the search for truth without interference from those who may not understand the objective or importance of their work.

PRACTICAL SUGGESTIONS

• Clear guidelines regarding academic freedom in each institution should be developed with faculty input.

An institution's policy and guidelines regarding academic freedom must be clear and specific so that both faculty and administration may understand the parameters within which they can operate. This is especially important when an institution has decided to restrict academic freedom in some way, as is the case with some private institutions. Specifically, a private religious college or university may restrict curriculum content and instructional methodology so as to be consistent with its mission and to preclude the endorsement of views that would go against its values and beliefs. An example would be the endorsement of abortion in a classroom lecture by a faculty member teaching in a Roman Catholic institution.

Although the concepts of academic freedom and freedom of speech apply only to public institutions unless incorporated contractually or by reference in private institutions, even public institutions may not be clear on the parameters of academic freedom and have policy or policies on the issue that are poorly worded. The lack of clarity is not surprising since the law provides scant guidance for administrators on this issue. This is especially true for private institutions, since the majority of the academic freedom cases have been based on constitutional decisions that apply only to public colleges and universities.

Kaplin and Lee (authors of a major work on the law in higher education), analyzing the decided cases, state: "Even the constitutional cases are sometimes incompletely reasoned or difficult to reconcile with one another. Because the decisions often depend heavily on a vague balancing of faculty and institutional interests in light of the peculiar facts of the case, it is difficult to generalize from one case or another."[100]

Both public and private institutions should include in their faculty handbooks or within the faculty contract an official institutional statement that details the scope of academic freedom within the institution, applicable restrictions, if any, and procedures that would be followed to grieve the infringement of academic freedom. Further, if the policy of the institution espouses the provisions of the AAUP "1940 Statement" and its later interpretations, it should so state, and a copy of the AAUP statement should be provided in full. Administrators must ensure that the policies are carefully worded in order to avoid overbroadness or vagueness.[101] A policy would be overbroad if it went beyond the reach of applicable law; a policy would be vague if it did not give clear notice of the actions that are prohibited.

Faculty and administrators should be actively involved in the development, periodic review, and revision of the institution's policy on academic freedom, and academic administrators in public institutions should become familiar with constitutional provisions and judicial precedents that affect individual as well as institutional academic freedom.[102] Faculty input in the creation and review of the institution's policy on academic freedom may be sought collegially by administrators or through collective bargaining. There should be periodic efforts to disseminate the policy through as convenient a vehicle as possible.[103]

- **Institutions should identify and disseminate mechanisms to handle artistic expression that has been found to be offensive or inappropriate.**

As is the case in freedom of speech, freedom of artistic expression applies in public institutions. Institutions may have rules as to what artistic work is deemed unprotected and inappropriate for display on campus, the location and placement of the art, and what alternate sites may be designated if the works to be displayed are potentially offensive, such as those with sexually explicit content. The AAUP has also suggested that institutions may "reasonably designate specific places as generally available or unavailable for exhibitions or performances."[104] Private institutions may go further than constitutional exceptions to free expression in designating works as inappropriate. The institution's guidelines should be made available to the university community and should provide a procedure for addressing complaints about breach of academic freedom.

In order to prevent misrepresentation and resulting complaints from the public as to the content or the intention of the artwork, institutions may post a statement indicating that the work is not endorsed by the institution and that the views expressed in its content are those of the artist and not necessarily those of the institution. Institutions may take advantage of the display of controversial works to spark debate and discussion on the content of the artistic expression.[105]

- **If an institution wishes to develop guidelines regarding political correctness and hate speech, they should be clear, published, and disseminated.**

Since the boundaries and definitions of political correctness and hate speech are still debatable, it is highly advisable that university or college administrators consult with counsel in the development or review of policies. Once the institution has decided to develop such a policy, it should make it available to the university community, and it should clearly state what procedures will be followed in the case of faculty or student misconduct and what penalties may be imposed. The policy may also be presented at personnel and student orientation sessions, followed by a discussion of positive and negative behaviors associated with academic freedom in general.[106]

- **Church-related institutions should clearly set forth the institution's stance on academic freedom and its limitations, if any.**

As stated previously, it is extremely important that private institutions, particularly religious schools, clearly articulate their academic mission and their policy on academic freedom, including any restrictions of that freedom. Such information should be part of the employee's contract. Details that operationalize the policy may be contained in a faculty handbook or other publication, and the policy should address the four component areas in the AAUP "1940 Statement" (freedom to teach, research, publish, and speak as a citizen) and how the institution's restrictions, if any, affect those four areas. If the institution endorses the AAUP "1940 Statement," and its later interpretative comments, or the academic freedom provisions of another entity, it should provide a full copy of the applicable statement or policies. Faculty contracts should also include reference to any other applicable policy on academic freedom,[107] if the length of the policy precludes including it in its entirety. If no policy exists within a religious institution, that should also be stated in the contract. Institutional members, and especially faculty members, must understand what they can and cannot say or do in and out of the classroom. If a private institution quotes the AAUP's "1940 Statement," it should also identify the limitations to academic freedom or state that there are no limitations.[108]

Examples of what would be stated in a limitation clause follows.

- For institutions affiliated with the Roman Catholic Church, professors may be required to adhere to the main precepts of the Church on issues such as birth control, abortion, the immortality of the soul, the infallibility of the Pope, the Trinity, and other Church teachings, by refraining from speaking against these core beliefs in the classroom.[109]

• An orthodox yeshiva institution may require that its faculty observe the Sabbath and the orthodox dietary laws.[110]

• Fundamentalist colleges may require instructors to teach or espouse the doctrine of Original Sin.[111]

All in all, clear policies help prevent confusion and threats to academic freedom in general. This is because the major threat to academic freedom has been identified by some as lack of unity among university constituencies (internal issues) and the external world.[112] The many challenges to academic freedom today include increasing external involvement in academia (e.g., by accrediting agencies, by public officials, and by those internal and external agencies whose function is assessing educational outcomes).[113] The most important skill an institution can have, therefore, is that of understanding the freedoms, responsibilities, and limitations under which the different constituencies operate. An institution that does not have a policy runs the risk of breaching both individual and institutional academic freedom by its lack of clarity and purpose.

ILLUSTRATIVE CASE

Description

According to the grievance procedures of Forrest College, a public institution offering bachelor of arts and bachelor of science degrees, a petition to the president of the college was the final appeal that a faculty member had regarding a charge of breach of academic freedom. William T. Avery, president of the college, was called upon to rule on the appeal of Dr. Robert Wisdom, an untenured professor in the Department of Business, regarding his nonreappointment. Dr. Wisdom had been with the college for four years and held the rank of assistant professor. Dr. Wisdom's department chairperson, Dr. Nancy Sterling, pursued the nonreappointment, based on Dr. Wisdom's unorthodox lectures and his speech in and out of the classroom. While teaching an accounting course, Dr. Wisdom had openly criticized the college's recent reorganization and made allegations that the vice president of Academic Affairs had appointed her brother-in-law as a faculty member in the Education Department without a search and made him chairperson immediately. Dr. Wisdom further questioned the institution's decision to buy adjacent land, which could not be built on, even though the needs of the college clearly were for more classroom and faculty office space. The faculty member was inciting students to speak out against the administration. Dr. Wisdom had also attended an informal gathering of the student government, in which he severely criticized the management skills of his department chairperson, calling his departmental meetings "The Bob and Nancy hour," since during those meetings, Dr. Wisdom had been the only faculty member questioning the chairperson extensively on departmental matters. That same semester, two female students and one male student had filed sexual harassment charges against the professor, offended by his frequent use of profanity and his unorthodox practice of embarrassing students who came in late. Once the class had started, Dr. Wisdom would kiss the last student who came into the class, saying, "So glad to see you, sweetie!" Dr. Wisdom kissed four female students and two male students. Two of the females and one of the males filed sexual harassment charges against the professor.

At the end of the semester, Dr. Wisdom was told that he would not be reappointed. The professor, irate at the action of the administration, claimed that he had been dismissed for criticizing the institution and that his occasional use of profanity in the classroom "was not something that these adult students, who are mostly over 18, have not heard before." Dr. Wisdom charged that his academic freedom and his First Amendment freedoms had been violated. He appealed the nonreappointment through the procedures available to him and detailed in the Faculty Handbook of the college. The statement on academic freedom found in the Faculty Handbook stated generally: "Forrest College is committed to the belief that the central purpose of an academic community is to promote knowledge through the search for truth, and to have the freedom to express such truth without undue interference or harassment. Faculty members are therefore entitled to freedom to teach and to discuss all matters which are not extraneous to their field, freedom to research and publish, provided their academic duties are adequately discharged, and the right to speak on nonacademic matters as ordinary citizens." The AAUP "1940 Statement of Principles on Academic Freedom and Tenure" (or its later interpretations) was not referenced in the policy of the college, and neither the college's own policy nor the AAUP "1940 Statement" was referenced in the faculty contract.

Analysis

• Meeting the requirements of law.

President Avery must decide whether to overturn Dr. Sterling's decision not to reappoint Professor Wisdom, a nontenured professor at Forrest College. In making this decision, President Avery must, as the voice of a public institution, uphold not only the institution's contracts, policies, and regulations but the constitutions of both the state and the country.

Nontenured professors are not entitled to a hearing upon nonreappointment, as they have neither a liberty nor property interest in their ongoing employment. The institution generally has no contractual obligation to a professor beyond the current expiration date of his or her contract of employment, unless there are provisions requiring more either in the contract or incorporated into the contract by reference. However, even without a contractual obligation, no personnel action may be taken by a public institution in violation of law or constitutional rights.

Forrest College, as a public institution, must safeguard the individual's academic freedom, a special concern of the First Amendment. In addition, Forrest College, in its employment handbook, incorporated into all contracts of employment, entitles all faculty (tenured and nontenured) to the freedom to teach and discuss all material not extraneous to the course of instruction and to the freedom to speak out as a citizen on nonacademic matters. Professor Wisdom is claiming that his nonreappointment is in violation of these academic freedoms and First Amendment rights.

Although we do not know the details and specifics supporting the institution's decision not to reappoint Dr. Wisdom, we know generally that the reasons related to his "unorthodox methods and lectures and his speech in and out of the classroom." The narrative tells us that while teaching, Dr. Wisdom discussed and criticized various administrative and institutional actions. By his own admission, he also used profanity in the classroom. Outside the classroom, in informal meetings of the student government, he was strongly critical of his department and was inciting the students to speak out against the administration. The narrative also relates that charges of sexual harassment were lodged against him for his profanity and for his practice of discouraging lateness by kissing the last student (male or female) who entered the classroom.

In order to determine whether the nonrenewal of the professor's contract was permissible, let us first determine whether Professor Wisdom's critical discussions about the administration, his profanity, and his unorthodox teaching methods in his classroom were protected by the Constitution or by contract. Addressing the contract provisions first, we see that Dr. Wisdom's freedom in the classroom extends to all matters not extraneous to his field (subject matter). Since his discussions about the administration were directed to its poor business practices and since we may assume that the subject of the class was business, it is arguable that his classroom speech was protected by his contract. On the other hand, his profanity and his method of ensuring promptness were extraneous to his subject matter and were, therefore, not protected by the contract. These issues could, therefore, serve as the basis for the nonrenewal of the professor's contract without violating any contractual obligation.

The Constitution, in this case, would probably not afford Professor Wisdom any more protection than his contract did, and perhaps less. The courts have given priority to the institution's academic freedom rights over that of the individual faculty member in the classroom and have supported the institution's right to determine what should be taught and how it should be taught. On this ground, Professor Wisdom might not have the right to include the institution's business practices in the curriculum if the institution were to determine that they did not want business taught in this manner. As for the professor's use of profanity unrelated to the course content, this also may not be protected. While profanity has been protected by the courts when it was part of the subject matter involved in the course, it has not received protection where it had no such connection to the curriculum. We would assume, therefore, that based on Professor Wisdom's classroom activities, the institution could probably decide not to renew his contract without violating his constitutional rights.

Next, we must determine whether Professor Wisdom's discussion of his department's activities with the student government is protected speech. The policy of the institution protects speech as an ordinary citizen but does not define this nor indicate if it includes speech as a member of the institution on matters relating to the institution. Even though Forrest College is a public institution, it is arguable that these internal management issues would be deemed personal rather than public concerns and not matters on which "ordinary citizens" would speak out. The court, when determining whether public employees could, under the Constitution, freely express themselves on matters concerning the institution, first require that the matter be of public concern rather than a personal concern. It would be hard to cast the professor's comments as being of public concern. Even if Professor Wisdom could meet this standard, the court would then require that the speech not impact the proper and efficient delivery of the educational services provided. Here it could be argued that the professor's comments to the students incite unrest and may in fact interfere with the efficient delivery of the service. Finally, the court supports a termination even where there has been protected speech if the termination would have occurred even without the speech in question. Although the charges of sexual harassment may not have survived a close examination, Professor Wisdom's use of the "kissing sanction" and profanity may have provided sufficient reason in themselves for the institution to decide not to reappoint him without it addressing his speech to the student government.

President Avery could, in view of the institution's disapproval of Professor Wisdom's classroom teaching methods and activities, and the applicable policy and law, support the decision not to reappoint him for another year at Forrest College.

• **Ethical considerations.**

Although legally permissible, is the nonreappointment of Professor Wisdom for his unorthodox methods and speech, in and out of the classroom, ethically sound, based on the principles valued by Forrest College? We know that academic freedom is valued by the institution. It is incorporated into all its contracts of employment. However, shielding students from abusive or harassing methods in the classroom could also be a value. Giving individuals respect and providing quality learning experiences are often core values in institutions of higher learning. Indeed, the survival of the institution could depend on how well Forrest College puts these core values into action. Consequently, President Avery, in weighing this situation, might ethically decide either to support the unlimited academic freedom of Professor Wisdom, if he believes academic freedom to be the primary value, or to limit Professor Wisdom's academic freedom in deference to other core values.

Would there be any competing value to limit Professor Wisdom's freedom to incite students to enter into his dispute with his department over its management and business practices? Some institutions would place a high value on student input into college matters as well as on the professor's freedom of expression. Other institutions might, however, deem Professor Wisdom's efforts to involve students in departmental matters to further his positions to be destructive to the main purpose of delivering and receiving educational services. President Avery's analysis of this issue would depend on his values and his assessment of the dominant values of his institution. As long as his decision on whether to renew Professor Wisdom's contract was based on a balancing of those values, he could ethically decide either way. An unethical determination would only result if he were to make his determination for reasons that were contrary or unrelated to those values.

• **Practical considerations.**

From a practical point of view, both Professor Wisdom and President Avery could have benefitted from a more detailed policy on academic freedom, including its limits, as well as from affirmative statements regarding the institution's values with regard to the role of the students and its role in providing teaching services. Such guidance may have altered Professor Wisdom's behavior and assisted President Avery in making a decision that truly reflected the consensus of values at his institution.

NOTES

1. Terence Leas and Charles J. Russo, "*Waters v. Churchill*: Autonomy for the Academy or Freedom for the Individual?" 93 *Ed. Law Rep.* 1099 (1994).

2. William A. Kaplin and Barbara A. Lee, *The Law of Higher Education: A Comprehensive Guide to Legal Implications of Administrative Decision Making*, 3rd ed. (San Francisco: Jossey-Bass, 1995), 299–300 (citing *Parowski v. Illinois Community College*, 759 F.2d 625 [7th Cir. 1985]).

3. Leas and Russo, 1099.

4. American Association of University Professors, "1940 Statement of Principles on Academic Freedom and Tenure, with 1970 Interpretive Comments," *AAUP Policy Documents and Reports* (Washington, DC: American Association of University Professors, 1995), 3–7; Richard H. Hiers, "Academic Freedom in Public Colleges and Universities: O Say, Does That Star-Spangled Banner Yet Wave?" 40 *Wayne Law Review* (Fall 1993): 1.

5. See Chapter 5, "Terminations, Nonrenewals, and Reductions in Force."

6. American Association of University Professors, supra note 4, at 3–7.

7. J. Louis Campbell III, "Academic Freedom and the First Amendment: Legal Entanglements," *ACA Bulletin*, no. 17 (August 1990): 53–62.

8. See Chapter 5, "Terminations, Nonrenewals, and Reductions in Force."

9. Kaplin and Lee, 301.

10. Ibid.

11. 342 U.S. 485 (1952).

12. Id. at 492.

13. Id. at 508–511.

14. 354 U.S. 234 (1957).

15. Id. at 250.

16. Id. at 263.

17. 385 U.S. 589 (1967).

18. Id. at 598.

19. Id. at 603.

20. Id.

21. Id. at 602.

22. *Wieman v. Updegraff*, 344 U.S. 183 (1952); *Shelton v. Tucker*, 364 U.S. 479 (1960); *Whitehill v. Elkins*, 389 U.S. 54 (1967).

23. 364 U.S. at 487.

24. 438 U.S. 265 (1978).

25. Id. at 312.

26. 454 U.S. 263 (1981).

27. Id. at 276.

28. 474 U.S. 214 (1985).

29. Id. at 226 fn.12.

30. Id. at 225–227.

31. Hiers, 1.

32. Robert K. Poch, *Academic Freedom in Higher Education: Rights, Responsibilities, and Limitations*, ASHE-ERIC Higher Education Report No. 4 (Washington, DC: George Washington University, School of Education and Human Development, 1993), 31.

33. Poch at 29, citing Kaplin at 192.

34. *Clark v. Holmes*, 474 F.2d 928, 931 (7th Cir. 1972); *Hetrick v. Martin*, 480 F.2d 705 (6th Cir. 1973).

35. *Lovelace v. Southeastern Massachusetts University*, 793 F.2d 419 (1st Cir. 1986).

36. *Clark*, 474 F.2d at 931.

37. *Bishop v. Aronov*, 926 F.2d 1066 (11th Cir. 1991).

38. *DiBona v. Matthews*, 269 Cal. Rptr. 882 (Cal. Ct. App. 4th Dist. 1990).

39. *Parate v. Isibor*, 868 F.2d 821 (6th Cir. 1984).

40. William H. Daughtry, "Legal Nature of Academic Freedom in United States Colleges and Universities," 25 *U. Rich. Law Review* 233, 255–258 (Winter 1991).

41. American Association of University Professors, supra note 4, at 3–7.

42. See, e.g., *Starsky v. Williams*, 353 F. Supp. 900 (D. Ariz. 1972); *Brown v. Board of Regents of the University of Nebraska*, 640 F. Supp. 674 (D. Neb. 1986); 269 Cal. Rptr. 882.

43. *Levin v. Harleston*, 770 F. Supp. 895 (S.D.N.Y. 1991), aff'd in part, 996 F.2d 85 (2d Cir. 1992).

44. *Jeffries v. Harleston*, 828 F. Supp. 1066 (S.D.N.Y. 1993), aff'd in part, 21 F.3d 1238 (2d Cir. 1994), cert granted, judgment vacated, 513, U.S. 996 (1994).

45. 888 F. Supp. 293 (D. New Hampshire 1994).

46. *Cohen v. San Bernadino Valley College*, 92 F.3d 968 (9th Cir. 1996).

47. *Miller v. California*, 413 U.S. 15 (1973).

48. *Martin v. Parrish*, 805 F.2d 583, 586 (5th Cir. 1986).

49. Poch, 42–43.

50. 413 U.S. 15 (1973).

51. Id. at 24.

52. *Close v. Lederle*, 424 F.2d 988 (1st Cir. 1970).

53. 391 U.S. 563 (1968).

54. 461 U.S. 138 (1983).

55. Id. at 147.

56. *Ayoub v. Texas A & M University*, 927 F.2d 834 (5th Cir. 1991).

57. 483 U.S. 378 (1987).

58. 439 U.S. 410 (1979).

59. 927 F.2d at 837.

60. *Mapes v. Martin*, 858 F.2d 1546, 1552 (11th Cir. 1988).

61. *Mt. Healthy Board of Education v. Doyle*, 429 U.S. 274, 285–287 (1977).

62. J. Graham Matherne, "Forced Disclosure of Academic Research," 37 *Vanderbilt Law Review* 5 (April 1984): 585, 594.

63. See Chapter 5, "Terminations, Nonrenewals, and Reductions in Force."

64. The AAUP standards, for example, require that faculty be accurate, show restraint, respect the opinion of others, and indicate that they do not speak for the institution.

65. Ronald Dworkin, "We Need a New Interpretation of Academic Freedom," *Academe* 82, no. 3 (May–June 1996): 11.

66. Lawrence Lee Oldaker, "Threats to Academic Freedom in Higher Education" (paper presented at the annual meeting of the National Organization on Legal Problems of Education National Conference, Scottsdale, AZ, November 21, 1992), ERIC No. ED 37778, 2.

67. Ibid., 18.

68. Joseph A. Raelin, "Academic Freedom and Control," *College Teaching* 39, no. 1 (Winter 1991): 26–29.

69. Ed Kellerman and Luke Cornelius, "Clothing Professors with Immunity: Points of Law on Academic Freedom" (January 1996), ERIC No. ED 402 874, 3.

70. American Association of University Professors, supra note 4, at 3–7.

71. Poch, 12.

72. American Association of University Professors, supra note 4, at 4.

73. Ibid., 3, 6.

74. Poch, 29, 35.

75. Donald Kennedy, *Academic Duty* (Cambridge, MA: Harvard University Press, 1997), 22.

76. Campbell, 58.

77. Kellerman and Cornelius, 2, 9.

78. Dworkin, 12–14.

79. Ibid.

80. Ibid., 12–13.

81. Ibid., 13–14.

82. Campbell, 56.

83. Ibid., 56–57.

84. Burton M. Leiser, "Threats to Academic Freedom and Tenure," 15 *Pace Law Review* (Fall 1994): 21.

85. Leiser, 20.

86. American Association of University Professors, "Academic Freedom and Artistic Expression," *AAUP Policy Documents and Reports* (Washington, DC: American Association of University Professors, 1995), 35–36.

87. Poch, 52–56.

88. Ibid., 54–56.

89. Ibid., 56–57.

90. Rodney A. Smolla, "Academic Freedom, Hate Speech, and the Idea of a University," *Law and Contemporary Problems* 53, no. 3 (Spring 1990): 216.

91. Poch, 57.

92. American Association of University Professors, supra note 4, at 6.

93. Poch, 60.

94. Leiser, 19.

95. American Association of University Professors, "Statement on Professional Ethics," *AAUP Policy Documents and Reports* (Washington, DC: American Association of University Professors, 1995), 105–106.

96. Kaplin and Lee, 328.

97. Oldaker, 11.

98. William W. May, ed., *Ethics and Higher Education* (New York: American Council on Education, Macmillan 1990), 308.

99. Ibid., 306.

100. Kaplin and Lee, 327.

101. Ibid.

102. Poch, 63, 73–74.

103. Oldaker, 31.

104. American Association of University Professors, supra note 86, at 36.

105. Poch, 51.

106. Ibid., 58.

107. Ibid., 67–68.

108. Ibid., 68.

109. Leiser, 19.

110. Ibid.

111. Ibid.

112. Oldaker, 23.

113. Charles M. Ambrose, "A Comparison of Faculty Members' and Administrators' Definitions of, and Attitudes Toward, Academic Freedom" (paper presented at the annual meeting of the Association for the Study of Higher Education, St. Louis, MO, November 3–6, 1988), ERIC No. ED 303087, 4.

Chapter 7

Student Disputes on Academic Matters

The courts defer to the educational institution in academic matters. There are, however, some limitations on the academic actions of the institution when grades, placement, academic dismissal, catalog offerings, or the advice of a faculty adviser are in dispute.

LEGAL PARAMETERS

- **Public institutions may not violate a student's constitutional rights or applicable laws and must provide students with due process procedures when they impinge on students' protected property or liberty interests. Fewer procedural due process requirements, however, are required for institutional actions based on academic matters than for those based on student misconduct. The court's substantive due process review of the institution's reason for its action has generally been limited to a determination of whether the institution's decision was arbitrary or capricious or whether it was based on an academic evaluation.**

The Constitution of the United States prohibits the government from affecting a person's property or liberty interest without due process of law. Due process is intended as a safeguard which minimizes the risk of error by the government.

Consequently, the public institution, which must meet constitutional requirements, cannot impact a student's property or liberty interests without providing the necessary due process. In the case of *Dixon v. Alabama State Board of Education*, the Fifth Circuit held that students in public schools have a property interest in their continued attendance and thus a due process right under the Fourteenth Amendment to notice and some opportunity to be heard before being dismissed for misconduct.[1] In higher education, a student's property right to continuing enrollment or to a degree can arise from a court's finding that the student had a contract with the institution or paid tuition.[2] The right to notice and hearing developed by the cases following *Dixon* is, however, limited to disciplinary decisions.[3] (See chapter 8 for a discussion of due process.) The district court in *Connelly v. University of Vt. & State Agricultural College*[4] declined to extend such due process rights to academic dismissals. That court asserted that schools had absolute discretion in actions based on academic judgments but that an arbitrary, capricious, or bad-faith dismissal was actionable.[5] Courts generally do not see themselves as equipped to review a student's academic progress with the expertise required and applied by the school.[6] Even when courts recognize a property interest in enrollment[7] or a liberty interest in protecting the student's reputation from damage as a result of institutional disparagement,[8] they have held that the institution's evaluation of a student's academic progress does not confer upon the student the due process rights they would be accorded if the issue were misbehavior.[9] Even where an institution has enunciated procedures and does not follow them, courts have frequently found that this in itself is not a violation of procedural due process.[10] In one case where a court held the institution to its enunciated procedures, the issue involved both academic and nonacademic matters.[11]

In two major cases involving academic decisions in public institutions, *Board of Curators of the Univ. of Mo. v. Horowitz*[12] and *The Regents of the University of Michigan v. Ewing*,[13] the plaintiff students were deemed to have received adequate procedural due process,[14] and the Supreme Court considered whether to also review the institutions' academic actions under a substantive due process standard. In both cases, the Court determined that the actions taken were based on academic evaluations and were not arbitrary and capricious, and thus a substantive due process review was not required.[15]

Courts have rarely found that academic judgments are arbitrary and capricious.[16] Based on *Horowitz* and *Ewing*, courts generally assume that a student has a protected liberty or property interest but conclude that the due process provided has been sufficient.[17]

* **A contractual relationship exists between the student and the institution. The terms of the contract may be found in the institution's published guidelines and oral representations. The court will not examine the substantive standards and**

evaluations of the institution but will only determine whether the institution met contractual requirements with good faith and fair dealing and did not render a decision that is arbitrary and capricious.

Courts generally have found an implied contractual relationship between the student and the college or university.[18] In public institutions, this serves as the basis for establishing a property right.[19] The terms of the contract are not in a single document that the parties have executed but are set out in the institution's published materials, such as catalogs, handbooks, and policy manuals, and the oral and written representations of students, teachers, and administrators.[20] The meaning of the terms of the contract are what the institution writing the provisions may reasonably expect the students to understand them to be.[21] While a student may terminate this contract with the institution at any time, the institution's termination of the contract (i.e., expulsion of the student) or other adverse academic action may be subject to examination by the courts.[22] If the action involves academic standards, the action may be reviewed to see if it is taken in good faith or if it is arbitrary or capricious.[23] Absent an arbitrary, capricious, or bad faith action, courts will not intervene in academic judgments made by the institution with reference to the student.[24] Even when the institution does not faithfully apply its guidelines, a decision based on the exercise of academic judgment is unlikely to be seen as arbitrary and capricious and a breach of contract.[25] In a case involving academic requirements, two students did not prevail in a breach of contract action when the catalog described a computer programming course as requiring only basic math skills, but was then taught at an advanced level and with a textbook aimed at computer programmers, scientists, and engineers.[26] Where, however, the matter is unrelated to academic standards, an institution may be held to its own rules and guidelines.[27] In the case of an obese student who was admitted to a nursing program and then dismissed after two successful years because of that obesity, the First Circuit, on remand, held that the student had substantially performed her part of the contract and that the dismissal put the school in breach of its contract with the student. The student was awarded damages.[28]

- **Where the institution has reserved the right to make changes, it may alter the catalog and course requirements even after a student has matriculated without being held in breach of contract, unless such change goes to the heart of the educational contract made with the student.**

Some courts have held that modifying and adding new requirements for students already enrolled is part of the institution's academic responsibility and can thus be reasonably expected.[29] Many colleges and universities specifically state in their catalogs that the requirements are subject to change, and based on these statements, courts have frequently rejected breach of contract claims instituted by students contesting changes made after enrollment.[30] In one case, however, the catalog in effect at matriculation specifically stated that the student could satisfy the requirements for graduation according to its terms or those of any subsequent catalog in effect during the student's registration at the university. There the Texas Appeals Court held that the university was in breach of contract when it dismissed the student on the basis of requirements that were not in the catalog at matriculation.[31] Institutions have also been held to be in breach of their implied contract with the student when changes made by the institution affect the ability of the student to be accredited or certified in the field of study in which they were accepted by the institution.[32]

- **Where specific representations are made by faculty or advisers upon which the student reasonably relies to his detriment, the court may hold the institution to those representations and estop the institution from applying the rules or requirements in effect.**

In *Blank v. Board of Higher Education*,[33] a student, relying on his adviser's advice, took the two remaining psychology courses toward his degree at Brooklyn College, without attending classes, while attending a distant law school. He successfully completed the assignments and took the exams in these psychology courses. At graduation, Brooklyn College attempted to deny the student his degree for failure to meet its residency requirement. The New York court held that the institution was estopped from denying the degree since the student had relied on those authorized by the college to give advice. Brooklyn College was bound by the acts and advice of its agents.[34] The authority of an institution's agents is not only that which is given by the institution but, with regard to third parties (students), that which the agent is held out to have by the institution.[35] Where, however, the court found that binding the institution by the acts of the agent might have resulted in an individual receiving an undeserved degree because of poor scholarship, the court rejected the estoppel claim.[36]

ETHICAL CONSIDERATIONS

As in the "Legal Parameters" section, issues discussed in this section will focus on academic matters and not student disciplinary actions.

- **What ethical issues are raised by changing academic requirements after a student has matriculated?**

Institutions can and usually do reserve the right to modify requirements "in midstream" regarding academic matters. Although such actions may be legal, they may not always be fair and just. When changing rules unilaterally, the institution should consider the consequences to the students who are "caught" in the transition. For example, if a curriculum requirement for a particular major or program listed and published in the catalog is changed substantially after the student has enrolled, and the student has chosen that major based on its content, substance, and/or length, as detailed in the catalog of the year in which the student was first admitted to the program, is the institution exercising fidelity to its word?[37]

Institutions have long been sensitive to this question, and as a result there is widespread use of the practice of "grandfathering/grandmothering" (e.g., allowing students who enter in the catalog of a specific year to complete their programs of study according to the "old" rules) or allowing each student a choice of the old or new rules/requirements. Although in most of these cases the institution *could* enforce the changes, especially if there is a disclaimer clause in the publication to this effect, the "grandfathering" option is an attempt by the institution to keep its perceived promise to the student. Naturally, institutions are free to make those choices only when the changes are not required by law or state regulations, such as teacher certification rules or regional accreditation mandates.

In making the decision to grandfather or allow students a choice of the old or new rules or curriculum, the institution may be seeking both fairness and fidelity, on the one hand, and utility (the greatest good for the greatest number), on the other hand. In making the changes, the institution clearly is acting on a utilitarian principle of providing the best program for all students, yet in allowing the student to continue the program as he or she entered it, the college or university is trying to meet the ideals of fairness and fidelity. Institutions that give students a choice are keeping their commitment to them and may also be striving to give the students some autonomy in making their own decisions,[38] as well as providing them with an opportunity to take advantage of an improved curriculum.

Certainly, if an institution imposes substantive changes that are not required by law, the institution (if the student were to grieve the change), should be able to prove that it did not act arbitrarily or capriciously and that the change is to the student's academic or educational benefit due to the changing nature of the discipline, needs/demands of employers in the field, or other good reasons. Institutional actions based on these principles not only meet the requirements of law as we saw in the "Legal Parameters" section; they also demonstrate the institution's desire to be fair and to deal with the student in good faith. The institution should also view any proposed change in academic requirements from the student's perspective, and acknowledging the rising costs of higher education, ask itself whether its reasons justify imposing requirements that will lengthen the student's program or change the nature or the content of the program that the institution, through its publications and oral representations, promised the student.

- **Which ethical principles should guide an administrator in the elimination of programs for students?**

The same ethical principles described in the preceding question apply to the elimination of programs (e.g., majors, minors, specializations, concentrations) when the final decision to discontinue a program has been made by the appropriate parties, most often a high-ranking administrator and, often, the governing board of the institution. Unless precluded by law or accreditation rules, institutions contemplating the elimination of programs usually opt for a plan that allows it to continue to serve the students already enrolled in the program and not accept new students as of a particular academic term. Especially in the case of a student who has enrolled for a particular course of study, it is ethically questionable, even if legally permissible, to deny the student the course of study which had been previously promised. Even in cases where practical considerations (e.g., lack of financial or human resources) affect the institution negatively, many colleges and universities, conscious of the ethical values of fidelity and fairness, do what is necessary to see the students through successful completion of programs the institutions have decided to discontinue.

When institutions close, it is a matter of ethics for representatives of the institution to counsel students and provide, whenever possible, as smooth a transition as possible into other institutions. Students' records, such as transcripts, must remain available to the students to facilitate their transfer into other institutions and/or employment opportunities. The American Association of Collegiate Registrars and Admissions Officers (AACRAO) can help an institution in the plans to secure its records and make them available to students through alternative means.

* **How flexible should an institution be regarding its standards for admissions? Is it ethical to admit a student, or allow a student to continue a degree program, if there is no reasonable expectation that he or she will complete it?**

An ethical issue often discussed is the propriety of admitting students who may lack the ability to benefit from, or the potential to succeed in, college-level study. This concern has particularly surfaced with student athletes and minorities. The National Collegiate Athletic Association (NCAA) has established guidelines for admissions and institutional responsibility for remediation of student athletes who are recruited and admitted with the university's knowledge that they are not educationally prepared to do college-level work. If the mission of a college or university is to educate, admitting a student to benefit from his or her ability to enhance an athletic team and therefore the institution's reputation when the student cannot succeed academically is ethically questionable. What remedial services does an institution owe to an academically weak student admitted for his or her athletic ability? Do fairness and honesty dictate that such a student should not be allowed to continue a degree program, or even attend, if it becomes clear that there is no possibility for success? Clearly, allowing a student to continue a degree program and then, right before graduation, denying that student a diploma raises ethical concerns.

- ## How much institutional support should be offered to assist a student in completing his or her program?

When the institution offers a program, it is effectively guaranteeing that those completing the program have acquired the competencies in a particular course of study. This guarantee impacts the integrity of the institution's degrees beyond the confines of the college or university. This does not necessarily mean that institutions cannot be faithful to a mission that includes access to higher education to those who, often through no fault of their own, do not favorably compare academically with the average student. Many institutions, especially those that espouse open admissions, believe that, in the interest of access, at-risk students should be given an opportunity to succeed. What matters, they claim, is assisting the students to succeed in mastering the competencies and skills in their programs of study.

Consequently, if we are to follow that line of reasoning, it is obvious that if academically qualified and educationally unprepared students are both admitted, those with the greatest potential to succeed are the ones who entered without educational deficits. Once any student is admitted, however, the responsibility for the academic success of that student lies not just with the student but also with the institution that has admitted him or her. Therefore, some contend that there is an ethical responsibility by the institution to provide the assistance necessary to ensure academic success for all its students. This assistance may take the form of counseling, tutoring, remedial courses, or adjustment of requirements. Early warning procedures will ensure honesty and fairness by communicating the student's deficiencies with sufficient time to remedy them.

How far does the institution's obligation go to assist the student in the successful completion of his or her chosen program? When an institution adjusts or lowers requirements for a particular student or group of students, the result may very well be that the students completing their program may *not* have mastered the competencies expected. Should the admitted students who have paid their tuition and have been allowed to continue in the program even though they are not achieving academically be given special consideration by bending the rules? Some say that this would only be fair to those students. However, the ethical dilemma arises in that by helping deficient students meet academic requirements by lowering standards for them, it hurts both the institution's reputation (the integrity of its degrees) and the other group of students who *have* achieved at the expected level. Awarding the same degree to students who have not achieved at the minimum level of expectation and to those who have makes the degree worth less to students who have met the standards. Consequently, many institutions adhere to their academic standards, while providing remedial help and other support to assist high-risk students in achieving those standards.

PRACTICAL SUGGESTIONS

- **The catalog and other documents which are or may be contractual obligations of the institution should be clear and must contain a provision for unilateral changes by the institution.**

Most colleges and universities realize that their catalogs may constitute a contractual commitment to the students. In order to provide needed flexibility to the institution, many catalogs contain a provision, that alerts the reader that unilateral changes may be made by the institution. This is an important provision, and the practice of including such a disclaimer is widely accepted by regional accrediting agencies as well as by the public. It is advisable that institutions engage counsel in the review of the catalog and especially of the wording in any and all disclaimers.

What many institutions fail to realize, however, is that other documents, such as student handbooks, college bulletins, student policy and procedure handbooks, faculty handbooks, forms signed by students, and course syllabi, may be deemed part of the contract with the student. It is imperative, therefore, that the catalog *and* other related published documents be as clear as possible. Although it may be impractical to have university counsel review all syllabi and handbooks, it is advisable that administrators, advisers, and even faculty be given guidelines and/or receive training in the importance of clarity in writing and reviewing these documents and in consistently applying the policies and procedures they contain. Further, it is crucial that these documents are consistent with, and do not contradict, one another. As stated in the "Legal Parameters" section of this chapter, courts have traditionally not passed judgment on the substantive standards and evaluations of the institution but may review whether the college or university has met its contractual obligations, has been consistent in the application of its own rules, and has acted in good faith and with fair dealing. Therefore, training of employees must include the importance of adherence to institutional policy and of keeping written documentation of the rationale for any exception from policy. Such documentation may be part of the evidence that the institution may have to submit in case of a student grievance, dispute, or legal action.

When a dispute between the student and the institution arises, and the institution lacks written policies and procedures, or has published documents that lack clarity or completeness, the courts and other outside parties will rely on academic custom and usage. Therefore, what the institution *consistently says and does* will be considered its policy, even when not written or published. Administrators, advisers/counselors, staff, and faculty should be informed that even when a policy is not reduced to writing, their statements and actions may well be considered policy and therefore should be fair and consistent.

- **Oral statements made by faculty and other personnel should be consistent with college or university policy. Any deviation from policy must be documented.**

Documentation is the key word when the institution must defend its position. Verbal representations by employees should be consistent with written or unwritten policy. Any deviation from normal institutional policy should be documented, even when made verbally. A memorandum or email communication to the student summarizing what was said will support oral statements and may be the deciding factor in helping the administrator, staff, or faculty member enforce policies and/or in supporting the institution's position in court. Staff training should therefore be geared to conveying the binding nature of oral representations by agents of the institution and the importance of consistency and the need for careful documentation of deviations from policy.

- **Careful planning that protects both the student and the institution is especially important in cases of program discontinuation or major changes in degree programs.**

When an institution is considering discontinuing a program or major, or making substantial changes in existing programs, careful planning should include how students currently enrolled in that program will be treated. When the decision to discontinue a program is made, an institution, through its administration and governing board, will most likely decide not to accept any new students into the program but continue to serve the students currently enrolled, even if and when there is a reduction in force of faculty or staff associated with the program. Rules may be relaxed—for example, allowing affected students a greater number of courses taken by independent study than is the normal policy of the department or institution.

When the curriculum of a program is substantially altered, students enrolled in the program at the time of the change may be offered the option of meeting the requirements of the "old" program or the new "revised" one. It is helpful when these options are put in writing and students are asked to indicate their choice by signing the document. Students entering the institution after the changes are made must abide by the new requirements. Advisers should become familiar with the options and plans available to students.

In cases such as these, it is even more important to develop a systematic advising process that places administrators, coordinators, advisers, and support personnel in constant collaboration. The following are practical recommendations for student advising:

(1) Promote concepts of shared responsibility for both students and the institution; (2) begin the advising relationship with an awareness of the larger purpose of advising, and move to an awareness of details; and (3) develop a collaborative environment where students can contact many members of the college community for answers to questions that arise in academic planning.[39]

ILLUSTRATIVE CASE

Professor John Joseph's duties as a faculty member included academic advisement in the Education Department of Fairfield University, an independent institution offering undergraduate and graduate degrees. Michael Scott was one of the students Professor Joseph advised. The student wanted to teach chemistry and mathematics at the secondary school level and was therefore majoring in chemistry, minoring in math, and taking the education courses necessary to become certified to teach in his state and school district. Mr. Scott was also engaged to be married and had counted on being able to get a teaching position in his school district before the wedding, which was to take place in September.

While advising the student during course selection for what would be Michael Scott's last semester of coursework, Professor Joseph had noticed that the student was missing a computer programming course that was required for his minor. Since the schedule of offerings of all of the computer courses that would meet the requirement conflicted with that of the teaching methods courses that the student needed to take, the professor suggested to the student that he take the missing course at a community college and transfer the resulting three credits into Fairfield. Michael Scott took the computer course at Coral Springs Community College, received a grade of "D" in the class, and sent a transcript showing completion of the course to Fairfield. During his last semester at Fairfield, and while completing his internship requirement, the student applied for graduation. Michael interviewed with his school district and received a job offer to teach in a high school near his home, contingent upon both the presentation of a final transcript with his degree posted and state teacher certification. Michael was pleased, since teaching positions in secondary schools were difficult to obtain and because the high school had a great academic reputation. Although Michael was to start teaching in August, the principal would even allow him to take a week off for his honeymoon and would approve a substitute for him. Michael Scott could not believe his good luck.

Two weeks before commencement, Michael received a letter from the registrar's office in Fairfield, indicating that he would not be graduating with his class. Although the student had fulfilled all course requirements for his major and minor, and had attained a 2.50 grade point average (GPA) in his major, he lacked a 2.25 GPA in his minor, which included the computer course he had taken at the community college. Michael immediately contacted the Education Department to argue that the grade for the computer course should not be included in his grade point average because Professor John Joseph had mentioned that Fairfield did not transfer in grades, but rather credits, from outside institutions. The catalog was silent on this specific matter. Without the transferred course, Michael's GPA in his minor was a 2.26. The registrar's office refused to hear Michael's case and told him he still could not graduate because his grade point average in his minor did not meet the minimum GPA requirement of Fairfield's degree completion policy. Michael demanded a hearing in the matter, claiming that he relied to his detriment on Professor Joseph's advice and that he would lose the job offer if he could not graduate. A further complication was his impending wedding, and Michael could not see how he could maintain a household without a teaching position, for which he needed the degree. Michael Scott demanded a hearing on his misadvising claim. Fairfield refused to hear Michael's case, stating that it was an academic matter and that the integrity of the degree would preclude the university from allowing any exception to published policy. The student entered the county's medical facility with an acute asthma attack and spent what would have been his graduation day in the hospital.

Analysis

* **Meeting the requirements of law.**

Was Fairfield correct in its adamant position that Michael Scott was not entitled to a hearing regarding Fairfield's decision to deny him graduation based on his failure to attain a 2.25 average in his minor course concentration? As a private, independent institution, Fairfield's actions do not have to meet constitutional due process standards, although they must be fundamentally fair (not arbitrary and capricious). Consequently, even if a hearing were required in a public institution, to protect Michael's property interest in the diploma he earned, it would not be required at Fairfield. In addition, the courts have held that academic matters, at public institutions, do not merit the procedural due process that should be accorded to misconduct issues. We may conclude, therefore, that in this matter—the failure to meet an academic standard—the institution, even if it were public, would probably not be required to provide the student with a due process hearing, and Fairfield was correct in its assessment about a hearing on these grounds.

The matter should also be examined to determine whether Michael might undertake legal action to challenge this decision on other grounds. For example, could this academic decision be overturned because of a claim that it is arbitrary or capricious or made in bad faith? This approach has little likelihood of success based on judicial history of deference to the institution's academic decisions. Also, the facts do not appear to support a claim that Michael met all the requirements for graduation and that the action by Fairfield in denying Michael his diploma was a breach of an implied or express contract to provide that diploma upon the completion of the course requirements. The facts suggest instead that Fairfield was applying a requirement that, if not fully and explicitly stated in the catalog, was consistent with its practice or interpretation of the catalog.

Michael's chances of success in a legal action might be stronger if he sought to challenge the decision on the ground that Professor Joseph, as Fairfield's agent, told him that only the credits, and not the grade, would be transferred into Fairfield from Coral Springs Community College. If the professor did state or reasonably imply that any passing grade would suffice and the catalog gave no notice that this was not the procedure, then the court might estop the university from denying Michael his diploma. Courts have determined that where the academic adviser, as an agent for the institution, gives advice upon which the student relies, then the institution will be held to that advice. It should be noted, however, that in a case where this would result in undermining the integrity of the degree, or where the student lost no right, the courts have not estopped the institution from taking the action it deems appropriate. If the institution, in this situation, believes that its diploma certifies to the world at large that the person has a greater expertise than is reflected by Michael's "D" grade, the court might well support the institution's action to protect the integrity of the diploma.

Although the narrative does not provide this information, Fairfield's catalog may have provided procedures and policies with reference to student complaints in academic matters. While a failure to follow all of the procedures provided by contract may not in itself be a failure of due process in a public institution, it may constitute, in either a public or a private institution, a breach of contract. The institution's governing documents should be examined in this matter to see if they afford Michael process or procedure that was not given.

• Ethical considerations.

From an ethical perspective, one might ask whether fairness demands that Fairfield give Michael an opportunity to be heard on this matter of crucial importance to his future. Allowing a student to state his case gives the student the sense that he or she has been heard and been dealt with justly, even if the result is not a favorable one. Providing a student with an opportunity to be heard also gives the institution a chance to assess the relevant facts and, based on those facts, take whatever corrective action it deems advisable. For example, in a hearing, Michael might offer to demonstrate that he has the needed competencies and claim that he did not meet certain course requirements because he believed them unnecessary based on the professor's advice. In such a case, the institution might be willing to test Michael and allow him to receive his diploma if he demonstrated the competency needed. Even if the institution decided that Michael could not, under any circumstances, have a diploma without the required grades, the hearing might indicate if there were a need to discipline or clarify matters with Professor Joseph or clarify and elaborate on Fairfield's written materials. In any event, hearing the matter can both serve the interests of fairness to the student and enhance the full and efficient functioning of the institution.

Would ethics dictate that the institution place fidelity to the word of its professor, upon which Michael relied, over adherence to its academic standards, or vice versa? Each course of action would be ethical if it served the institution's priorities and values. Fairfield's adherence to the academic standard that its diploma had come to represent and on which the community could rely, was neither surprising nor unethical.

• Practical considerations.

The narrative demonstrates that professors, especially those with advising responsibilities, need to be clear on the policies of the institution and that the written materials should be revised to clearly reflect the policy in place. Explicit detailed policies are a protection against the type of problem encountered in this case.

If a professor/adviser seeks to change an accepted written policy, such change should be undertaken pursuant to a written procedure. Approvals should be sought and obtained before a student embarks on a course of action which deviates from the requirements for graduation.

NOTES

1. 294 F.2d 150 (5th Cir. 1961), cert. denied, 368 U.S. 930 (1961).

2. William A. Kaplin and Barbara A. Lee, *The Law of Higher Education: A Comprehensive Guide to Legal Implications of Administrative Decision Making*, 3rd ed. (San Francisco: Jossey-Bass, 1995), 380–382.

3. *Mahavongsanan v. Hall*, 529 F.2d 448, 449 (5th Cir. 1976).

4. 244 F. Supp. 156 (D. Vt. 1965).

5. Id. at 160–161.

6. *Gaspar v. Bruton*, 513 F.2d 843 (10th Cir. 1975).

7. E.g., id. (paid enrollment fee).

8. *Greenhill v. Bailey*, 519 F.2d 5 (8th Cir. 1975).

9. *Mahavongsanan*, 529 F.2d at 449.

10. *Moire v. Temple University School of Medicine*, 613 F. Supp. 1360, 1375 (E.D. Pa. 1985), aff'd, 800 F.2d 1136 (3rd Cir. 1986).

11. Thomas A. Schweitzer, "Academic Challenge Cases: Should Judicial Review Extend to Academic Evaluations of Students?" 41 *American University Law Review* 267 (1962): 329, citing *Tedeschi v. Wagner College*, 404 N.E.2d 1302 (N.Y. 1980).

12. 435 U.S. 78 (1980).

13. 474 U.S. 214 (1985).

14. Schweitzer, 322.

15. *Ewing* at 221–227; *Hershowitz* at 92.

16. Schweitzer, 308.

17. Ibid., 322.

18. See, e.g., *DeMarco v. University of Health Sciences*, 480, 352 N.E.2d 356, 366 (1976). But see *Love v. Duke University*, 776 F. Supp. 1070, 1074 (M.D. N.C. 1991), aff'd, 959 F.2d 231 (4th Cir. 1992), wherein the court held that the academic bulletin did not create a binding contract.

19. *Ross v. Pennsylvania State University*, 445 F. Supp. 147, 152 (M.D.Pa. 1978).

20. Daniel P. Rafferty, "Technical Foul: *Ross v. Creighton University* Allows Courts to Penalize Universities Which Do Not Perform Specific Promises Made to Student-Athletes," *South Dakota Law Review* 38 (1993): 180; see, e.g., *Zumbrun v. University of Southern California*, 25 Cal.App. 3d 1, 10 (2nd Cir. 1972) 1976.

21. *Giles v. Howard University*, 428 F. Supp. 603, 605 (D.D.C. 1977).

22. See, e.g., *Russell v. Salve Regina College*, 938 F.2d 315 (1st Cir. 1991).

23. *Tedeschi* at 1304 (N.Y. 1980).

24. Schweitzer, 268 n.7, citing *Susan M. v. New York Law School*, 149 A.D.2d 69, 544 N.Y.S.2d 829 (1990).

25. See, e.g., *Heisler v. New York Medical College*, 453 N.Y.S.2d 196, aff'd, 459 N.Y.S.2d 27 (1982).

26. *Andre v. Pace University*, 655 N.Y.S. 2d 277 (1996).

27. See *Tedeschi* at 1306.

28. *Russell*, 938 F.2d 315.

29. *Mahavongsanan*, 529 F.2d 448.

30. See, e.g., *Hammond v. Auburn University*, 669 F. Supp. 1555, 1559 (M.D. Ala. 1987), aff'd, 858 F.2d 744 (11th Cir. 1988), cert. denied, 489 U.S. 1017 (1989).

31. *University of Texas Health Science Center at Houston v. Babb*, 646 S.W.2d 502, 505 (Texas Ct. App. 1982).

32. See, e.g., *Behrend v. State*, 379 N.E.2d 617 (Ohio Ct. App. 1977).

33. 273 N.Y.S.2d 796 (Sup. Ct. 1966).

34. Id. at 801.

35. *Healy v. Larsson*, 323 N.Y.S.2d 625 (Sup. Ct. 1971).

36. See, e.g., *Olsson v. Board of Higher Education*, 426 N.Y.S. 248, 252 (1980).

37. Marc Lowenstein and Thomas J. Grites, "Ethics in Academic Advising," *NACADA Journal* 13, no. 1 (Spring 1993): 53–54.

38. Ibid., 54–56.

39. Susan H. Frost, "Academic Advising for Student Success," ERIC Clearinghouse on Higher Education (Washington, DC, November 1991), *ERIC Digest*, ED 340274, HE025122, 2.

Chapter 8

Transcript and Degree Issues

A primary responsibility of an institution of higher education is to provide instruction to its students. In support of this undertaking, the institution keeps an official record of the student's progress in the form of a transcript. When the student successfully completes a course of study, the institution also awards a diploma that "certifies to the world-at-large of the recipient's educational achievement and fulfillment of the institution's standards."[1] Access to the transcript is regulated by both state and federal law. Under the federal law known as the Family Educational Rights and Privacy Act, commonly referred to as FERPA or the "Buckley Amendment," the transcript may be used internally by school officials, including teachers, who have "legitimate educational interests"[2] in the academic record of a student. FERPA also states that the transcript may be provided to officials of other schools or school systems in which the student seeks to enroll; to accrediting agencies and certain organizations conducting studies for the institution; to certain government officials; to the parents of a dependent student; to persons designated in a Federal grand jury subpoena or other subpoena issued for law enforcement purposes; and to third parties at the parents' or student's request.[3]

The accuracy of student records is clearly of great importance. Their contents serve as the basis for decisions about the student by the institution or others that can determine the student's subsequent educational opportunities and employment. They can also affect the weight accorded to the student's opinions and performance in the future. Hence, the institution must strive for accuracy to maintain public confidence in the integrity of its records. This includes the obligation to employ procedures that assure the accuracy of their records and, when indicated, to investigate and correct errors.

In situations in which inaccurate diplomas or transcripts result from fraud, plagiarism, or other wrongdoing by the student or an employee, the institution not only must correct its records but must also discipline the perpetrator based on educational, legal, ethical, and practical considerations. Perhaps most challenging to the institution are those situations in which it discovers that a degree has been awarded to a student who has not earned it.

LEGAL PARAMETERS

- **Federal law, and many state laws,[4] require that students (or their parents, if they are under 18 and are dependents under federal income tax law) have the right to examine and challenge the content of student records via a university procedure to ensure that they are not inaccurate, misleading, or a violation of the student's right to privacy.**

Among other things, Title 20, Section 1232g of the United States Code, the Family Educational Rights and Privacy Act, provides that parents and students have a right to access student records and be heard if they wish to challenge their contents. Failure of the institution to comply can result in a loss of federal funds. Unless the challenge is to correct a ministerial error in a student's record, there is no private right of action allowing parents or students to sue the institution for failure to permit access and hearing.[5]

The student's right of access does not permit students in postsecondary institutions access to the financial records of their parents. Further, a student who has signed a waiver of his or her access rights with regard to references or recommendations he or she has requested may not access those records.[6]

It should also be noted that the following are not considered educational records and are, therefore, not open to parental or student inspection: records of instructional, supervisory, and administrative personnel that are kept in the sole possession of the maker and are available only to a substitute; records of a law enforcement unit of the educational institution made by the law enforcement unit for law enforcement purposes; records that relate to a person solely in his or her capacity as an employee of the institution; and medical and psychological records of a student 18 years of age or older or one who is in attendance at a postsecondary institution, which are made in connection with treatment and are only available to persons providing treatment. The medical and psychological records described can be reviewed by a doctor or appropriate professional of the student's choice.[7]

- **Courts have held that universities have the power, for good cause, to revoke or rescind a degree previously granted.**

The question of whether an institution may revoke or rescind a degree it previously awarded has not come before the courts frequently. When it has, the courts have most often found that universities, both public and private, have the power to revoke a degree for good cause if the degree holder is afforded a fair hearing.[8]

The power to revoke a degree has been deemed by the courts to be implicit in the power to confer a degree. In the case of a public institution, such power is given directly or indirectly by statute. One commentator, while recognizing that contract law cannot be strictly applied to the relationship between a student and the institution, has opined that the private institution can also look to contract law and the remedy of rescission (i.e., the nullification of the contract) for its power to rescind a degree that has been awarded as the result of a fraud or misrepresentation by the student.[9]

With reference to the showing of good cause the courts have required for revocation, the Supreme Court of Ohio, in *Waliga v. Board of Trustees of Kent State University*, stated that good cause for revocation includes fraud, deceit, and error.[10] In that case, Kent State University revoked the degrees of George A. Waliga and Kent L. Taylor when it was discovered that their records were incorrect and that these students had failed to complete their degree requirements. The court held that the university, a public institution, had the power to revoke degrees where there was such error. In another case, a federal appeals court upheld the University of Michigan's revocation of a degree when a student fraudulently obtained that degree by fabricating the data he used in his master's thesis.[11] Furthermore, the Court of Appeals of Tennessee noted that plagiarism, even when condoned by the student's faculty adviser, was deemed sufficient justification for the revocation of a student's degree by the University of Tennessee.[12]

Ralph D. Mawdsley, in his commentary on degree revocation has stated that he believes the courts have erred in allowing a person who is no longer a student to be subject to the university's internal academic procedures with reference to such a significant property interest as a degree. He believes that legal judgments must be made and recommends that the courts and not the university determine whether or not to revoke or rescind a degree previously conferred after full legal process.[13] To date, however, the courts have not agreed with Mawdsley.

• A public institution must provide for due process in its degree revocation procedures.

Both student misconduct and constitutional rights are involved in a revocation and both require that the student affected be afforded procedural safeguards. Courts have held that disciplinary actions by the institution based on student misconduct require more due process than those based strictly on academic evaluations.[14] In addition, the Fourteenth Amendment to the Constitution, applicable to public institutions, provides that a person cannot be deprived of property or liberty without due process.[15] A degree is a property interest. Consequently, its revocation triggers due process rights.[16] Revocation may also implicate a liberty interest (such as when the revocation involves reputational damage that can impact the student's freedom to take advantage of other opportunities) thus providing an additional basis for requiring due process.[17]

In determining the procedural due process necessary, the courts have deemed that public institutions must provide a student with notice of the action contemplated by the institution and the charges against the student as well as the basis for those charges and that action. The student must also be given an opportunity to be heard.[18] The opportunity to be heard has been held to include the right to present evidence before an impartial decision maker.[19] While confrontation and cross-examination have not been required in every case, some cases have indicated that such confrontation may be advisable when serious interests are at issue. Most courts have not required that the student be represented by counsel in disciplinary proceedings.[20] Where there are serious consequences, as in a revocation, allowing the student to have counsel present to advise, but not actually participate, appears to be most consistent with due process requirements.[21] A federal court has also held that the student is entitled to counsel if the institution proceeds through its counsel.[22]

In addition to providing procedural due process, courts have also reviewed revocation actions under a substantive due process standard to determine if there is a rational basis for the decision. Courts are unwilling to substitute their judgment for the judgment of the institution in academic matters unless the decision maker has clearly deviated from accepted academic norms, (did not have clear and convincing evidence, did not exercise professional judgment, or was arbitrary and capricious).[23] Where the issue also concerns misconduct, as is the case in a degree revocation, the argument for a substantive review by the court is stronger. An institution can avoid being seen as arbitrary and capricious by having clear standards, consistently applied.

- **A private institution must provide and adhere to fair procedures in the rescission of a degree.**

Although not circumscribed in its rescission procedures and actions by constitutional limitations, unless a nexus between the state and the action is found to justify considering that state action is involved, the courts have nevertheless required that private institutions maintain and follow fair procedures.[24] As discussed above, fair procedures include clear standards, notice, and the opportunity to be heard before an impartial decision maker. The opportunity to confront and question witnesses and to have an attorney present (though not participating) is also advisable. Courts will ordinarily support a decision to rescind a degree that is not arbitrary and that is arrived at through a fundamentally fair procedure. Private institutions wishing to pass judicial scrutiny should strictly adhere to their procedures and employ the substantive and procedural due process standards applicable to the public institution.[25]

• **Only the body within the institution that is empowered to
grant the degree may revoke or rescind it.**

A degree may only be revoked or rescinded by the institutional body that is empowered to grant the degree. In a case addressing this issue, *Hand v. Match-ett*,[26] the federal appeals court voided the revocation of a doctoral student's degree even though his dissertation contained plagiarized material. The board of regents had delegated the revocation to faculty and administrators. The court stated that the statute at issue gave the board of regents exclusive power to confer degrees and that it therefore assumed that to the extent a power to revoke degrees was recognized, it too was vested exclusively in the regents, and no statute gave it the power to delegate this responsibility. The board of regents had to exercise final authority in the revocation process.[27]

ETHICAL CONSIDERATIONS

Society needs to trust higher education to accomplish its mission of producing educated citizens, and higher education needs the public's trust in order to remain viable. Part of developing this trust is the ability of the community at large to be relatively certain that the holders of an institution's academic degrees truly possess the skills its faculty has certified and the board of trustees has conferred upon them. Institutions have an ethical obligation to uphold that trust.

• **In cases of diploma or transcript fraud, what is the primary
obligation of the institution?**

If we agree that the search for truth and the survival of the institution are fundamental values in the operation of a college or university, the primary obligation of the institution ought to be the integrity of its records. As a seeker of truth, an institution cannot knowingly permit inaccurate records. Moreover, to ensure its survival, an institution must maintain public confidence in the accuracy of its certifications and records. For these two fundamental reasons, records found to be erroneous must be corrected.

• **What should govern the institution's responses to the student
culprit in the case of transcript or diploma fraud?**

The institution is charged with the responsibility of educating the student and enforcing the rules and regulations that apply to student conduct. The institutional response should, therefore, enforce its code of conduct by applying appropriate sanctions as well as by instructing the student on acceptable behavior.

In meeting its primary obligation of protecting the integrity of its records, the institution may take any one of a number of actions, such as changing a grade, rejecting a plagiarized work, or rescinding a degree. These actions not only correct but also maintain standards and both educate and punish the student by disallowing the sought-after reward. Are further sanctions needed?

Sanctions should be determined by the nature of the offense, the mitigating circumstances, if any, and institutional policy and precedent. Sanctions that are more severe than necessary to instruct the student, correct the errors, and enforce regulations should be carefully scrutinized and their value or purpose clearly enunciated and approved before being imposed. Lack of fairness or consistency in applying sanctions should be avoided, as such action may impair the institution's reputation and can raise legal questions of discrimination.

The questions of intent, previous performance, and consistency should be relevant to the sanctions meted out. Consider, however, the case of *Napolitano v. Trustees of Princeton University*.[28] In that case, the university applied a more severe sanction than it had in other similar cases. It chose to withhold the award of Ms. Napolitano's undergraduate degree for one year, despite her desire to go to law school, because of a finding of plagiarism on a term paper submitted for a course in Spanish. The student, who had an otherwise spotless record and a high academic average, admitted to quoting without attribution. However, the student also asserted that this occurred because of poor use of the rules of attribution and not because she had any *intent* to deceive her professor.

The court, examining the university's student handbook, found there was sufficient evidence to support a conclusion of plagiarism as it was defined and a penalty of the withholding of Ms. Napolitano's degree for one year. However, the court also found that in previous disciplinary cases the university imposed varying degrees of penalties that seemed to have been applied on an ad hoc basis. Withholding a senior's degree for one year was the exception rather than the rule.

The court nonetheless upheld the university's actions, asserting that it could not substitute its own views of greater leniency in this case for those of a "duly constituted administrative body within a private institution."[29] Compassion, noted the court, cannot be mandated.

Although in this case there was no legal requirement for the institution to be consistent with its past practice, should it have been? In this and other similar cases, the institution should determine if the punishment is congruent with the university's obligations and values, if there is justification for a severe response, if the punishment serves a purpose, if there are mitigating circumstances, if the punishment appears fair, if the punishment fits the crime, and if the best interests of the student and the institution are well served.

- ### • Whom should the institution notify of the existence of a corrected record?

Once the decision has been made to correct the inaccuracies, whom should be notified? Common sense appears to require that all who received inaccurate information should be provided with the correct information. Under FERPA, however, an institution may not send transcripts to anyone without the written consent of the student. It is legally unclear whether an institution may send a corrected transcript to all those to whom transcripts were sent at the student's request prior to the record being rectified.

Consider also instances where transcripts were not issued to third parties directly but the institution has reason to believe that the third party is in possession of, or has acted on the basis of, inaccurate records issued to the student by the institution. Ethical concerns may indicate that the institution should attempt to correct those records to meet its obligations to accuracy but such action could violate FERPA. To protect the institution from violating the law, legal counsel should be consulted before sending any corrected transcript without the written consent of the student involved.

PRACTICAL SUGGESTIONS

An institution can take measures that will clarify its position; communicate its standards to students, faculty, and staff; and protect its records. Among these are the following.

- **There should be a clear student academic conduct code, properly disseminated to students and faculty and consistently enforced.**

An academic conduct code should be formulated through a participatory process that involves students, faculty, and administrators. Students should receive a copy of the code at an orientation or advising meeting, at registration, or as part of a student handbook or other publication. Many institutions have students acknowledge their familiarity with the academic conduct code by signing a statement that is kept in the student file. Whenever possible, an explanation of the code with examples of appropriate and inappropriate behaviors should supplement the written document. Faculty and academic administrators should also be familiar with the contents of the code, since they are responsible for its proper implementation.

All higher education institutions should encourage close faculty supervision and proper mentor oversight,[30] in addition to having a clear definition of plagiarism. Again, examples of what constitutes plagiarism should be provided to students. In this age of computers, World Wide Web, Internet, and other electronic devices and sources, institutions must address computer and software ethics and issues regarding intellectual property. Faculty and administration should instruct students, through orientation sessions, in research courses, and through any other means that the institution may choose what plagiarism consists of and how to avoid it.

- **Access to academic records and paraphernalia should be safeguarded, and there should also be clear written rules regarding such access.**

Written rules regarding who has access to academic records (hardcopy, computerized, or in any other form) are important to safeguard the records against tampering or inadvertent errors. In addition to adherence to FERPA regulations, each institution should establish its own rules regarding input and retrieval of information from the records. For example, many institutions prohibit student workers from handling student records, require employees to utilize individual passwords to access the database, and utilize other security measures to ensure accountability. It is advisable to conduct periodic audits of the records and of the system.

It is strongly advisable that transcript and diploma papers, the software used for the creation of actual diplomas and transcripts, and institutional seals and signature stamps be secured. Checks and balances in access procedures should also be utilized. This security is especially important because the advent of the computer, scanner, sophisticated printers, and other technological advances has made it easier for those who would falsify documents to scan and copy official institutional seals and signatures. Desktop publishing and laser and color printers can create official-looking transcripts and diplomas. Consequently, a college or university should review the possibilities of enhancing the security of its transcripts and diplomas by purchasing special paper (such as SCRIP-SAFE paper) that greatly reduces the opportunity for alteration. Comparatively recent practices such as electronic transmission and instant student academic record acknowledgment increase the security of transcript transmission among universities, colleges, and high schools.[31]

- **If a transcript from another institution does not appear to be genuine, looks altered, or has been hand delivered, telephone or contact the college or university that allegedly issued the document to seek verification. If an institution finds an altered document, the college or university that purportedly produced the diploma or transcript should be notified immediately.**

Examine all transcripts to determine their authenticity. There are a number of observations that are pertinent to this process. For example, the postmark on the envelope is of interest. Normally, transcripts are mailed from the registrar at the issuing institution, unless the student is delivering the document in person or mailing it himself or herself. The postmark should therefore match the city of the issuing institution or student domicile. If the transcript was supposed to originate at the issuing institution, the envelope would most likely also bear an institutional meter mark rather than a postage stamp. The date of issuance is also of concern. A transcript with a date of issuance that is more than a few weeks prior to date of receipt could mean that the transcript was not mailed directly from the issuing institution. Next, examine the registrar's signature and institutional seal for clarity and authenticity. The type of font and format should also be consistent.[32]

A common mistake made by those who counterfeit transcripts is to add the hours earned or attempted and the quality points incorrectly. They also bungle the calculation of the grade point average. In fraudulent diplomas, the names of the individuals who sign them may be fictitious, or names of real people may be misspelled.

An institution that receives an altered document should, after verifying that it is false, share the information with the institution that is being misrepresented. This will afford the institution the opportunity to investigate how the fraud was perpetrated, determine whether there was internal involvement, and attempt to prevent a reoccurrence.

Also, when in doubt about the authenticity of a foreign diploma, or of its issuing institution, seek the help of the American Association of Collegiate Registrars and Admissions Officers or one of a number of professional associations that specialize in the verification and evaluation of foreign credentials.

- **When transcript or diploma fraud is uncovered, a careful audit of the systems in place at the institution should be undertaken immediately to prevent further incidents. Cases of diploma or transcript fraud should be dealt with according to the institution's policies and procedures.**

Colleges and universities should establish and periodically revise internal policies and procedures in the handling of these cases, including due process procedures for those accused and remedial actions to be sure that they conform to legal and ethical principles. These procedures need not be published in their catalogs but, as described above, should be available for students to examine. Students should be notified that such policies and procedures exist.

Does the security of the institution's records merit significant expenditures and attention? To what extent must the university protect itself? There is no one answer for all institutions and all circumstances. All university actions involve some costs. The economic impact of each action must be measured against the institution's purpose; each institution must decide when the costs are appropriate. The integrity of the institution's certifications merit reasonable expenditure because of the devastating effects incorrect records may have on the institution's reputation and perhaps even on its survival.

ILLUSTRATIVE CASE

Description

An audit of registrar's records has uncovered that student BG has been given credit for courses she did not take at Our Lady of Lourdes University. In fact, about one fourth of all the courses she took for her undergraduate degree were fraudulently added to her transcript. As a result of the fraud, the student had been awarded an undergraduate degree one year before the audit discovered the alterations. As is customary, a notation was made on her transcript that the degree had been awarded, along with the date and major, and a diploma was issued by the university.

It was discovered through a review of computer records that an employee of the registrar's office modified her transcripts, adding the extra courses and posting the undergraduate degree. The employee was confronted with the facts and was terminated when he was unable to provide a satisfactory explanation for the erroneous transcript.

The university then contacted student BG and asked her to explain the courses on her transcripts that, according to university records, either were not taken by her or were not offered by the university in the semester indicated on the transcript. The student disavowed any knowledge that those courses or the degree were noted on her transcript. The university's records showed that the student had requested and signed for transcripts of her work after the fraudulent degree was awarded. When confronted with this fact, the student claimed that she had picked them up in a sealed envelope to be delivered to third parties and that she had not looked at the transcript. The registrar's records showed transcripts were requested by and prepared for the student herself, and no other transcript requests were on file. The student reported her work location was at an elementary school and listed herself as a full-time teacher. In the state in which this private religious university was operating, no teacher could be hired without an undergraduate degree, so the chief academic officer of the university assumed that the transcript bearing the "degree awarded" notation was sent to the state capitol for teacher certification purposes by the student in a sealed envelope that she retrieved herself from the registrar's office. When questioned about this, the student refused to answer.

Following an informal hearing before the chief academic officer, the chairperson of the student's academic department, and the university counsel, the student (who declined to bring an advocate or counsel) was notified in writing that her transcript would be corrected, her undergraduate degree would be rescinded, and a corrected transcript would be sent to her. She was given an opportunity for an appeal hearing before the president of the university, but she declined the offer.

The university moved to revoke the student's undergraduate degree and corrected her transcript to show only actual coursework completed by the student. The same entities who signed the student's diploma when it was issued (president, vice president, dean, and chairman of the university's board of trustees) also affixed their signatures to a document revoking the degree. The student was sent a corrected copy of the transcript and a copy of the document revoking her undergraduate degree.

The university sent a corrected transcript to the state's Office of Teacher

Certification. The university undertook no formal legal action against the dismissed employee.

Analysis

• **Meeting the requirements of law.**

Under existing case law, the university probably had the power to revoke the degree awarded to BG. Fraud, error, and deceit, one or more of which was present in the circumstances described, have been cited by some courts as constituting the good cause required to revoke.

The power to revoke also requires that the student be given an opportunity to be heard. While the university's procedures do not have to pass constitutional muster on this point, a fair hearing must be, and was, provided. The university gave the student notice and a hearing before an impartial decision maker. The student was also afforded the opportunity to bring counsel and appeal the decision, though she chose not to do either.

In conformance with the case law on this issue, the same institutional body that awarded the degree to BG revoked the degree.

The university may well have violated FERPA when it sent a corrected transcript to the state's Office of Teacher Certification without BG's consent. The law requires the written consent of the student before his or her transcript may be sent to a third party. However, in this case the institution knew that it had issued the erroneous transcript to BG, which she must have sent to the Office of Teacher Certification in order to get her license. The institution might argue, therefore, that it had a duty to the integrity of its documents to correct any errors discovered in the transcript, particularly when the public good might be affected.

• **Ethical considerations.**

The revocation of the degree obtained through fraud, deceit, or error was clearly a demonstration of the institution's action to meet its basic obligation to truth, to the integrity of its records, and to the public—all necessary to ensure its survival. The institution's duty to educate and discipline the student was addressed by the correction of her transcript and the revocation of her degree. She was, no doubt, punished and educated by her failure to benefit from the fraud and by having her record and possibly her future tainted by this incident.

One might argue, as did Ralph D. Mawdsley,[33] that the institution at which she was no longer a student should not have judged a matter of such significance, which required the evaluation of evidence and the drawing of legal conclusions. On the other hand, others might argue that the institution's duty to protect its records merited this action.

• **Practical considerations.**

Budget considerations, as well as issues of proof and the allocation of resources, may have been responsible for the university's decision not to pursue a legal action against its former employee who allegedly falsified records. The university's records were obviously vulnerable. The institution should undertake further audits to determine if there were any other alterations made to the records and should promptly correct all errors discovered. There may be a possibility that this was not an isolated case or that the dismissed employee was not acting alone. Next, the institution must determine if access to records in the registrar's office was and is now properly controlled, if employee standards and supervision were and are now appropriate, and if it has proper procedures in place to guard against alterations of transcripts. Finally, a plan needs to be developed to avoid the possibility of a recurrence in the future, thereby ensuring the accuracy of its certifications, and the continuing trust of the public in the integrity of its records.

NOTES

1. *Waliga v. Board of Trustees of Kent State University*, 488 N.E.2d 850, 852 (Ohio 1986).
2. 20 U.S.C.A. § 1232g (b) (1) (A) (West 1998).
3. 20 U.S.C.A. § 1232g (b) (1) (West 1998).
4. Administrators should check the requirements of state law as well as federal law on student records.
5. *Tarka v. Cunningham*, 917 F.2d 890 (5th Cir. 1990); but see *Fay v. South Colonie Cent. School District*, 802 F.2d 21 (1986). (FERPA does not itself give rise to a private cause of action, but it creates an interest that may be vindicated in a 1983 action.)
6. 20 U.S.C.A. § 1232g (a) (1) (C) (West 1998).
7. 20 U.S.C.A. § 1232g (a) (A) (West 1998).
8. *Waliga*, 488 N.E.2d 850; see *Crook v. Baker*, 813 F.2d 88, 93 (6th Cir. 1987), citing unreported case of *Abalkhail v. Claremont University Center*, No. B014012 (Cal. Ct. App. Feb. 27, 1986, cert. denied, 107 S.Ct. 186 [1986]).
9. Bernard D. Reams, Jr., "Revocation of Academic Degrees by Colleges and Universities," *Journal of College and University Law* 14 (Fall 1987): 183, 285–288.
10. 488 N.E.2d at 852.
11. *Crook v. Baker*, 813 F.2d 88.
12. *Faulkner v. University of Tennessee*, 1994 WL 642765 (Tenn. App.).
13. Ralph D. Mawdsley, "Judicial Deference: A Doctrine Misapplied in Degree Revocations," *Ed. Law Rep.* 70 (1992): 1043.
14. See *Board of Curators of the University of Missouri v. Horowitz*, 435 U.S. 78 (1978); *Ross v. University of Minnesota*, 439 N.W. 2d 28 (Minn. App. 1989).
15. *U.S. Const.* Amend. XIV, § 1.
16. See *Crook v. Baker*, 813 F.2d 88, 96.
17. *Greenhill v. Bailey*, 519 F.2d 5 (8th Cir. 1975).
18. See *Crook v. Baker*, 813 F.2d at 97.
19. Id. at 97.
20. *Hall v. Medical College of Ohio at Toledo*, 742 F.2d 299 (6th Cir. 1984).

21. *Gabrilowitz v. Newman*, 582 F.2d 100 (1st Cir. 1978).

22. *French v. Bashful*, 303 F. Supp. 1333 (E.D. La. 1969), app. dismissed, 425 F.2d 182 (5th Cir.), cert. denied, 400 U.S. 941 (1970).

23. See *Crook v. Baker*, 813 F.2d 88, 99–100.

24. *Napolitano v. Trustees of Princeton*, 453 A.2d 279 (N.J. Super. Ct. 1982); Bernard D. Reams, Jr., "Recovation of Academic Degrees by Colleges and Universities," *Journal of College and University Law* (1987): 14, 283.

25. See *Napolitano* at 283.

26. 957 F.2d 791 (10th Cir. 1992).

27. Id.

28. 453 A.2d 279.

29. Id.

30. Ralph D. Mawdsley, "Plagiarism Problems in Higher Education," *Journal of College and University Law* (1986): 13, 65.

31. "EDI in Academia: Salle Mae Brings Electronics to the Ivory Tower," *Corporate EFT Report*, August 12, 1992.

32. Bruce T. Shutt, "Summary of Spoken Comments as Testimony on Fraudulent Records," *College and University: The Journal of the American Association of Collegiate Registrars* (Spring 1986): 206–211. (Summary of testimony before the Subcommittee on Health and Long-Term Care of the U.S. House of Representatives, December 11, 1985.)

33. Mawdsley, supra note 14 at 1043.

Appendix 1

Values Audit Process

Several colleges and universities performed their own values audits in the 1980s, many in cooperation with the Society for Values in Higher Education. Various professional associations have also undergone the process, which may take anywhere from three to nine months.[1] The procedure for the audit starts by compiling an explicit values inventory from a variety of sources, such as an institution's mission statement, handbook, catalog(s). The resulting list is then compared to the implicit values revealed in surveys, analyses of institutional history, and discussions. The next step is an analysis of the values inherent in the inventories as they relate to recent decisions that the institution has made. This analysis may reveal which values are in conflict when there are ethical dilemmas or when tough issues are involved. An audit report is developed as a third step. As a final step, new procedures are institutionalized that will strive to mitigate incongruencies and reinforce behavior that exemplifies the agreed-upon values. At this point, a commitment of institutional resources to support the plan may be made.[2]

NOTES

1. David Charles Smith, "Program Improvement Through Values Audits," in *Evaluation for Program Improvement*, ed. D. Deshler (San Francisco: Jossey-Bass, 1984), 44.
2. Ibid.

Appendix 2

AAUP "Statement
on Professional Ethics"

The statement which follows, a revision of a statement originally adopted
in 1966, was approved by the Association's Committee B on Professional
Ethics, adopted by the Association's Council in June 1987, and endorsed
by the Seventy-third Annual Meeting.

INTRODUCTION

From its inception, the American Association of University Professors has recognized that membership in the academic profession carries with it special responsibilities. The Association has consistently affirmed these responsibilities in
major policy statements, providing guidance to professors in such matters as
their utterances as citizens, the exercise of their responsibilities to students and
colleagues, and their conduct when resigning from an institution or when undertaking sponsored research. The *Statement on Professional Ethics* that follows
sets forth those general standards that serve as a reminder of the variety of
responsibilities assumed by all members of the profession.

In the enforcement of ethical standards, the academic profession differs from
those of law and medicine, whose associations act to ensure the integrity of
members engaged in private practice. In the academic profession the individual
institution of higher learning provides this assurance and so should normally
handle questions concerning propriety of conduct within its own framework by
reference to a faculty group. The Association supports such local action and

stands ready, through the general secretary and Committee B, to counsel with members of the academic community concerning questions of professional ethics and to inquire into complaints when local consideration is impossible or inappropriate. If the alleged offense is deemed sufficiently serious to raise the possibility of adverse action, the procedures should be in accordance with the 1940 *Statement of Principles on Academic Freedom and Tenure*, the 1958 *Statement on Procedural Standards in Faculty Dismissal Proceedings*, or the applicable provisions of the Association's *Recommended Institutional Regulations on Academic Freedom and Tenure*.

THE STATEMENT

I. Professors, guided by a deep conviction of the worth and dignity of the advancement of knowledge, recognize the special responsibilities placed upon them. Their primary responsibility to their subject is to seek and to state the truth as they see it. To this end professors devote their energies to developing and improving their scholarly competence. They accept the obligation to exercise critical self-discipline and judgment in using, extending, and transmitting knowledge. They practice intellectual honesty. Although professors may follow subsidiary interests, these interests must never seriously hamper or compromise their freedom of inquiry.

II. As teachers, professors encourage the free pursuit of learning in their students. They hold before them the best scholarly and ethical standards of their discipline. Professors demonstrate respect for students as individuals and adhere to their proper roles as intellectual guides and counselors. Professors make every reasonable effort to foster honest academic conduct and to ensure that their evaluations of students reflect each student's true merit. They respect the confidential nature of the relationship between professor and student. They avoid any exploitation, harassment, or discriminatory treatment of students. They acknowledge significant academic or scholarly assistance from them. They protect their academic freedom.

III. As colleagues, professors have obligations that derive from common membership in the community of scholars. Professors do not discriminate or harass colleagues. They respect and defend the free inquiry of associates. In the exchange of criticism and ideas professors show due respect for the opinions of others. Professors acknowledge academic debt and strive to be objective in their professional judgment of colleagues. Professors accept their share of faculty responsibilities for the governance of their institution.

IV. As members of an academic institution, professors seek above all to be effective teachers and scholars. Although professors observe the stated regulations of the institution, provided the regulations do not contravene academic freedom, they maintain their right to criticize and seek revision. Professors give due regard to their paramount responsibilities within their institution in determining the amount and character of work done outside it. When considering the interruption or termination of their service, professors recognize the effect of their decision upon the program of the institution and give due notice of their intentions.

V. As members of their community, professors have the rights and obligations of other citizens. Professors measure the urgency of these obligations in the light of their responsibilities to their subject, to their students, to their profession, and to their institution. When they speak or act as private persons they avoid creating the impression of speaking or acting for their college or university. As citizens engaged in a profession that depends upon freedom for its health and integrity, professors have a particular obligation to promote conditions of free inquiry and to further public understanding of academic freedom.

NOTE

Reproduced with permission from American Association of University Professors, "Statement on Professional Ethics," *AAUP Policy Documents and Reports* (Washington, DC: American Association of University Professors, 1995), 105–106.

Appendix 3

AAUA "Mission Statement and Professional Standards"

THE MISSION OF THE AAUA

The AAUA develops and advances the standards for the profession of higher education administration.

The AAUA emphasizes through its policy statements, programs and services the responsibility of administrators, at all levels, to demonstrate moral and ethical leadership in the exercise of their duties.

The AAUA provides, through programs and services, opportunities for the professional development of its members, whether they be employed by colleges, universities, specialized institutions or professional associations.

PROFESSIONAL STANDARDS OF THE AAUA

In 1975, the AAUA developed a set of professional standards, which embody the principles of moral and ethical leadership and which define the rights and responsibilities of administrators in higher education. These professional standards were revised in 1994.

The revision process began in October 1992. The Professional Standards Committee, working with the AAUA's General Counsel, developed a series of draft revisions that were reviewed and amended by the Board of Directors at its regular meetings, and by the AAUA membership at National Assembly XXII, in June 1993. In November 1993, Draft IV of the revised standards was mailed to all members of the AAUA with a questionnaire, the responses to which were included in Draft V. Draft V of the revised standards was approved, with amendments, by the Board of Directors of National Assembly XXIII, in June 1994.

1. Non-discrimination

(a) An applicant for employment or promotion as an Administrator has the right to consideration without being discriminated against on the grounds of race, gender, sexual orientation, religion (except where exempt by Title VII of the 1964 Civil Rights Act, or other statute), national origin, age or disability.

(b) An Administrator has the responsibility to perform the duties of his or her office in such a way as to not discriminate on the grounds of race, gender, sexual orientation, religion (except where exempt by Title VII of the 1964 Civil Rights Act, or other statute), national origin, age or disability.

2. Written Terms of Employment

(a) An Administrator has the right to a written statement of the terms of his or her employment, including, but not limited to, statements on salary and fringe benefits, term of office, process of review, and responsibilities of the position.

(b) An Administrator has the responsibility to perform the duties of his or her office as defined in the written statement of the terms of employment, or as defined in an official handbook of the institution.

3. Institutional Authority and Support

(a) An Administrator has the right to the authority necessary to fulfill the responsibilities of his or her office, and to a supportive institutional environment.

(b) An Administrator has the responsibility to use the authority of his or her office, and the support provided by the institution, to fulfill the responsibilities of his or her office.

4. Availability and Use of Resources

(a) An Administrator has the right to the financial, physical and human resources necessary to fulfill the responsibilities of his or her office.

(b) An Administrator has the responsibility to use the financial, physical and human resources of his or her office in a way that is consistent with the policies and priorities set by the institution's governing board; and has the responsibility to develop, allocate, and preserve the resources of the institution that are within the limits of his or her office.

5. Policy Development and Implementation

(a) An Administrator has the right to participate in the development and implementation of those institutional policies that relate to the authority and responsibilities of his or her office.

(b) An Administrator has the responsibility to participate in the development and implementation of those institutional policies that relate to the authority and responsibilities of his or her office.

6. Speaking for the Institution

(a) An Administrator has the right to act as a spokesperson of the institution within the limits of his or her office, and subject to the policies of the institution.

(b) An Administrator has the responsibility to act as a spokesperson for the institution within the limits of his or her office, insofar as that function is a requirement of the office.

7. Professional Growth and Development

(a) An Administrator has the right to support for his or her professional growth and development, by means such as participation in professional activities and attendance at professional meetings, and by sharing in sabbaticals, leaves of absence and other developmental programs of the institution.

(b) An Administrator has the responsibility to improve his or her professional skills, abilities and performance, by means such as participation in professional activities and attendance at professional meetings, and by sharing in sabbaticals, leaves of absence and other developmental programs of the institution.

8. Job Performance Evaluation

(a) An Administrator has the right to regular formal evaluation of his or her job performance, to participation in the evaluation process, and to timely receipts of the results of those evaluations.

(b) An Administrator has the responsibility for ensuring that his or her subordinates receive regular job performance evaluations, that they participate in the evaluation process, and that they receive, in a timely manner, the results of those evaluations.

9. Advancement Within the Institution

(a) An Administrator has the right to be considered for career advancement opportunities within the institution.

(b) An Administrator has the responsibility, when positions become available that are within the limits of his or her office, to post those positions within the institution and to give consideration to candidates from within the institution.

10. Academic Freedom

(a) An Administrator has the right to enjoy the benefits of academic freedom, insofar as the concept of academic freedom (as defined by the institution) is applicable to his or her duties.

(b) An Administrator has the responsibility to perform the duties of his or her office in a way that maintains and secures the academic freedom of faculty, students, and administrators, and that maintains and secures the academic freedom of the institution.

11. Expression of Personal Opinion

(a) An Administrator has the right, subject to the policies of the institution, to express personal opinions on issues that are related to the institution and on issues that are not related to the institution.

(b) An Administrator has the responsibility, when expressing personal opinions on issues that are related to the institution, to make clear that he or she is speaking as a private person, and not as a representative of the institution.

12. Harassment Free Environment

(a) An Administrator has the right to perform the responsibilities of his or her office without being harassed.

(b) An Administrator has the responsibility to perform the duties of his or her office in a way that creates and maintains an environment in which each person is able to perform his or her responsibilities without being harassed.

13. Personal Privacy

(a) An Administrator has the right to privacy in all personal matters, including, but not limited to, financial information, religious beliefs, and political views and affiliations, unless this right is specifically limited by statute or the conditions of the particular office.

(b) An Administrator has the responsibility to respect the right of privacy of others, in all personal matters including, but not limited to, financial information, religious beliefs, and political views and affiliations, except where this right of others is specifically limited by statute or the conditions of their office.

14. Participation in Associations and Support of Causes

(a) An Administrator has the right to participate in associations and to support causes of his or her choice, subject only to the constraints imposed by institutional responsibilities or conflict of interest considerations.

(b) An Administrator has the responsibility to respect the right of his or her subordinates to participate in associations and support causes, subject to the constraints imposed by institutional responsibilities or conflict of interest considerations.

15. Fair and Equitable Treatment

(a) An Administrator has the right to fair and equitable treatment by his or her superiors, and by the institution's administrators and governing board; and to receive treatment that is free from arbitrary or capricious action.

(b) An Administrator has the responsibility to treat subordinates fairly and equitably, and to avoid arbitrary or capricious actions, especially in situations relating to performance evaluations, promotions, demotions and, or, the termination of employment.

16. Reappointment and Termination

(a) An Administrator has the right to receive a copy of the institution's policies and procedures relating to the timely notification of reappointment and termination actions, prior to his or her appointment. When these policies and procedures are amended, an administrator has the right to receive the amended policies and procedures.

(b) An Administrator has the responsibility to respect his or her subordinates' rights contained in the institution's policies and procedures relating to the timely notification of reappointment and termination actions.

17. Post Employment Support

(a) An Administrator has the right, when his or her termination of employment is for reasons other than for cause, to receive professional and technical support from the institution in seeking new employment.

(b) An Administrator has the responsibility, within limits of his or her office, to provide professional and technical support to subordinates whose employment is terminated for reasons other than for cause.

18. Post Employment References

(a) An Administrator has the right, when ending his or her employment or subsequent to ending his or her employment, to receive a written statement from the institution that reflects clearly and accurately his or her job performance evaluation and the reason for his or her termination of employment.

(b) An Administrator has the responsibility, when requested by a subordinate or former subordinate, for providing a written statement from the institution that reflects clearly and accurately the performance evaluation and the reason for termination of employment of that subordinate or former subordinate.

NOTE

Reproduced with permission from American Association of University Administrators, "Mission Statement and Professional Standards" (Tuscaloosa, AL: American Association of University Administrators, 1994).

Appendix 4

AAUP "Statement on Conflicts of Interest"

The statement that follows was approved for publication by the Association's Committee B on Professional Ethics in June 1990.

American universities and colleges have long been engaged with the institutions of the wider society, to their mutual benefit. Universities have trained ministers, teachers, corporate leaders, and public servants, and have taken on wider responsibilities in research and administration for state and federal governments. The years after World War II brought both quantitative and qualitative change in this relationship as a result of the world responsibilities assumed by the United States and of the strikingly new importance attained by science. This change was symbolized and advanced by an immense increase in federal and state funding for higher education and in investment by private foundations. Now, as universities enter an era of more stringent budgetary limitations, yet another major shift seems certain—to greater reliance on private funding and to a closer symbiosis between universities and industry.

The many opportunities offered to both university researchers and the private sector by sweeping developments in certain areas of science and technology have led to new concerns in both universities and government. One such concern, about freedom to do research and to publish the results, has rightly exercised universities in deliberations about whether or not to undertake such joint efforts and on what terms. More recently, the question of conflict of interest has been raised anew, with regard to the pressures that financial interests of faculty members participating in extra-university enterprises may exert, consciously or not, on the design and the outcome of the research.

The American Association of University Professors has addressed these questions in the past, and we believe it important to reaffirm the 1965 joint statement of the AAUP and the American Council on Education, *On Preventing Conflicts of Interest in Government-Sponsored Research at Universities*, and to commend the 1983 report of an Association subcommittee on *Corporate Funding of Academic Research*. The latter report, avowedly tentative and anticipating a fuller statement at a later time, properly assumed that the initiative must lie with university faculties for drawing up such conflict-of-interest guidelines as are appropriate to each campus, with due regard for the proper disclosure of a faculty member's involvement in off-campus enterprises, in terms of investment, ownership, or consultative status; for the use of university personnel, including students; and for the disposition of potential profits.

Recent developments have suggested the following considerations to be taken into account by faculties involved in developing or revising such guidelines.

Government draft proposals for policing possible conflicts of interest have been overwhelmingly rejected by the academic community as involving a massive, unneeded enlargement of the government's role on the campus. Faculties must be careful, however, to ensure that they do not defensively propose a similar bureaucratic burden differing only in the locus of administration. Any requirements for disclosure of potential conflicts of interest should be carefully focused on legitimate areas of concern and not improperly interfere with the privacy rights of faculty members and their families.

Because the central business of the university remains teaching and research unfettered by extra-university dictates, faculties should ensure that any cooperative venture between members of the faculty and outside agencies, whether public or private, respects the primacy of the university's principal mission, with regard to the choice of subjects of research and the reaching and publication of results.

Faculties should make certain that the pursuit of such joint ventures does not become an end in itself and so introduce distortions into traditional university understandings and arrangements. Private and public agencies have a direct interest in only a few fields of research and in only certain questions within those fields. Accordingly, external interests should not be allowed to shift the balance of academic priorities in a university without thorough debate about the consequences and without the considered judgment of appropriate faculty bodies. So, too, care must be taken to avoid contravening a commitment to fairness by widening disparities—in teaching loads, student supervision, or budgetary allocation—between departments engaged in such outside activity and those not less central to the nature of a university, which have, or can have, no such engagement.

The ability to procure private or government funding may in certain circumstances be an appropriate consideration in making judgments about salaries, tenure, and promotion, but it must be kept in proper proportion and be consistent with criteria established by the faculty. Guidelines concerning intra-university research support should guard against making its availability dependent, solely or predominantly, on the likelihood that the research so supported will result in obtaining outside funding.

NOTE

Reproduced with permission from American Association of University Professors, "Statement on Conflicts of Interest," *AAUP Policy Documents and Reports* (Washington, DC: American Association of University Professors, 1995), 119–120.

Appendix 5

AAUP "On Preventing Conflicts of Interest in Government-Sponsored Research at Universities"

The many complex problems that have developed in connection with the extensive sponsored research programs of the federal government have been of concern to the government, the academic community, and private industry. The Association, through its Council, and the American Council on Education, working in cooperation with the president's science advisor and the Federal Council of Science and Technology, in 1965 developed a statement of principles formulating basic standards and guidelines in this problematic area.

An underlying premise of the statement is that responsibility for determining standards affecting the academic community rests with that community and that conflict-of-interest problems are best handled by administration and faculty in cooperative effort. In addition to providing guidelines, the statement seeks to identify and alert administration and faculty to the types of situations that have proved troublesome. Throughout, it seeks to protect the integrity of the objectives and needs of the cooperating institutions and their faculties, as well as of sponsoring agencies.

In April 1990, the Council of the American Association of University Professors adopted several changes in language in order to remove gender-specific references from the original text.

The increasingly necessary and complex relationships among universities, government, and industry call for more intensive attention to standards of procedure and conduct in government-sponsored research. The clarification and application of such standards must be designed to serve the purposes and needs of the projects and the public interest involved in them and to protect the integrity of the cooperating institutions as agencies of higher education.

The government and institutions of higher education, as the contracting parties, have an obligation to see that adequate standards and procedures are developed and applied; to inform one another of their respective requirements; and to ensure that all individuals participating in their respective behalves are informed of and apply the standards and procedures that are so developed.

Consulting relationships between university staff members and industry serve the interests of research and education in the university. Likewise, the transfer of technical knowledge and skill from the university to industry contributes to technological advance. Such relationships are desirable, but certain potential hazards should be recognized.

A. CONFLICT SITUATIONS

1. Favoring of Outside Interests. When a university staff member (administrator, faculty member, professional staff member, or employee) undertaking or engaging in government-sponsored work has a significant financial interest in, or a consulting arrangement with, a private business concern, it is important to avoid actual or apparent conflicts of interest between government-sponsored university research obligations and outside interests and other obligations. Situations in or from which conflicts of interest may arise are:

a. the undertaking or orientation of the staff member's university research to serve the research or other needs of the private firm without disclosure of such undertaking or orientation to the university and to the sponsoring agency;

b. the purchase of major equipment, instruments, materials, or other items for university research from the private firm in which the staff member has the interest without disclosure of such interest;

c. the transmission to the private firm or other use for personal gain of government-sponsored work products, results, materials, records, or information that are not made generally available (this would not necessarily preclude appropriate licensing arrangements for inventions, or consulting on the basis of government-sponsored research results where there is significant additional work by the staff member independent of the government-sponsored research);

d. the use for personal gain or other authorized use of privileged information acquired in connection with the staff member's government-sponsored activities (the term "privileged information" incudes, but is not limited to, medical, personnel, or security records of individuals; anticipated materials requirements or price actions; possible new sites for government operations; and knowledge of forthcoming programs or of selection of contractors or subcontractors in advance of official announcements);

e. the negotiation or influence upon the negotiation of contracts relating to the staff member's government-sponsored research between the university and private organizations with which the staff member has consulting or other significant relationships;

f. the acceptance of gratuities or special favors from private organizations with which the university does, or may conduct, business in connection with a government-sponsored research project, or extension of gratuities or special favors to employees of the sponsoring government agency, under circumstances which might reasonably be interpreted as an attempt to influence the recipients in the conduct of their duties.

2. Distribution of Effort. There are competing demands on the energies of faculty members (for example, research, teaching, committee work, outside consulting). The way in which a faculty member divides his or her effort among these various functions does not raise ethical questions unless the government agency supporting the research is misled in its understanding of the amount of intellectual effort the faculty member is actually devoting to the research in question. A system of precise time accounting is incompatible with the inherent character of the work of faculty members, since the various functions they perform are closely interrelated and do not conform to any meaningful division of a standard work week. On the other hand, if the research agreement contemplates that a faculty member will devote a certain fraction of effort to the government-sponsored research, or the faculty member agrees to assume responsibility in relation to such research, a demonstrable relationship between the indicated effort or responsibility and the actual extent of the faculty member's involvement is to be expected. Each university, therefore, should—through joint consultation of administration and faculty—develop procedures to ensure that proposals are responsibly made and complied with.

3. Consulting for Government Agencies or Their Contractors. When the staff member engaged in government-sponsored research also serves as a consultant to a federal agency, such conduct is subject to the provisions of the Conflict of Interest Statutes (18 U.S.C. 202–209 as amended) and the president's memorandum of May 2, 1963, *Preventing Conflicts of Interest on the Part of Special Government Employees.* When the staff member consults for one or more government contractors, or prospective contractors, in the same technical field as the staff member's research project, care must be taken to avoid giving advice that may be of questionable objectivity because of its possible bearing on the individual's other interests. In undertaking and performing consulting services, the staff member should make full disclosure of such interests to the university and to the contractor insofar as they may appear to relate to the work at the university or for the contractor. Conflict-of-interest problems could arise, for example, in the participation of a staff member of the university in an evaluation for the government agency or its contractor of some technical aspect of the work of another organization with which the staff member has a consulting or employment relationship or a significant financial interest, or in an evaluation of a competitor to such other organization.

B. UNIVERSITY RESPONSIBILITY

Each university participating in government-sponsored research should make known to the sponsoring government agencies:

1. the steps it is taking to ensure an understanding on the part of the university administration and staff members of the possible conflicts of interest or other problems that may develop in the foregoing types of situation, and

2. the organizational and administrative actions it has taken or is taking to avoid such problems, including:

   a. accounting procedures to be used to ensure that government funds are expended for the purposes for which they have been provided, and that all services which are required in return for these funds are supplied;

   b. procedures that enable it to be aware of the outside professional work of staff members participating in government-sponsored research, if such outside work related in any way to the government-sponsored research;

   c. the formulation of standards to guide the individual university staff members in governing their conduct in relation to outside interests that might raise questions of conflicts of interest; and

   d. the provision within the university of an informed source of advice and guidance to its staff members for advance consultation on questions they wish to raise concerning the problems that may or do develop as a result of their outside financial or consulting interests, as they relate to their participation in government-sponsored university research. The university may wish to discuss such problems with the contracting officer or other appropriate government official in those cases that appear to raise questions regarding conflicts of interest.

The above process of disclosure and consultation is the obligation assumed by the university when it accepts government funds for research. The process must, of course, be carried out in a manner that does not infringe on the legitimate freedoms and flexibility of action of the university and its staff members that have traditionally characterized a university. It is desirable that standards and procedures of the kind discussed be formulated and administered by members of the university community themselves, through their joint initiative and responsibility, for it is they who are the best judges of the conditions which can most effectively stimulate the search for knowledge and preserve the requirements of academic freedom. Experience indicates that such standards and procedures should be developed and specified by joint administration-faculty action.

NOTE

Reproduced with permission from American Association of University Professors, "On Preventing Conflicts of Interest in Government-Sponsored Research at Universities," *AAUP Policy Documents and Reports* (Washington, DC: American Association of University Professors, 1995), 116–118.

Appendix 6

AAUP "1940 Statement of Principles on Academic Freedom and Tenure, with 1970 Interpretive Comments"

In 1940, following a series of joint conferences begun in 1934, representatives of the American Association of University Professors and of the Association of American Colleges (now the Association of American Colleges and Universities) agreed upon a restatement of principles set forth in the *1925 Conference Statement on Academic Freedom and Tenure*. This restatement is known to the profession as the *1940 Statement of Principles on Academic Freedom and Tenure*.

The 1940 Statement is printed below, followed by Interpretive Comments as developed by representatives of the American Association of University Professors and the Association of American Colleges in 1969. The governing bodies of the two associations, meeting respectively in November 1989 and January 1990, adopted several changes in language in order to remove gender-specific references from the original text.

The purpose of this statement is to promote public understanding and support of academic freedom and tenure and agreement upon the procedures to ensure them in colleges and universities. Institutions of higher education are conducted for the common good and not to further the interest of either the individual teacher* or the institution as a whole. The common good depends upon the free search for truth and its free exposition.

---

*The word "teacher" as used in this document is understood to include the investigator who is attached to an academic institution without teaching duties.

Academic Freedom is essential to these purposes and applies to both teaching and research. Freedom in research is fundamental to the advancement of truth. Academic freedom in its teaching aspect is fundamental for the protection of the rights of the teacher in teaching and of the student to freedom in learning. It carries with it duties correlative with rights.[1]**

Tenure is a means to certain ends; specifically: (1) freedom of teaching and research and of extramural activities, and (2) a sufficient degree of economic security to make the profession attractive to men and women of ability. Freedom and economic security, hence, tenure, are indispensable to the success of an institution in fulfilling its obligations to its students and to society.

ACADEMIC FREEDOM

(a) Teachers are entitled to full freedom in research and in the publication of the results, subject to the adequate performance of their other academic duties; but research for pecuniary return should be based upon an understanding with the authorities of the institution.

(b) Teachers are entitled to freedom in the classroom in discussing their subject, but they should be careful not to introduce into their teaching controversial matter which has no relation to their subject.[2] Limitations of academic freedom because of religious or other aims of the institution should be clearly stated in writing at the time of the appointment.[3]

(c) College and university teachers are citizens, members of a learned profession, and officers of an educational institution. When they speak or write as citizens, they should be free from institutional censorship or discipline, but their special position in the community imposes special obligations. As scholars and educational officers, they should remember that the public may judge their profession and their institution by their utterances. Hence they should at all times be accurate, should exercise appropriate restraint, should show respect for the opinions of others, and should make every effort to indicate that they are not speaking for the institution.[4]

ACADEMIC TENURE

After the expiration of a probationary period, teachers or investigators should have permanent or continuous tenure, and their service should be terminated only for adequate cause, except in the case of retirement for age, or under extraordinary circumstances because of financial exigencies.

In the interpretation of this principle it is understood that the following represents acceptable academic practice:

1. The precise terms and conditions of every appointment should be stated in writing and be in the possession of both institution and teacher before the appointment is consummated.

**Bold-face numbers in brackets refer to Interpretive Comments which follow.

2. Beginning with the appointment to the rank of full-time instructor or a higher rank, [5] the probationary period should not exceed seven years, including within this period full-time service in all institutions of higher education; but subject to the proviso that when, after a term of probationary service of more than three years in one or more institutions, a teacher is called to another institution, it may be agreed in writing that the new appointment is for a probationary period of not more than four years, even though thereby the person's total probationary period in the academic profession is extended beyond the normal maximum of seven years.[6] Notice should be given at least one year prior to the expiration of the probationary period if the teacher is not to be continued in service after the expiration of that period.[7]

3. During the probationary period a teacher should have the academic freedom that all other members of the faculty have.[8]

4. Termination for cause of a continuous appointment, or the dismissal for cause of a teacher previous to the expiration of a term appointment, should, if possible, be considered by both a faculty committee and the governing board of the institution. In all cases where the facts are in dispute, the accused teacher should be informed before the hearing in writing of the charges and should have the opportunity to be heard in his or her own defense by all bodies that pass judgment upon the case. The teacher should be permitted to be accompanied by an advisor of his or her own choosing who may act as counsel. There should be a full stenographic record of the hearing available to the parties concerned. In the hearing of charges of incompetence the testimony should include that of teachers and other scholars, either from the teacher's own and from other institutions. Teachers on continuous appointment who are dismissed for reasons not involving moral turpitude should receive their salaries for at least a year from the date of notification of dismissal whether or not they are continued in their duties at the institution.[9]

5. Termination of a continuous appointment because of financial exigency should be demonstrably *bona fide*.

1940 INTERPRETATIONS

At the conference of representatives of the American Association of University Professors and of the Association of American Colleges on November 7–8, 1940, the following interpretations of the *1940 Statement of Principles on Academic Freedom and Tenure* were agreed upon:

1. That its operation should not be retroactive.

2. That all tenure claims of teachers appointed prior to the endorsement should be determined in accordance with the principles set forth in the 1925 *Conference Statement on Academic Freedom and Tenure*.

3. If the administration of a college or university feels that a teacher has not observed the admonitions of paragraph (c) of the section on Academic Freedom and believes

that the extramural utterances of the teacher have been such as to raise grave doubts concerning the teacher's fitness for his or her position, it may proceed to file charges under paragraph (a)(4) of the section on Academic Tenure. In pressing such charges the administration should remember that teachers are citizens and should be accorded the freedom of citizens. In such cases the administration must assume full responsibility, and the American Association of University Professors and the Association of American Colleges are free to make an investigation.

1970 INTERPRETIVE COMMENTS

Following extensive discussions on the *1940 Statement of Principles of Academic Freedom and Tenure* with leading educational associations and with individual faculty members and administrators, a joint committee of the AAUP and the Association of American Colleges met during 1969 to reevaluate this key policy statement. On the basis of the comments received, and the discussions that ensued, the joint committee felt the preferable approach was to formulate interpretations of the *Statement* in the terms of the experience gained in implementing and applying the *Statement* for over thirty years and of adapting it to current needs.

The committee submitted to the two associations for their consideration the following "Interpretive Comments." These interpretations were adopted by the Council of the American Association of University Professors in April 1970 and endorsed by the Fifty-sixth Annual Meeting of Association policy.

In the thirty years since their promulgation, the principles of the *1940 Statement of Principles on Academic Freedom and Tenure* have undergone a substantial amount of refinement. This has evolved through a variety of processes, including customary acceptance, understandings mutually arrived at between institutions and professors or their representatives, investigations and reports by the American Association of University Professors, and formulations of statements by that association either alone or in conjunction with the Association of American Colleges. These comments represent the attempt of the two associations, as the original sponsors of the *1940 Statement*, to formulate the most important of these refinements. Their incorporation here as Interpretive Comments is based upon the premise that the *1940 Statement* is not a static code but a fundamental document designed to set a framework of norms to guide adaptations to changing times and circumstances.

Also, there have been relevant developments in the law itself reflecting a growing insistence by the courts on due process within the academic community which parallels the essential concepts of the *1940 Statement*; particularly relevant is the identification by the Supreme Court of academic freedom as a right protected by the First Amendment. As the Supreme Court said in *Keyishian v. Board of Regents* 385 U.S. 589 (1967), ''Our Nation is deeply committed to safeguarding academic freedom, which is of transcendent value to all of us and not merely to the teachers concerned. That freedom is therefore a special concern of the First Amendment, which does not tolerate laws that cast a pall of orthodoxy over the classroom.''

The numbers refer to the designated portion of the *1940 Statement* on which interpretive comment is made.

1. The Association of American Colleges and the American Association of University Professors have long recognized that membership in the academic profession carries with it special responsibilities. Both associations either separately or jointly have consistently affirmed these responsibilities in major policy statements, providing guidance to professors in their utterances as citizens, in the exercise of their responsibilities to the institution and to students, and in their conduct when resigning from their institution or when undertaking government-sponsored research. Of particular relevance is the *Statement on Professional Ethics*, adopted in 1966 as Association policy. (A revision, adopted in 1987, was published in *Academe: Bulletin of the AAUP* 73 [July–August 1987]: 49.)

2. The intent of this statement is not to discourage what is ''controversial.'' Controversy is at the heart of the free academic inquiry which the entire statement is designed to foster. The passage serves to underscore the need for teachers to avoid persistently intruding material which has no relation to their subject.

3. Most church-related institutions no longer need or desire the departure from the principle of academic freedom implied in the *1940 Statement*, and we do not now endorse such a departure.

4. This paragraph is the subject of an interpretation adopted by the sponsors of the 1940 *Statement* immediately following its endorsement which reads as follows:

If the administration of a college or university feels that a teacher has not observed the admonitions of paragraph (c) of the section on Academic Freedom and believes that the extramural utterances of the teacher have been such as to raise grave doubts concerning the teacher's fitness for his or her position, it may proceed to file charges under paragraph (a)(4) of the section on Academic Tenure. In pressing such charges the administration should remember that teachers are citizens and should be accorded the freedom of citizens. In such cases the administration must assume full responsibility, and the American Association of University Professors and the Association of American Colleges are free to make an investigation.

Paragraph (c) of the section on Academic Freedom in the 1940 *Statement* should also be interpreted in keeping with the 1964 ''Committee A Statement on Extramural Utterances'' (*AAUP Bulletin* 51 [1965]: 29), which states *inter alia*: ''The controlling principle is that a faculty member's expression of opinion as a citizen cannot constitute grounds for dismissal unless it clearly demonstrates the faculty member's unfitness for his or her position. Extramural utterances rarely bear upon the faculty member's unfitness for his or her position. More-

over, a final decision should take into account the faculty member's entire record
as a teacher and scholar."

Paragraph V of the *Statement on Professional Ethics* also deals with the nature
of the "special obligations" of the teacher. The paragraph reads as follows:

As members of their community, professors have the rights and obligations of other
citizens. Professors measure the urgency of other obligations in the light of their responsibilities to their subject, to their students, to their profession, and to their institution.
When they speak or act as private persons they avoid creating the impression of speaking
or acting for their college or university. As citizens engaged in a profession that depends
upon freedom for its health and integrity professors have a particular obligation to promote conditions of free inquiry and to further public understanding of academic freedom.

Both the protection of academic freedom and the requirements of academic
responsibility apply not only to the full-time probationary and the tenured
teacher, but also to all others, such as part-time faculty and teaching assistants,
who exercise teaching responsibilities.

5. The concept of "rank of full-time instructor or a higher rank" is intended
to include any person who teaches a full-time load regardless of the teacher's
specific title.*

6. In calling for an agreement "in writing" on the amount of credit given
for a faculty member's prior service at other institutions, the *Statement* furthers
the general policy of full understanding by the professor of the terms and conditions of the appointment. It does not necessarily follow that a professor's
tenure rights have been violated because of the absence of a written agreement
on this matter. Nonetheless, especially because of the variation in permissible
institutional practices, a written understanding concerning these matters at the
time of appointment is particularly appropriate and advantageous to both the
individual and the institution.**

7. The effect of this subparagraph is that a decision on tenure, favorable or
unfavorable, must be made at least twelve months prior to the completion of
the probationary period. If the decision is negative, the appointment for the
following year becomes a terminal one. If the decision is affirmative, the provisions in the *1940 Statement* with respect to the termination of service of teachers or investigators after the expiration of a probationary period should apply
from the date when the favorable decision is made.

The general principle of notice contained in this paragraph is developed with
greater specificity in the *Standards for Notice of Nonreappointment*, endorsed
by the Fiftieth Annual Meeting of the American Association of University Professors (1964). These standards are:

*For a discussion of this question, see the "Report of the Special Committee on Academic Personnel
Ineligible for Tenure," *AAUP Bulletin* 52 (1966): 280–82.
**For a more detailed statement on this question, see "On Crediting Prior Service Elsewhere as
Part of the Probationary Period," *AAUP Bulletin* 64 (1978): 274–75.

Notice of nonreappointment, or of intention not to recommend reappointment to the governing board, should be given in writing in accordance with the following standards:

(1) *Not later than March 1 of the first academic year of service,* if the appointment expires at the end of that year; or, if a one-year appointment terminates during an academic year, at least three months in advance of its termination.

(2) *Not later than December 15 of the second academic year of service,* if the appointment expires at the end of that year; or, if an initial two-year appointment terminates during an academic year, at least six months in advance of its termination.

(3) At least twelve months before the expiration of an appointment after two or more years in the institution.

Other obligations, both of institutions and of individuals, are described in the *Statement on Recruitment and Resignation of Faculty Members,* as endorsed by the Association of American Colleges and the American Association of University Professors in 1961.

8. The freedom of probationary teachers is enhanced by the establishment of a regular procedure for the periodic evaluation and assessment of the teacher's academic performance during probationary status. Provision should be made for regularized procedures for the consideration of complaints by probationary teachers that their academic freedom has been violated. One suggested procedure to serve these purposes is contained in the *Recommended Institutional Regulations on Academic Freedom and Tenure,* prepared by the American Association of University Professors.

9. A further specification of the academic due process to which the teacher is entitled under this paragraph is contained in the *Statement on Procedural Standards in Faculty Dismissal Proceedings,* jointly approved by the American Association of University Professors and the Association of American Colleges in 1958. This interpretive document deals with the issue of suspension, about which the 1940 *Statement* is silent.

The 1958 *Statement* provides: "Suspension of the faculty member during the proceedings is justified only if immediate harm to the faculty member or others is threatened by the faculty member's continuance. Unless legal considerations forbid, any such suspension should be with pay." A suspension which is not followed by either reinstatement or the opportunity for a hearing is in effect a summary dismissal in violation of academic due process.

The concept of "moral turpitude" identifies the exceptional case in which the professor may be denied a year's teaching or pay in whole or in part. The statement applies to that kind of behavior which goes beyond simply warranting discharge and is so utterly blameworthy as to make it inappropriate to require the offering of a year's teaching or pay. The standard is not that the moral sensibilities of persons in the particular community have been affronted. The standard is behavior that would evoke condemnation by the academic community generally.

ENDORSERS

[The list of 170 endorsers with the corresponding year of endorsement has been omitted from this appendix.]

NOTE

Reproduced with permission from American Association of University Professors, "1940 Statement of Principles on Academic Freedom and Tenure, with 1970 Interpretive Comments" *AAUP Policy Documents and Reports* (Washington, DC: American Association of University Professors, 1995), 3–7.

Appendix 7

AAUP "Statement on Procedural Standards in Faculty Dismissal Proceedings"

The following statement was prepared by a joint committee representing the Association of Colleges (now the Association of American Colleges and Universities) and the American Association of University Professors and was approved by these two associations at their annual meetings in 1958. It supplements the *1940 Statement of Principles on Academic Freedom and Tenure* by providing a formulation of the "academic due process" that should be observed in dismissal proceedings. The exact procedural standards here set forth, however, "are not intended to establish a norm in the same manner as the 1940 Statement of Principles on Academic Freedom and Tenure, but are presented rather as a guide . . ."

The governing bodies of the American Association of University Professors and the Association of American Colleges, meeting, respectively, in November 1989 and January 1990, adopted several changes in language in order to remove gender-specific references from the original text.

INTRODUCTORY COMMENTS

Any approach toward settling the difficulties which have beset dismissal proceedings on many American campuses must look beyond procedure into setting and cause. A dismissal proceeding is a symptom of failure; no amount of use of removal process will help strengthen higher education as much as will the cultivation of conditions in which dismissals rarely if ever need occur.

Just as the board of control or other governing body is the legal and fiscal corporation of the college, the faculty is the academic entity. Historically, the academic corporation is the older. Faculties were formed in the Middle Ages, with managerial affairs either self-arranged or handled in course by the parent church. Modern college faculties, on the other hand, are part of a complex and extensive structure requiring legal incorporation, with stewards and managers specifically appointed to discharge certain functions.

Nonetheless, the faculty of a modern college constitutes an entity as real as that of the faculties of medieval times, in terms of collective purpose and function. A necessary precondition of a strong faculty is that it have first-hand concern with its own membership. This is properly reflected both in appointments to and in separations from the faculty body.

A well-organized institution will reflect sympathetic understanding by trustees and teachers alike of their respective and complementary roles. These should be spelled out carefully in writing and made available to all. Trustees and faculty should understand and agree on their several functions in determining who shall join and who shall remain on the faculty. One of the prime duties of the administrator is to help preserve understanding of those functions. It seems clear on the American college scene that a close positive relationship exists between the excellence of colleges, the strength of their faculties, and the extent of faculty responsibility in determining faculty membership. Such a condition is in no way inconsistent with full faculty awareness of institutional factors with which governing boards must be primarily concerned.

In the effective college, a dismissal proceeding involving a faculty member on tenure, or one occurring during the term of an appointment, will be a rare exception, caused by individual human weakness and not by an unhealthful setting. When it does come, however, the college should be prepared for it, so that both institutional integrity and individual human rights may be preserved during the process of resolving the trouble. The faculty must be willing to recommend the dismissal of a colleague when necessary. By the same token, presidents and governing boards must be willing to give full weight to a faculty judgment favorable to a colleague.

One persistent source of difficulty is the definition of adequate cause for the dismissal of a faculty member. Despite the 1940 *Statement of Principles on Academic Freedom and Tenure* and subsequent attempts to build upon it, considerable ambiguity and misunderstanding persist throughout higher education, especially in the respective conceptions of governing boards, administrative officers, and faculties concerning this matter. The present statement assumes that individual institutions will have formulated their own definitions of adequate cause for dismissal, bearing in mind the 1940 *Statement* and standards which have developed in the experience of academic institutions.

This statement deals with procedural standards. Those recommended are not intended to establish a norm in the same manner as the 1940 *Statement of Principles on Academic Freedom and Tenure*, but are presented rather as a guide to be used according to the nature and traditions of particular institutions in giving effect to both faculty tenure rights and the obligations of faculty members in the academic community.

PROCEDURAL RECOMMENDATIONS

1. Preliminary Proceedings Concerning the Fitness of a Faculty Member

When reasons arise to question the fitness of a college or university faculty member who has tenure or whose term appointment has not expired, the appropriate administrative officers should ordinarily discuss the matter with the faculty member in personal conference. The matter may be terminated by mutual consent at this point; but if an adjustment does not result, a standing or *ad hoc* committee elected by the faculty and charged with the function of rendering confidential advice in such situations should informally inquire into the situation, to effect an adjustment, if possible, and, if none is effected, to determine whether in its view formal proceedings to consider the faculty member's dismissal should be instituted. If the committee recommends that such proceedings should be begun, or if the president of the institution, even after considering a recommendation of the committee favorable to the faculty member, expresses the conviction that a proceeding should be undertaken, action should be commenced under the procedures which follow. Except where there is a disagreement, a statement with reasonable particularity of the grounds proposed for the dismissal should then be jointly formulated by the president and the faculty committee; if there is a disagreement, the president or the president's representative should formulate the statement.

2. Commencement of Formal Proceedings

The formal proceedings should be commenced by a communication addressed to the faculty member by the president of the institution, informing the faculty member of the statement formulated, and informing the faculty member that, at the faculty member's request, a hearing will be conducted by a faculty committee at a specified time and place to determine whether he or she should be removed from the faculty position on the grounds stated. In setting the date of the hearing, sufficient time should be allowed the faculty member to prepare a defense. The faculty member should be informed, in detail or by reference to published regulations, of the procedural rights that will be accorded. The faculty member should state in reply whether he or she wishes a hearing, and, if so, should answer in writing, not less than one week before the date set for the hearing, the statements in the president's letter.

3. Suspension of the Faculty Member

Suspension of the faculty member during the proceedings is justified only if immediate harm to the faculty member or others is threatened by the faculty member's continuance. Unless legal considerations forbid, any such suspension should be with pay.

4. Hearing Committee

The committee of faculty members to conduct the hearing and reach a decision should be either an elected standing committee not previously concerned with the case or a committee established as soon as possible after the president's letter to the faculty member has been sent. The choice of members of the hearing committee should be on the basis of their objectivity and competence and of the regard in which they are held in the academic community. The committee should elect its own chair.

5. Committee Proceeding

The committee should proceed by considering the statement of grounds for dismissal already formulated, and the faculty member's response written before the time of the hearing. If the faculty member has not requested a hearing, the committee should consider the case on the basis of the obtainable information and decide whether the faculty member should be removed; otherwise the hearing should go forward. The committee, in consultation with the president and the faculty member, should exercise its judgment as to whether the hearing should be public or private. If any facts are in dispute, the testimony of witness and other evidence concerning the matter set forth in the president's letter to the faculty member should be received.

The president should have the option of attendance during the hearing. The president may designate an appropriate representative to assist in developing the case; but the committee should determine the order of proof, should normally conduct the questioning of witnesses, and, if necessary, should secure the presentation of evidence important to the case.

The faculty member should have the option of assistance by counsel, whose functions should be similar to those of the representative chosen by the president. The faculty member should have the additional procedural rights set forth in the 1940 *Statement of Principles on Academic Freedom and Tenure*, and should have the aid of the committee, when needed, in securing the attendance of witnesses. The faculty member or the faculty member's counsel and the representative designated by the president should have the right, within reasonable limits, to question all witnesses who testify orally. The faculty member should have the opportunity to be confronted by all adverse witnesses. Where unusual and urgent reasons move the hearing committee to withhold this right, or where the witness cannot appear, the identity of the witness, as well as the statements of the witness, should nevertheless be disclosed to the faculty member. Subject to these safeguards, statements may, when necessary, be taken outside the hearing and reported to it. All of the evidence should be duly recorded. Unless special circumstances warrant, it should not be necessary to follow formal rules of court procedure.

6. Consideration by Hearing Committee

The committee should reach its decision in conference, on the basis of the hearing. Before doing so, it should give opportunity to the faculty member or the faculty member's counsel and the representative designated by the president to argue orally before it. If written briefs would be helpful, the committee may request them. The committee may proceed to decision promptly, without having the record of the hearing transcribed, where its feels that a just decision can be reached by this means; or it may await the availability of a transcript of the hearing if its decision would be aided thereby. It should make explicit findings with respect to each of the grounds of removal presented, and a reasoned opinion may be desirable. Publicity concerning the committee's decision may properly be withheld until consideration has been given to the case by the governing body of the institution. The president and the faculty member should be notified of the decision in writing and should be given a copy of the record of the hearing. Any release to the public should be made through the president's office.

7. Consideration by Governing Body

The president should transmit to the governing body the full report of the hearing committee, stating its action. On the assumption that the governing board has accepted the principle of the faculty hearing committee, acceptance of the committee's decision would normally be expected. If the governing body chooses to review the case, its review should be based on the record of the previous hearing, accompanied by opportunity for argument, oral or written or both, by the principals at the hearing or their representatives. The decision of the hearing committee should either be sustained or the proceeding be returned to the committees with objections specified. In such a case the committee should reconsider, taking account of the stated objections and receiving new evidence if necessary. It should frame its decision and communicate it in the same manner as before. Only after study of the committee's reconsideration should the governing body make a final decision overruling the committee.

8. Publicity

Except for such simple announcements as may be required, covering the time of the hearing and similar matters, public statements about the case by either the faculty member or administrative officers should be avoided so far as possible until the proceedings have been completed. Announcement of the final decision should include a statement of the hearing committee's original action, if this has not previously been made known.

NOTE

Reproduced with permission from American Association of University Professors, "Statement on Procedural Standards in Faculty Dismissal Proceedings," *AAUP Policy Documents and Reports* (Washington, DC: American Association of University Professors, 1995), 11–14.

Appendix 8

AAUP "Academic Freedom and Artistic Expression"

The statement which follows was adopted by the participants in the 1990 Wolf Trap Conference on Academic Freedom and Artistic Expression, sponsored by the American Association of University Professors, the American Council on Education, the Association of Governing Boards of Universities and Colleges, and the Wolf Trap Foundation. The statement was endorsed by AAUP's Committee A on Academic Freedom and Tenure and by its Council at their meetings in June 1990.

Attempts to curtail artistic presentations at academic institutions on grounds that the works are offensive to some members of the campus community and of the general public occur with disturbing frequency. Those who support restrictions argue that works presented to the public rather than in the classroom or in other entirely intramural settings should conform to their view of the prevailing community standard rather than to standards of academic freedom. We believe that, "essential as freedom is for the relation and judgment of facts, it is even more indispensable to the imagination."* In our judgment academic freedom in the creation and presentation of works in the visual and the performing arts, by ensuring greater opportunity for imaginative exploration and expression, best serves the public and the academy.

The following proposed policies are designed to assist academic institutions

*Helen C. White, "Our Most Urgent Professional Task," *AAUP Bulletin* 45 (March 1959): 282.

to respond to the issues that may arise from the presentation of artistic works to the public and to do so in a manner which preserves academic freedom:

1. *Academic Freedom in Artistic Expression.* Faculty members and students engaged in the creation and presentation of works of the visual and the performing arts are as much engaged in pursuing the mission of the college or university as are those who write, teach, and study in other academic disciplines. Works of the visual and the performing arts are important both in their own right and because they can enhance our understanding of social institutions and the human condition. Artistic expression in the classroom, the studio, and the workshop therefore merits the same assurance of academic freedom that is accorded to other scholarly and teaching activities. Since faculty and student artistic presentations to the public are integral to their teaching, learning, and scholarship, these presentations merit no less protection. Educational and artistic criteria should be used by all who participate in the selection and presentation of artistic works. Reasonable content-neutral regulation of the "time, place, and manner" of presentations should be developed and maintained. Academic institutions are obliged to ensure that regulations and procedures do not impair freedom of expression or discourage creativity by subjecting artistic work to tests of propriety or ideology.

2. *Accountability.* Artistic performances and exhibitions in academic institutions encourage artistic creativity, expression, learning, and appreciation. The institutions do not thereby endorse the specific artistic presentations, nor do the presentations necessarily represent the institution. This principle of institutional neutrality does not relieve institutions of general responsibility for maintaining professional and educational standards, but it does mean that institutions are not responsible for the views or the attitudes expressed in specific artistic works any more than they would be for the content of other instruction, scholarly publication, or invited speeches. Correspondingly, those who present artistic work should not represent themselves or their work as speaking for the institution and should otherwise fulfill their educational and professional responsibilities.

3. *The Audience.* When academic institutions offer exhibitions or performances to the public, they should ensure that the rights of the presenters and of the audience are not impaired by a "heckler's veto" from those who may be offended by the presentation. Academic institutions should ensure that those who choose to view an exhibition or attend a performance may do so without interference. Mere presentation in a public place does not create a "captive audience." Institutions may reasonably designate specific places as generally available or unavailable for exhibitions or performances.

4. *Public Funding.* Public funding for artistic presentations and for academic institutions does not diminish (and indeed may heighten) the responsibility of the university community to ensure academic freedom and of the public to respect the integrity of the academic institutions. Government imposition on artistic expression of a test of propriety, ideology, or religion is an act of cen-

sorship which impermissibly denies the academic freedom to explore, to teach, and to learn.

NOTE

Reproduced with permission from American Association of University Professors, "Academic Freedom and Artistic Expression," *AAUP Policy Documents and Reports* (Washington, DC: American Association of University Professors, 1995), 35–36.

Table of Cases

Selected Bibliography

Allen, F. C. L. "Indicators of Academic Excellence: Is There a Link Between Merit and Reward?" *Australian Journal of Education* 34, no. 1 (1990): 87–98.

American Association of University Administrators. "Mission Statement and Professional Standards." Tuscaloosa, AL: American Association of University Administrators, 1994.

American Association of University Professors. "Academic Freedom and Artistic Expression." *AAUP Policy Documents and Reports*. Washington, DC: American Association of University Professors, 1995, 35–36.

American Association of University Professors. "1940 Statement of Principles on Academic Freedom and Tenure, with 1970 Interpretive Comments." *AAUP Policy Documents and Reports*. Washington, DC: American Association of University Professors, 1995, 3–7.

American Association of University Professors. "On Preventing Conflicts of Interest in Government-Sponsored Research at Universities." *AAUP Policy Documents and Reports*. Washington, DC: American Association of University Professors, 1995, 116–118.

American Association of University Professors. "Statement on Conflicts of Interest." *AAUP Policy Documents and Reports*. Washington, DC: American Association of University Professors, 1995, 119–120.

American Association of University Professors. "Statement on Procedural Standards in Faculty Dismissal Proceedings." *AAUP Policy Documents and Reports*. Washington, DC: American Association of University Professors, 1995, 11–14.

American Association of University Professors. "Statement on Professional Ethics."

AAUP Policy Documents and Reports. Washington, DC: American Association of University Professors, 1995, 105–106.

Andrews, Hans A. "Expanding Merit Recognition Plans in Community Colleges." *Community College Review* 20, no. 5 (1993): 50–58.

Baez, Benjamin, and John A. Centra. *Tenure, Promotion, and Reappointment: Legal and Administrative Implications.* ASHE-ERIC Higher Education Report No. 1. Washington, DC: George Washington University, School of Education and Human Development, 1995.

Barrow, Clisby Louise Hall. "Academic Freedom and the University Title VII Suit After *University of Pennsylvania v. EEOC and Brown v. Trustees of Boston University.*" 43 *Vanderbilt Law Review* n.3 (October 1990): 1571–1606.

Black, Dennis R., and Matt Gilson. *Perspectives and Principles: A College Administrator's Guide to Staying Out of Court.* Madison, WI: Magna Publications, 1988.

Black's Law Dictionary. 6th ed. St. Paul, MN: West, 1990.

Boyer, Carol M., and Darrell R. Lewis. *And on the Seventh Day: Faculty Consulting and Supplemental Income.* ASHE-ERIC Higher Education Report No. 3. Washington, DC: George Washington University, 1985.

Cahn, Steven M. *Saints and Scamps: Ethics in Academia.* Lanham, MD: Rowman & Littlefield, 1994.

Campbell, J. Louis, III. "Academic Freedom and the First Amendment: Legal Entanglements." *ACA Bulletin*, no. 17 (August 1990): 53–62.

Canon, Harry J., and Robert D. Brown, eds. *Applied Ethics in Student Services.* San Francisco: Jossey-Bass, 1985.

Daughtry, William H. "Legal Nature of Academic Freedom in United States Colleges and Universities." 25 *U. Rich. Law Review* 233–271 (Winter 1991).

Diamond, Robert M. *Serving on Promotion and Tenure Committees: A Faculty Guide.* Boston, MA: Anker, 1994.

Dworkin, Ronald. "We Need a New Interpretation of Academic Freedom." *Academe* 82, no. 3 (May–June 1996): 10–15.

Farmer, Donald W. "Designing a Reward System to Promote the Career Development of Senior Faculty." *New Directions for Teaching and Learning*, No. 55 (1993): 43–53.

Hendrickson, R. M., and B. A. Lee. *Academic Employment and Retrenchment: Judicial Review and Administrative Action.* ASHE-ERIC Higher Education Report No. 8. Washington, DC: Association for the Study of Higher Education, 1983, ED 240 972.

Hiers, Richard H. "Academic Freedom in Public Colleges and Universities: O Say, Does That Star-Spangled First Amendment Banner Yet Wave?" 40 *Wayne L. Rev.* 1 (Fall 1993): 1–107.

Hunnicutt, Garland G., Rush Lesher Taylor, and Michael J. Keeffe. "An Exploratory Examination of Faculty Evaluation and Merit Compensation Systems in Texas Colleges and Universities." *CUPA Journal* (Spring 1991): 13–21.

Ingram, Richard T. "A Board's Guide to Conflict-of-Interest and Disclosure Issues." *Trusteeship* (March–April 1993): 23–26.

Kaplin, William A., and Barbara A. Lee. *The Law of Higher Education: A Comprehensive Guide to Legal Implications of Administrative Decision Making.* 3rd ed. San Francisco: Jossey-Bass, 1995.

Keeton, W. Page, ed. *Prosser and Keeton on the Law of Torts.* 5th ed. St. Paul, MN: West, 1984.

Kennedy, Donald. *Academic Duty.* Cambridge, MA: Harvard University Press, 1997.

Kingsley, Marcie. "Honest Hiring: What Should We Tell Job Candidates About Personnel Problems?" *Journal of Library Administration* 14, no. 3 (1992): 55–63.

Kramer, George R. "Title VII on Campus: Judicial Review of University Employment Decisions." 82 *Columbia Law Review* 1206–1234 (October 1982).

Lauer, A. Lawrence. "Searching for Answers: Should Universities Create Merit Pay Systems?" *NACUBO Business Officer* (November 1991): 52–54.

Lawler, Edward E., III. *From the Ground Up: Six Principles for Building the New Logic Corporation.* San Francisco: Jossey-Bass, 1996.

Leap, Terry L. *Tenure, Discrimination, and the Courts.* 2nd ed. Ithaca, NY: ILR Press, 1995.

Leas, Terence, and Charles J. Russo. "*Waters v. Churchill*: Autonomy for the Academy or Freedom for the Individual?" 93 *Ed. Law Rep.* 1099 (1994).

Lee, John. "Tenure." *Update: NEA Higher Education Research Center* 1, no. 3 (1995): 1–6.

Leiser, Burton M. "Threats to Academic Freedom and Tenure." 15 *Pace Law Review* (1994): 15–67.

Lovain, Timothy B. "Grounds for Dismissing Tenured Postsecondary Faculty for Cause." *Journal of College and University Law* 10 (1983): 419–421.

Lowenstein, Marc, and Thomas J. Grites. "Ethics in Academic Advising." *NACADA Journal* 13, no. 1 (Spring 1993): 53–54.

Magnusen, Karl O. "Faculty Evaluation, Performance, and Pay: Application and Issues." *Journal of Higher Education* 58 (1987): 516–529.

Marchant, Gregory J., and Isadore Newman. "Faculty Evaluation and Reward Procedures: Views from Education Administrators." *Assessment and Evaluation in Higher Education* 19, no. 2 (1994): 145–152.

Matherne, J. Graham. "Forced Disclosure of Academic Research." *Vanderbilt Law Review* 37, no. 5 (April 1984): 585–594.

Mawdsley, Ralph D. "Judicial Deference: A Doctrine Misapplied in Degree Revocations." 70 *Ed. Law Rep.* 1043 (1992).

Mawdsley, Ralph D. "Plagiarism Problems in Higher Education." *Journal of College and University Law* 13 (1986): 65.

May, William W., ed. *Ethics and Higher Education.* New York: American Council on Education, Macmillan, 1990.

McLaughlin, Judith Block. "Plugging Search Committee Leaks." *AGB Reports* 27, no. 3 (May–June 1985): 24–30.

Miller, Keith T. "Merit Pay from the Faculty's Perspective." *CUPA Journal* (Fall 1992): 7–16.

Moore, Kathryn M., and Marilyn J. Amey. *Making Sense of the Dollars: The Costs and Uses of Faculty Compensation.* ASHE-ERIC Higher Education Report No. 5. Washington, DC: George Washington University, School of Education and Human Development, 1993.

Mullaney, John W., and Elizabeth M. Timberlake. "University Tenure and the Legal System: Procedures, Conflicts, and Resolutions." *Journal of Social Work Education* 30, no. 2 (Spring–Summer 1994): 172–184.

Oakley, Francis. "Apocalypse Now in U.S. Higher Education." *America* 160, no. 12 (April 1, 1989): 286–287, 308.

Olivas, Michael A. *The Law and Higher Education: Cases and Materials on Colleges in Court.* 2nd ed. Durham, NC: Carolina Academic Press, 1997.

Olswang, Steven, and Barbara A. Lee. *Faculty Freedoms and Institutional Accountability: Interactions and Conflicts.* ASHE-ERIC Higher Education Research Report No. 5. Washington, DC: George Washington University, 1984.

Pacholski, Susan L. "Title VII in the University: The Difference Academic Freedom Makes." 59 *University of Chicago Law Review* (1992): 1317–1336.

Poch, Robert K. *Academic Freedom in Higher Education: Rights, Responsibilities, and Limitations.* ASHE-ERIC Higher Education Report No. 4. Washington, DC: George Washington University, School of Education and Human Development, 1993.

Raelin, Joseph A. "Academic Freedom and Control." *College Teaching* 39, no. 1 (Winter 1991): 26–29.

Rafferty, Daniel P. "Technical Foul: *Ross v. Creighton University* Allows Courts to Penalize Universities Which Do Not Perform Specific Promises Made to Student-Athletes." *South Dakota Law Review* 38 (1993): 180.

Reams, Bernard D., Jr. "Revocation of Academic Degrees by Colleges and Universities." *Journal of College and University Law* 14 (Fall 1987): 283–302.

Rosenfeld, Lawrence B., and Beverly Whitaker Long. "An Evaluation System for Measuring Faculty Performance." *ACA Bulletin* 79 (1992): 36–44.

Schweitzer, Thomas A. "Academic Challenge Cases: Should Judicial Review Extend to Academic Evaluations of Students?" 41 *Am. U.L. Rev.* 267 (1962): 329.

Shutt, Bruce T. "Summary of Spoken Comments as Testimony on Fraudulent Records." *College and University: The Journal of the American Association of Collegiate Registrars* (Spring 1986): 206–211. (Summary of testimony before the Subcommittee on Health and Long-Term Care of the U.S. House of Representatives, December 11, 1985.)

Smolla, Rodney A. "Academic Freedom, Hate Speech, and the Idea of a University." *Law and Contemporary Problems* 53, no. 3 (Spring 1990): 195–226.

Thomas, James. "Ethics and Methods of Employment References." *ACA Bulletin* 80 (April 1992): 19–22.

Tierney, William G., and Robert A. Rhoads. *Faculty Socialization as a Cultural Process: A Mirror of Institutional Commitment.* ASHE-ERIC Higher Education Report No. 93–6. Washington, DC: George Washington University, School of Education and Human Development, 1994.

Vaughan, George B., ed. *Dilemmas of Leadership: Decision-Making and Ethics in the Community College.* San Francisco: Jossey-Bass, 1992.

Wilcox, John R., and Susan L. Ebbs. *The Leadership Compass: Values and Ethics in Higher Education.* ASHE-ERIC Higher Education Report No. 1. Washington, DC: George Washington University, School of Education and Human Development, 1992.

Wilcox, John R., and Susan L. Ebbs. "Promoting an Ethical Climate on Campus: The Values Audit." *NASPA Journal* 29, no. 4 (1992): 253–260.

Williams, Gwen B., and Perry A. Zirkel. "Academic Penetration in Faculty Collective Bargaining Contracts in Higher Education." *Research in Higher Education* 28, no. 1 (1988): 76–95.

Index

About the Authors

NORMA M. GOONEN is Dean of the Farquhar Center for Undergraduate Studies at Nova Southeastern University. An academic administrator whose experience in higher education spans two decades, Dr. Goonen previously served as Vice President for Academic Affairs at St. Thomas University and Associate Dean of Undergraduate Studies at Florida International University. She has taught on the high school and university levels and written extensively on education topics.

RACHEL S. BLECHMAN is a partner in the Miami office of the law firm of Holland & Knight LLP. Since 1982 she has focused a portion of her legal practice on the representation of colleges and universities. Ms. Blechman has provided legal services to public and private institutions in matters involving governance, student affairs, academic affairs, administration and finance, and employment law.